$10.25

Barney Fowler

Adirondack
Album BY BARNEY FOWLER

Presenting Volume No. 2 of Adirondack Album and continuing an unusual view of New York State's Adirondack Region by a veteran reporter-photographer, containing text and illustrations of present and past. Hopefully it will prove pleasant reading.

A toast of mountain air, of beauty to behold and enjoy, to the Adirondacks and to those dearest of friends, living and dead, from every walk of life, of all ages, who made this effort not only possible but a reality.

Copyright 1980
Published by Outdoor Associates
1279 Dean Street
Schenectady, N.Y. 12309

Printed by Benche, Inc.
31 Lafayette Street
Schenectady, N.Y. 12301

ISBN
0-9605556-0-9

TABLE OF CONTENTS

From the author:

Volume No. 1 of Adirondack Album contained these remarks:

"The author is not partial to hard-to-read small type. Nor is he partial to photographs compressed into sizes where details are not adequately portrayed.

"As a result, this book has been designed for easy reading and its pages are eight-and-one-half by eleven inches for better display of photographs. The type used is 11 pt. Press Roman medium, and captions are in 10 pt. Press Roman italics.

"The paper is chosen to eliminate glare, and the finish is vellum."

That was part of the Introduction of Volume No. 1. It still holds. The basic price, out of sheer necessity, has risen slightly, but quality of materials used has not diminished one whit.

INTRODUCTION

Gearing up for Volume No. 2 of Adirondack Album has proved most pleasant.

And one turns many things over in mind.

The basic purpose of this book remains identical with that of the previous one: To present the six-million-acre Adirondack Park in a different manner — from a newspaperman's view.

It is one thing, for instance, to note that Gen. Montcalm, the French fighter, was a great figure in Adirondack early history. To me the astonishing aspect is what happened to his remains after death at the Battle of Quebec. This is a story unto itself; is explained in the chapter called "The Skull," researched in the Ursuline Convent in the old section of Quebec.

All of us use radios; most drivers use snow tires; most assuredly all use pencils and electric motors in daily routines. Yet their association with the Adirondacks has never, to my knowledge, been told in a collective manner. The chapter, "Mountain Genius," may be the answer. I found research of tremendous fascination.

And so it went during additional research for what I call the "human interest" themes which abound in the North Country. Higley Flow is a man-made reservoir known to thousands. How it all started and what happened after the impoundment began its remarkable life will, I am sure, be of interest.

So will the story of what John Hickey found when he hunted for a honey bee tree in Keene Valley; hopefully, so will a startling tale of a giant python which "lived" in the mountains and ate goats and bears — believable (perhaps) only to the author who wrote it. I didn't, I hastily add.

This is a book based not upon only one geographical section. The effort has been made to make it general, to confine it to the Adirondack region, with, possibly, a spill-over now and then.

I have hiked, camped, canoed and fished the Adirondacks for more than fifty years. In the 1930's when organized skiing began at North Creek (minus state help) I skied that area and assisted in planning the first snow train out of Schenectady, working with G. Stanley Martin.

The viewing of this magnificent country always has been tempered with the task of gathering material for stories. The combination of physical exertion and academic interest has been productive, and I feel some personal observations, made over a period of years, might not be amiss in this introduction.

Among the most interesting of recent happenstances occurred during the 1980 Winter Olympics at Lake Placid. During a three-day stay, bedding down in Winkelman's Motel, Wilmington with other Capital Newspapers reporters, I had occasion to note the Russians were not only coming but had arrived. They were, of course, Soviet newsmen from Moscow; of the six I met at the Wilderness Inn at Wilmington, run by Clay and Francis Walton, one spoke English and acted as interpreter. He was from Tass in New York City.

They were gusty lot, given easily to laughter. Afghanistan was not mentioned. The Soviets did express some amazement at treatment accorded political leaders by American newsmen. And when they were asked why they didn't treat their own leaders in similar fashion, this was the answer:

"There is no need. Our leadership does not merit criticism!"

Conversation involved many subjects, fishing, boating, Russia's vast forests, oil and gas reserves (of gas they said they had plenty), and the Olympics themselves. At this point in speaking of the American victory over the Russian hockey team I said casually:

"Of course your team is stronger. But our boys showed that enthusiasm can win. It would be good if we exchanged blows only with hockey sticks and battled only in sports."

I had no idea the phrase would travel, but it did. My amazement was complete only two days later when Pravda, the official Communist Party newspaper quoted that same phrase, and the New York Times, in a dispatch from Moscow, reprinted it nationally! How it appeared in Russian is printed herein.

— Это была честная равная игра. Конечно, ваша команда сильнее. Но наши ребята показали, что энтузиазм может победить. Хорошо, если мы всегда будем обмениваться «ударами» только клюшек, «воевать» только в спорте,— сказал нам обозреватель газеты «Олбани тайм юнион» (Барни Фоллу).

How the Communist Party newspaper, Pravda, put the author's words in Russian.

I think, however, the most important subject the Soviets and this writer agreed upon was that the Adirondack Mountains geologically and scenically, are superb ranges, and they had no hesitation in so stating.

They were, and are, correct.

These mountains of ours have been abused and neglected in the past, but times have changed. The Adirondack Forest Preserve, which as of this writing, is 2,350,000 acres big, and which nestles amid private holdings of more than three million additional acres, remains totally innovative in concept — a region by law immune to the lumbermen and developer of "inner cities."

The balance of animal life has changed. Once moose and elk roamed the hills and valleys. The elk is gone. The moose is no longer considered a permanent resident — as a later chapter will explain.

Long gone are the days in the late 1800's when Vermonters crossed Lake Champlain with dogs and guns to raid New York's deer herd. One Vermont hunter during the so-called "hounding season" returned with thirty carcasses for the restaurant market!

Methods of killing have changed. A hotel operator in the North Country said that in 1893 a total of eighteen deer were killed in one day by driving them into the waters of two lakes near his resort — where they were shot like fish in a barrel or, possibly, the method called "pole noosing" was used. In this barbaric gesture, a noose at the end of a long pole was slipped over a swimming deer's head, and death arrived at the convenience of the courageous hunter.

Many Adirondackers in the early days lived on venison; during the winter those who raided deer yards were called "crusters," and the reason is obvious; they walked on frozen crust while deer hoofs sank through, immobilizing the frightened and weather-weakened animals. This too joins memory.

If all this sounds as though deer were plentiful, they were. Lumbering of the Adirondacks had cut deeply into virgin growth; areas were clear cut and that left wide-open spaces for new growth. All of which was perfect for the deer. These animals are browsers, not grazers as are horses or cattle. They consume leaves and twigs as well as beechnuts and acorns.

A "mature" forest with its heavy canopy such as the Adirondacks of the 1700's and early 1800's before lumbering became unrestricted, allowed little or no new growth in the shade of the giant trees. Deer lived in the more open valleys. But as lumbermen clear cut, and new growth appeared, the deer population went up as the animals moved in. If the lumbermen did their slashing job well, so did forest fires which were left in most cases to burn themselves out.

Sparks from lumber locomotives caused many of the fires; so did lightning — which still does. Honey seekers caused more as they set smudge fires to smoke bees away from their treasure. And in one case, a major fire was caused by a guide simply because he wanted to build the "biggest damned bonfire" the mountains had ever seen. He was Elijah Simonds who set fire to the top of a mountain named Nippletop and his "monument" remained for years, a blackened, bald mountain pate.

Whitetail sizes were impressive as the herd found more space, more food. A buck shot by John T. Denny,

near Meacham Lake, Franklin County, in 1877, weighed 357 pounds. Albert H. Thomas, Warrensburg, a former Warren County treasurer, shot a buck during the late 1800's in Essex County and that animal ran a full 350 pounds.

In 1890 James M. Patterson of West Stony Creek, Warren County, commented to the Glens Falls newspaper, "Morning Star":

"I have seen accounts published in your paper of large deer but I think yesterday, Oct. 11, Henry Ordway killed the king of all bucks. I weighed and measured it myself before witnesses. The weight before being dressed was 388 pounds.

"The height over the withers was four-feet, three-inches. There were nine prongs on one antler and ten on the other. Length of the antlers was thirty-two inches; distance between antlers, twenty-six inches; length of deer, from tip of nose to tip of tail, was nine-feet, seven-inches!

"The Lake House, of which Oscar W. Ordway, father of Henry Ordway, is proprietor, is within two miles of Mud Lake, where deer are thicker than in any spot in the Adirondacks. Thirteen deer have been killed the past week, all within two miles of the house."

Hunter control came slowly. Today a person who kills illegally can be fined $2,000, given a one-year term in jail — or both. The same penalty now holds for killing a moose, as mentioned, a non-resident. A bill setting this penalty for shooting a moose into oblivion was sparked by Assemblyman Neil Kelleher, Troy, and became law in March, 1980.

One might add here that it is also illegal to shoot two additional species of non-residents, the caribou and the antelope.

While lumbermen on private tracts do their bit to open the woods, there are many who today say the Forest Preserve should be opened by selective cutting to increase browse for deer. And there are those who oppose such a move. One novel idea of creating more open space would involve no human nor the touch of the axe or chainsaw, but would involve the amphibious rodent called the beaver, whose building of dams create flowed lands, or shallow inland lakes and ponds, and thus kill timber by inundation. Beaver eat bark, twigs and leaves; they are ever busy simply because they could be killed by their own teeth if they changed food habits; the teeth continue growing; nary a beaver has sought dentures in the history of beaverdom.

It is the idea of Paul Schaefer of Schenectady, long active in conservation circles, to set aside areas where trapping of beaver would be forbidden over periods of time. In this way more open space would be generated by the animals themselves and no constitutional amendment would be needed to change the timber protective clause in the state constitution because beaver, unlike man, can destroy trees without penalty.

Thus, in a way, certain selected areas would return to early days when beaver were abundant and unmolested. Today they are reasonably abundant after having almost

Paul Schaefer, photographed while on a trip through the Moose River Plains area before it became state-owned.

been trapped out of existence, and often live near humans. In the area near the home of Charles Severance on Peaceful Valley Road, Town of Johnsburg, for instance, near where Ross and Chatiemac Creeks join to form North Creek, beaver have been in the area for many years. In the Long Lake area a colony was established by the animals in full view of motorists traveling the highway twixt Blue Mt. Lake and Long Lake.

Several years ago while canoeing the Oswegatchie River upstream from Inlet to High Falls, I found it necessary to bull the craft over fifteen dams. Schaefer's idea might be well worth the try, particularly in the wilderness areas created by edict where no motorized traffic of any kind is allowed.

These "new mountains from old rocks" (Chapter 1) have seen unusual sights, have witnessed unusual feats.

On May 26, 1976, to give an example, Tom Wiley of Hagaman, Montgomery County, started climbing 4,098-foot-high Cascade Mountain with a package in his arms. He moved upward with extreme care and for good reason; he was carrying a two-tiered wedding cake. Upon arrival at the summit, the cake was placed on a stone and there it remained until William A. Kozel and Kathleen Ann Lynch, Schenectady, were joined in marriage by The Rev. Philip L. Giles, son of Rev. and Mrs. David A. Giles of Trinity Methodist Church, Albany.

In this mountain-top ceremony Tom acted as best man and Jeannine, his wife, as matron of honor. A friend, Matt Pollak, Johnstown, recorded the notable event on film, and among spectators wishing the couple well was a person long noted for her interest in con-

serving the Adirondacks, Grace Hudowalski of Albany and Schroon Lake. Grace is a member of the famous and highly exclusive club known as the 46'ers; to join it one must have climbed the mountains' 46 highest peaks — some without trails.

A novel note after the ceremony. No confetti was tossed at the couple. Birdseed was. And our feathered friends dined well that day. The couple and the wedding party descended Cascade, dinnered in Lake Placid.

Not quite as fortunate insofar as a climbing experience is concerned was Michael Ford, son of former President Ford during the same month of May. He and his party were marooned on Nye Mountain, which reaches upward some 4,895 feet, after a freak snowstorm battered the area with fourteen inches. No public advance notice was given of the trip by Ford and his party of students and faculty members of Gordon Cornwall Seminary in Massachusetts for security reasons.

The thirteen-man safari began at Heart Lake on the Indian Pass trail near Lake Placid on Sunday, May 16. EnCon did, however, receive official notice.

For three days events moved smoothly and the group, equipped with portable radios, one with the Whiteface Mt. frequency and another with the frequency used by EnCon aircraft, kept in touch. Then came the snow, which even the Secret Service couldn't prevent. Nye Mountain held a miserable group on May 19, and on the 20th, EnCon Conservation Officer D.R. Jarvas contacted the party at 6 a.m. and told members a relief group would be on its way.

Jarvas manned his radio at Adirondack Loj at Heart Lake while Officers H.E. Karaka, C.W. Reynolds, D.C. Scudder, G.A. Mulverhill and J.T. Flynn split into two teams. The Ford group was located and assisted to the Loj, run by the Adirondack Mountain Club, and members were dried out and fed.

The compulsion to climb mountains is a powerful one. Some try to set a speed record. At 6:18 p.m. August 16, 1972, John (Sharpe) Swan, Jr., of Brookfield Center, Connecticut, and Edward Palen of Verona, New Jersey, both counselors at Camp Pok-O-Moonshine, Willsboro, established a record for the completion of the 46 peaks — a feat which I doubt has been excelled since. If it has, I'd like to hear of it.

Swan and Palen, both 17 at the time, finished their grueling marathon trek over the 46 peaks atop Whiteface Mt., Wilmington, after six days, eighteen hours and eighteen minutes! William Penn couldn't have done better when his Indian friends said he could keep all the land he walked for one full day.

Before this, the record of nine days was held by Norman Grieg of Red Hook, N.Y., and was made in 1969. Ed Palen and John Swan, in achieving their record, returned it to Pok-O-Moonshine whose counselor, Pete Welles of Elmira, N.Y., had established the first one of eleven days in 1962.

To give you an idea of the effort put forth in he new record: Swan and Palen started on August 10, at 12:01 a.m., and on August 10 alone climbed Seymour,

Seward, Donaldson, Emmons, Couchsachrage, Panther and Santanoni. On August 11 they climbed Allen, Cliff, Redfield, Gray, Skylight and Marcy; on August 12 Haystack, Basin, Saddleback, Sawtooth, Gothics, Armstrong, Upper Wolf Jaws, Lower Wolf Jaws and Big Slide. And they finished off the others in the remaining days!

These young men were lucky in a way; an older climber in "excellent physical condiition" lost his life on Marcy in June of 1972 as he attempted to set a 46'er record.

Marcy, in all its moods, is not a charitable mountain. One merely has to ask P.F. Loope, former executive secretary of the Adirondack Mountain Club; he climbed this peak more than 60 times, in all seasons, in all weather; with ordinary gear during spring, summer and fall, and in winter on snowshoes and skis, the latter equipped with sealskin, held under the ski, to prevent backsliding. The grain of the fur was directed for forward movement; if the ski started backwards, the ruffled fur stopped the motion.

In commenting on the two Pok-O-Moonshine counselor's victory, Tim Tefft, camper and counselor at the camp, said this in part, when a person tossed criticism at the feat:

"They hoped to attain neither glory nor notoriety. For them, as for others, it was for personal reasons. . . Perhaps one peak forty-six times is a far more sensible challenge, but this is the sort of achievement impossible to justify in terms of sensibility. Like a mountain peak itself, men will attempt to break a record not because it's sensible, but rather, because it is there. It is, in part, explanation of the human spirit. We each achieve personal triumph in different ways."

I have found if one grows happy with rugged achievement, there is happiness in less spectacular things. Happiness is in learning and benefiting from the interest generated therefrom. Nobody knows all there is about the Adirondacks; new things are learned constantly. I, for instance, learned to my astonishment that at one time fresh water pearls from the Grasse River in St. Lawrence County once sold for as much as $1,400.

That fact was unearthed by Heidi Fuge who researched various industries which once existed in he Adirondacks, in behalf of the ever-growing library of the Adirondack Museum at Blue Mt. Lake.

A small, fresh water pearl business flourished briefly in Russell, she found, and before the supply ran out,

one such pearl sold for the sum mentioned at Tiffany's in New York City. The pearl industry, if one may call it that, began about 1890 when a gentleman named M.C. Rowe discovered such an offering in a fresh water clam scooped from Frost Brook, a tributary of the Grasse River. Four years later not only were the clams exhausted, but so was the constant supply, and from 1915 to 1920, the search for pearls continued at a much slower pace. During the period mentioned a buyer was driven from the railroad station at DeKalb to Russell by Floyd Conant. On his very last trip, the buyer presented Mr. Conant a stick pin set with Grasse River pearls. That pin passed into the hands of Floyd's brother, Leland who, with his wife, presented it to the Adirondack Museum.

Pearl hunters had better luck than seekers of gold and silver riches. Traces have been found, but nothing to make one excited.

Most assuredly stories vary in the North Country and for a change of pace, let's swing over to the John Brown farm near Lake Placid, considered a memorial of sorts to the noted abolitionist. An interesting fact brought out by the well known Adirondack author, Maitland C. De Sormo of Saranac Lake, in his book, "Old Times in the Adirondacks," involved Watson Brown, son of John. Watson was wounded in the Harper's Ferry raid and died October 19, 1859. Death did not stop the travels of his body.

He remained unburied for nearly twenty-three years. This is what happened: The state of Virginia, following Watson's death, still considered the corpse a criminal, and his body was given to the Medical College at Winchester, and there the cadaver was preserved as an anatomical specimen. All this despite the fervent pleas of Watson's mother, who wished a decent burial.

She was refused consistently. Then the Union forces occupied Winchester and an Indiana surgeon decided to claim the body as a "curiosity." He kept the corpse until 1882 when finally, in a spirit of generosity, he informed survivors he had the body. From Indiana the cadaver was shipped to the mother in Ohio and finally it was transported to the Brown Farm near Placid and on October 22, 1882, it was interred near the leader of the Brown clan. Watson was 24 when he died.

One could go on, but there is a book to be read. It is the author's hope the content will be enjoyed in its reading as much as enjoyment was produced in its creation.

TALES FROM TALL PEAKS

"The tall, bald-headed man just stood there, occasionally with his hands in his pockets, spinning off stories, yarns and tales of the Adirondacks like a stand up comedian at a night club.

"And he had 'em laughing. He had 'em clapping. He even had 'em asking for more at the end."

The above was the lead to a story written by James D. Phillips of the Watertown Times after I spoke before the Clinton-Essex-Franklin Counties Library System at its annual meeting in Moira, a community between Malone and Massena.

I must admit that for a moment after reading that introduction I had the uncomfortable thought I should have topped my noggin with a hair piece, preferably of bear hide. But the Phillips story advanced an idea. Why not, for instance, expand some of those stories into a full chapter?

Why not indeed?

The Adirondack region, all six million acres of it, is one vast fountainhead of stories, numbering in the thousands; people stories, animal stories, some of tragedy, some of outlandish humor; many of historical significance. All together, a most bewildering array of ammunition for a writer and awesome to anyone who attempts to organize and select.

One absorbs much in traveling through the mountains over a period of many years, and in talking to residents, conservation officers, rangers, politicians, seasonal visitors, hunters and fishermen and other observers of the rugged scene.

Let's take just the mountains and animal life for this chapter. But first the scene must be set and to do that consider what I hold to be a comparatively new version of the origin of the Adirondacks.

Tranquility and beauty can be found within the area. But the mountains are not geologically passive. They are rising. The growth at the "dome," or crest, a few miles from Lake Placid, and including the High Peak region, is three millimeters a year, or approximately one-and-one- quarter inches every decade. The actual crest might be considered in the MacIntyre Range.

Now that's not enough of a heave to shake you off your feet if you're scrambling up Mt. Marcy, but is enough to astonish, particularly in view of the fact that the Dome Center is rising three times as fast as the Swiss Alps. How high the peaks will eventually reach in ages to come cannot be forecast. Nobody, as yet, has mastered the art of measuring the longevity of the enormous, incalculable pressures beneath this specific Northeastern section of the United States.

That there are pressures is not to be denied; an uneasy crust has produced minor earthquakes; even the Lake George area has felt their impacts. And the Blue Mt. Lake area is most assuredly not immune. Instruments to measure internal shocks were placed in the vicinity of the Adirondack Museum several years ago.

Are the mountains themselves young? An interesting question. Once upon a time the Adirondacks were referred to as the "oldest mountains in the world." That's partly correct, partly wrong.

Dr. Donald W. Fisher, Dr. Yngvar W. Isachsen and Dr. Philip R. Whitney, members of the New York State Geological Survey, State Education Department, say that the mentioned uplift, "plus the general radial drainage pattern, suggests that the present Adirondack Mountains are geologically very young, perhaps as little as five million years old."

That pertains to the mountains themselves. But the rock variety in them goes back a billion or more years, some of them born in a hell's fire far below, surpassing anything conjured by Dante.

1

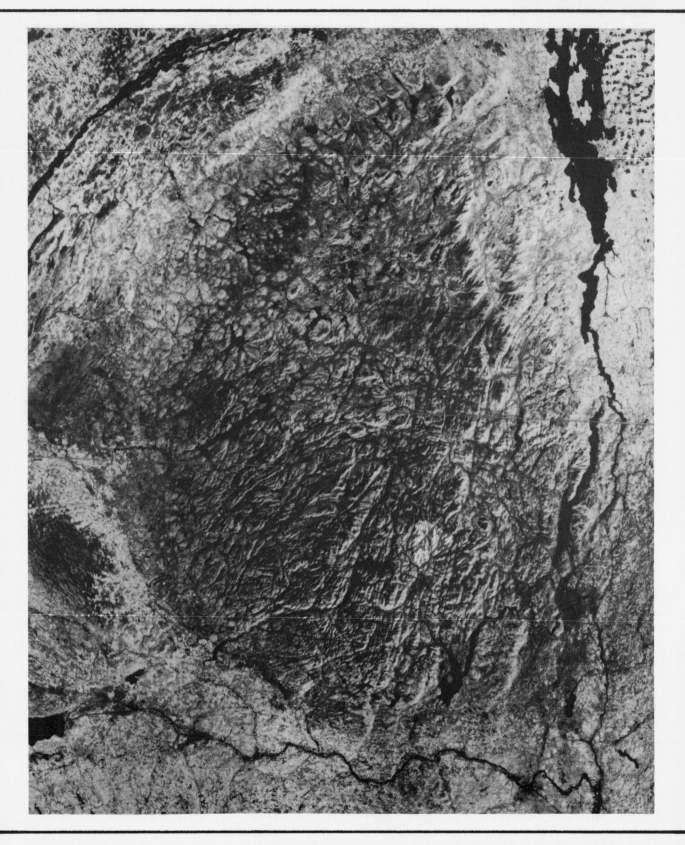

This U.S. government photo is remarkable in that it portrays in mosaic fashion the entire Adirondack Mountain region. Water appears black and the large body at top right is Lake Champlain. South of this lake is Lake George, and southwest of Lake George is the Sacandaga Reservoir.

The river at bottom of photo is the Mohawk and the lake to the lower left is Oneida Lake, part of the Erie Division of the Barge Canal. The junction of the Mohawk and Hudson is at lower right. The river at top left is the St. Lawrence. Slightly right, upper center, would mark the dome or crest area of the growing Adirondacks.

It should be noted at this point there is one basic aspect of Nature. She has no sense of hurry. If she ran a production line of something other than rabbits and field mice, she'd bankrupt her firm. But she's not. In this case, she is building peaks. Egyptian pharoahs and their pyramids were novices by comparison.

Five million years ago the mountain area was comparatively flat. It was covered with a shallow, warm water sea. This enormous water area withdrew, then returned some fifty million years later. Fossil forms prove the existence of these liquid blankets. The seas retreated as the land mass began to grow upward and the power that thrust up buried strata of rock is attributed to "hot spots" deep beneath.

These spots have muscle, plenty of it, and the muscle still is being used. Thus rock, which ordinarily would have remained far down in the earth's crust, was lifted and exposed. Some of that rock is of igneous origin, born of unbelievable heat. Granite, for instance. Anorthosite is another. Gneiss is still another; this rock is a metamorphic one.

One might think, if seas once covered the region, fossil forms would be plentiful. Not so. Such evidence of life is found in what is called sedimentary rock, such as limestone or sandstone.

Not too much of this type of rock is found because while once it did exist, and possibly capped mountains, vast glaciers ripped it to shreds and kidnapped it to parts unknown. But the glaciers missed some spots. These are called outliers. Original fossil forms exist therein.

One such outlier is in the Wells area of Hamilton County. Another can be seen by the motorist driving in the Chestertown section of the Northway; it is an outcropping between the south and northbound lanes. This is a mixture of limestone and dolostone. But outliers remain limited in number.

No prehistoric footprints of any dinosaur have been found along with fossil forms in the mountains, al-

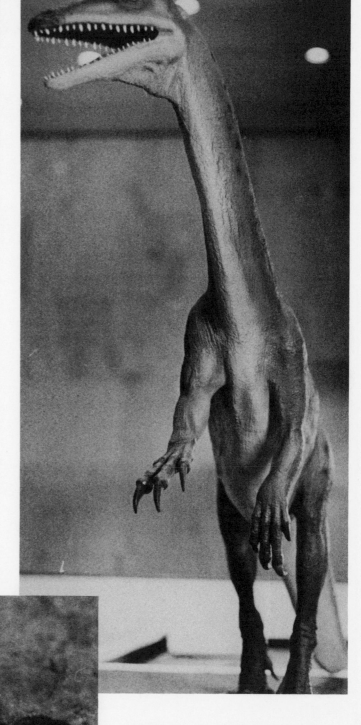

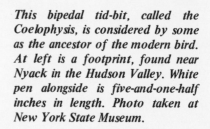

This bipedal tid-bit, called the Coelophysis, is considered by some as the ancestor of the modern bird. At left is a footprint, found near Nyack in the Hudson Valley. White pen alongside is five-and-one-half inches in length. Photo taken at New York State Museum.

3

though there is the possibility that a creature known as Coelophysis might have been one of the tail dragging dinosaurs which roamed the region.

Coelophysis is interesting, and the New York State Museum reproduced one in form and size and displayed it for several months in the museum lobby where boggle-eyed youngsters and adults could marvel at a part of the state's past.

The creature was a meat eating bipedal dinosaur and thus far it is the only dinosaur which has left its mark in New York State. Footprints of this 100-120 pound predator were found in the Nyack region along Hudson's River, solidified in ancient rock. The beast is believed to have prowled the Northeast 200 million years ago.

It was hollow-boned, as are all flying birds, and some paleontologists believe coelosaurian dinosaurs may have been the ancestors of our feathered friends of today, which would include everything from the ubiquitious chicadee to the eagle, turkey buzzard, raven and headache-immune woodpecker.

One artistic version of a mastodon, different from that which appears on the next page. This could very well be a picturization of a mammoth as well because of its tusk structure. The mammoth, as well as the mastodon, once roamed the Adirondack region, where remains have been found.

Is the modern bird, such as this small nuthatch, also called a nutbreaker, nutjobber and nutpecker, a descendant of coelosaurian dinosaurs? Some paleontologists believe it might be true. The 'hatch is noted for its ability to break and eat hazelnuts, but also is an insect consumer.

As a matter of fact, there are paleontologists who consider modern birds the "dinosaurs" of today! All of which means not one whit to such an organization as the High Peaks Audubon Society; birds are birds, no matter what the evolutionary form, and deserve to be studied, protected and encouraged.

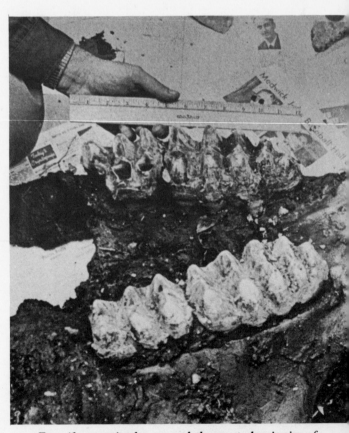

Few, if any animal surpassed the mastodon in size of teeth. The molars, shown above, run a foot in length!

You're looking at a reconstruction of probably the most famous behemoth in New York State, the Cohoes Mastodon, remains of which were found in September, 1866, during construction of the Harmony Mills at Cohoes. Remains of this big tusker probably floated down the ancient Iro-Mohawk, and the carcass snagged in a giant pothole. For scores of years it was a favorite exhibit in the old State Museum; is now in the Human Resources Center, Cohoes, Canvass and Mohawk Streets, to which place it was transported in sections. It is a familiar relic to millions.

While no such reptilian evidence as Coelophysis has been found in the North County, more luck was had by those who have searched for mammalian evidence. It is known mastodons once roamed the region, probably 20,000 or so years ago.

It is believed the giant mammoth did the same; one leg bone of this behemoth of long gone days was reportedly excavated in southern Warren County.

Musk ox evidence has been uncovered in Jefferson County. Prehistoric elk remains have been discovered in Clinton County. In that same county once lived the seal, and the lively presence of this adept swimmer would not be unusual. At the end of the Ice Age salt water moved from the Atlantic into what was called the "Champlain Sea," and with the salt water came varieties of life living within it.

While caribou probably existed in the Northeast along with the bison and the horse, remains of these species have been found farther south. Caribou remains were found in Schenectady County; bison in Albany County, and evidence of the prehistoric horse was uncovered along the border of Albany and Greene Counties. The horse of this age was not the small, almost dog-like creature often portrayed as the ultimate ancestor, but the size of the animal today.

One might presume, and this is presumption only, that the giant beaver, six feet long from nose to tail's end, also chomped his way into oblivion.

A large area such as this, heavily forested, populated with a wide variety of animal life, was bound to produce unusual wildlife stories, particularly during the past century-and-one-half, when tourists, hunters, fishermen, lumbermen and the gentry of high finance and little ecological consideration began to invade.

The reading mood will, I am sure, change with the presentation of some of these.

In the sprawling Cranberry Lake area in the Northwestern portion of the Adirondacks, west of Tupper Lake, through which flows the famous Oswegatchie River, a resident was awakened one 2 a.m. by the noise of his grindstone being turned in his yard. Tossing a beam of lantern light into the blackness, he promptly squinted with surprise.

Before him were beaver. One was turning the wheel. One was sharpening his teeth. And behind him, lined up patiently awaiting their turn, were a dozen others!

That one I won't vouch for. Sounds too much like the old gentleman who lived along the Cedar River during the 1800's, and who would feed trout off his dock daily. Eventually the fish got accustomed to the free menu, and became quite tame. So tame that when the old man was hungry, he could reach down gently, tickle their bellies, thus throwing them into a happy stupor and eventually tossing them into a frying pan.

I think other stories are on more solid ground.

Some years back, a hunter out for bear and armed with a Winchester 30-30, parked his car alongside Route 73 in the Keene Valley section, and tramped sturdily and hopefully into the wilderness where, after a day of

Once again the magic of Walter Schoonmaker's artistic hand is seen in the above sketch of a bear, an animal much involved in tales of the North Country.

back-breaking bush whacking, he neither found nor heard anything save the cheerful twittering of birds. He returned with sadness, his weapon unfired, his manhood manifest but untested.

But he did find, to his consternation, that he had left the door on the driver's side of his car slighly ajar. And a bear had accepted the preferred hospitality, had entered and was sound asleep behind the wheel!

The hunter, possessed of no desire to shoot the bear and spatter blood, called conservation department personnel. At this point he found one of the difficulties of life was trying to explain two things, 1, that he was sober, and 2, how a bear managed to get behind his wheel.

The problem was solved by the animal, which snored itself awake and departed. My own opinion is that the hunter was lucky he hadn't left keys in the ignition. Keene Valley valley residents, who have seen unusual sights, might not have believed that one!

The bear is an animal well adapted to stories, some a bit on the wild side. Known is that in early days they were trapped because of suspected damage to livestock. They were also trapped for hides and food. Known also is that many a trapper had frightening experiences with a bruin with a foot held in iron jaws. Friendliness does not sprout easily in such situations. Pound for pound, I was once told, the Adirondack black bear is the strongest animal on the North American continent.

The fact that one once crushed the skull of a horse on a farm in northern Franklin County is proof enough of the strength in its blows.

Stories about them show wide variety. About two years ago, Paws, the German Shepherd trained at the New York State Police Academy in Albany for use by the Department of Environmental Conservation in sniffing out illegal venison, was with his handler, Conservation Officer Richard Matzell of Colton, St. Lawrence County, and Lt. Larry Kring. Paws had been transported to the town dump at Cranberry Lake for a reason: The bear season was about to begin and some "hunters" choose dumps where bears come to feed for a head start on anticipated rugs. Shooting before a season begins is frowned upon mightily by The Law.

A parked car was spotted. No driver. Paws, sniffing dutifully, brought Matzell and Kring to a specific spot in a heap of garbage. The top of a hat was seen. So was the muzzle of a rifle. Buried in the ripeness was a gallant "hunter" who at first refused commands to come forth and be seen.

Conservation Officer Richard Matzell, with EnCon's German Shepherd, Paws, trained, among many things, to sniff out illegal venison and in tracking poachers.

That reluctance was speedily rectified; Paws was put on the "alert," and growled. The confined gentleman changed his mind and, dripping garbage and dispensing several varieties of malodorous scents, came topside and was ordered forthwith before a town justice. He drove his own car, followed by the officers, which was understandable. He learned his fate. A fine.

The Tale of the Drunken Bear is worth repeating. A big bruin broke into a farmer's pig pen up Malone way and the porkers therein scooted thereout, leaving the big visitor busy at the food trough. The irate farmer barricaded the pen, called for official action, but before conservation officers arrived, a couple hunters wandered by.

Both were apparently well supplied with an unknown but potent brand of whiskey or bourbon and the brand proved its power when poured into the mixture in the trough. The bear got crocked. Had it blown into a Breathalyzer, that interesting device would have shattered. And when officers arrived, the bartenders were gone and the bear was seated on its haunches, rocking back and forth, with tears streaming from its eyes. On

Trap above, from the Adirondack Museum collection, was used for bear; in 1953 one was found, still set, on Prospect Mt. at Lake George, where it probably had lain for more than a half century. Below is another variety – a man trap – used in England when knights were bold, and poachers killed deer on private preserves. Note claws!

Life had its frightening moments for early trappers, particularly when a bruin got its dander up to protest entrapment. No photographs exist to show what such a confrontation between trapper and bear might have looked like, but my friend, the late Walter J. Schoonmaker, zoologist, photographer and artist, put his own impression in charcoal. (Note photos of both bear and man traps in this chapter.)

occasion there was a soft groan. The bear had, for the first time in its life, tasted civilization.

The ending to this story? The CO's took one look and decided to draw the straws of death. Neither had the heart to perform the inevitable shooting, but the deed had to be done. It was.

There can be a different kind of sadness to an animal story. Deer can, and have, broken through thin ice and drowned while within sight of solid ground. I have seen herons whose necks have been caught in the crotch of trees, where they dangled, strangled. I have seen "hung" deer on fences, barriers which snagged them in mid leap, where they remained helpless until slow death took over. And I have seen a homesick bear which was killed when less than 100 miles from the home to which it sought return.

Many times in public campsite areas, "nuisance" bears are tranquilized by EnCon personnel and transported into another region, such as from the Adiron-

dacks into the Catskills. At the Lewey Lake campsite between Speculator and Indian Lake, a female was trapped and moved to the Windham area in Greene County, south of Albany.

This sow possessed an uncanny homing instinct, however; determined to hike to more familiar surroundings and thus began a long, oft interrupted journey, during which time she reportedly swam across Hudson's River twice before reaching the Northway. Nobody knows why she crossed the river.

But she finally made it into the Town of Colonie. That town was her own Little Big Horn, her last stand. She was shot. At least the end was mercifully fast. She wasn't crippled by a car, as some have been, only to die with slowness and pain.

While many hunters — most of them, actually — prefer the more edible whitetail deer to bear, some will kill the bruins for no reason at all. In one grisly incident, a bear was killed, transported to the Albany area, and dumped into a phone booth.

Hunting bear can produce more than a rug. Robert A. Geandreau of Indian Lake, who operates Geandreau's cabins, found that out when he shot a bruin. Embedded in a shoulder blade was a three-bladed, razor-sharp broadhead of the type used on hunting arrows. In other photo, a close-up of point of impact shows how bone grew around and through arrowhead. The bear shot by Geandreau may have carried this bit of toxophilitic "shrapnel" for as long as two years and lived in normal fashion!

This unusual 42-point buck was mentioned in a report shortly around the turn of the century, only a few years after the Forest Preserve became reality. It was killed in Franklin County, and to the best of knowledge, no buck since has displayed such an unusual rack. The whereabouts of the mounting — if it still exists — is unknown. It may have been destroyed by fire. Points were distributed in this fashion: Twenty on one rack, twenty-two on the other.

Deer hunting offers its own special yarns. The Catskills, earlier settled than the Adirondacks, were shot free of deer. North Country whitetails were trapped around the turn of the century, sent southward to start a new herd. The effort obviously proved successful and in many cases the size and weight of southern zone deer are greater than their northern cousins. Much of this, of course, is based upon food and food value.

However, I doubt if any modern deer hunter, anywhere in the state, ever obtained the trophy killed near Paul Smith's in Franklin County around 1900. This astonishing prize was a forty-two pointer, that is, there were forty-two prongs or "points" on its antlers!

I have tried to track down this mounting, but the effort has not been successful. At one time I heard this novel head had been displayed in a North Country hotel for many years, but was destroyed along with the hotel when fire registered as an unwelcome guest. The name of the hunter remains unknown.

Not all hunters are so fortunate in gaining trophies. One gentleman in the Bloomingdale area near Saranac Lake, shot a prime buck (a designation of a male deer which eventually became a monetary trade mark) and, since it possessed an excellent rack, decided he'd include himself in a photo.

He arranged the deer in suitable pose, then placed his spanking new and expensive rifle across its antlers. He

10

then walked to his camera to set the self timer, a device which delays release of the instrument's shutter for several seconds, thus allowing the camera owner to enter the scene for posterity to behold.

While setting the timer, he was startled by a snort. It was the "dead" deer heaving itself into running position. And run the whitetail did — far, far into the woods, with the rifle still held securely in its antlers!

Poaching, or illegal killing, is not uncommon. Sometimes even a gentleman of the medical profession will make an attempt. A physician from downstate, roaming the Long Lake forest area of Hamilton County, killed a doe, which was decidedly illegal. As a surgeon he figured he could repair the dismal situation neatly by creating a buck.

He obtained a set of spike horns (single growths about six inches long, both of which were embedded in a portion of a male skull) and with operating room technique did what one might call a cranial transplant. He inserted the spikes into the doe's head, carefully stitching the hide to avoid all trace of having removed part of the doe's skull for insertion of the buck's.

The venison chops for which he so mightily yearned never materialized, because conservation personnel, attempting to lift the gutted-out carcass by the horns at a checking station, found the transplant moved. Never having come across a deer whose head possessed a lid, they investigated further. Appropriate legal action followed. EnCon, I gather, considered this a form of wildlife malpractice.

I once did a night patrol with two officers east of Schroon Lake. We stationed ourselves about three miles in from the highway, leaving our car sufficiently distant from the trail's head so it would not be discovered. Our lookout point was near a pond and swamp where deer jackers were known to enjoy their trade.

About 2 a.m. a powerful beam of light suddenly illuminated a deer standing in shallow water. A shot followed. The deer collapsed. The light was extinguished.

My party cut back to the highway where the trail to the swamp began, and we did it without lights; how, I still can't quite figure. There we found a parked car. There we waited for at least three hours. And there we heard, finally, a group approaching.

Twenty feet from the car the officers shed light on the scene. One of the men had a carcass slung over his shoulders. Two others in the group were also bloodied from assisting in dressing out the animal.

With an oath of disgust, the gentleman carrying the carcass tossed it to the ground. Group members were arrested.

Later I asked Dwinal Kerste, one of the officers, why the arrest wasn't made at the scene of the killing. His answer made sense.

"In that case," he replied, "we probably would have had to carry out the evidence!"

While deer stories are numerous, moose yarns are not; this huge member of the deer family was shot out of existence, and restocking attempts have failed. The killing of these animals was relentless. Even failing numbers didn't stop the slaughter.

Two were killed in 1851 by John Constable, a "well known sportsman," near Independence Creek, Herkimer County, and a year later he shot one west of Charley Pond. That same season Alonzo Wood and Edward

How did the monetary term "buck" originate? It goes back into the early period of the fur trade. When trappers brought pelts to a trader he gave them shiny brass tokens with the figure of a male deer, or buck, in bas relief, of the type seen above left. These could be redeemed for needed goods such as blankets, guns or ammunition. The buck token was the size of the silver dollar and, at times, both could be used as chips in gambling; thus buck and dollar became interchangeable. Tokens were widely used in the old West as poker chips. (Buck token pictured is from collection of Mayor Erastus Corning, 2nd, Albany.)

Arnold shot two in the Seventh Lake area of Hamilton County. In 1855 the last moose captured alive was taken by Charles L. Phelps, who killed a cow in Brown's Tract and brought her calf out of the woods with him. Within a year it was dead.

Gov. Horatio Seymour was thought to have killed the last Adirondack moose, but not so. He did shoot a bull in 1859, not far from West Canada Creek in Herkimer County, but in 1860 Alva Dunning, a guide, killed several on West Canada Creek. The last family of these animals was destroyed at Raquette Lake in 1861, and, from all accounts, the last single remnant of this species was shot along the Marion River by a man named Palmer, a guide who was shepherding a group of sportsmen in canoes. Several of the group discharged their rifles; all missed. Palmer thus gained the "honor" of killing the last known native of the mountains. It was a cow.

Efforts to restock by private park owners, notably Edward H. Litchfield, failed. If these giants are seen today, they are wanderers, and are protected. The last known of these was killed in the Broadalbin area about two years ago. It was a bull. The law against shooting the animals has been strengthened considerably since.

The fine art of fishing has produced a horde of yarns.

Up Lake George way one day, two conservation officers on boat patrol in The Narrows, saw in the distance what appeared to be "hippy" types on the shore of an island. They also saw a big "red-headed son-of-a-gun," perched on a rock, fishing. A most curious sight. They moved their craft nearer.

What they saw was hard to digest.

Squatting on a rock, with fish pole in hand, was an orangutan, an anthropoid ape, which in structure

Lake George fisherman

resembles Man. Such a creature can grow to five feet and may run 150-200 pounds in its stocking feet. This one had no stockings, however, but it did wear shorts, bright red shorts. And it was not only "red-headed," but possessed a fine growth of reddish hair over its body.

Lake George is hardly the spot for an ape usually more at home in Borneo or Sumatra or a zoo. The animal is not listed in any book of wildlife as an avid fisherman, or should the term be fisherape?

But that's what this big one was doing. The hook was baited by the men on shore, later found to be its owners. The bait was lowered into the lake and when a nibble was noted, the simian jerked the line upward and backward. The men then removed the fish from the hook, cleaned, scaled it and tossed it into a frying pan.

The officer who told me this story upon his retirement did not file an official report.

"Why not?" I inquired innocently. He replied:

"Who the hell would believe it?"

I'll believe. The orangutan has an IQ of a child of six.

In talking of real fishermen, and good ones, one must consider Peter Dubuc, whom I interviewed in Albany several years ago. He caught the world record northern pike out of the Sacandaga Reservoir in 1940 in the Batchlerville area. The monster weighed in at forty-six pounds, two ounces. Mr. Dubuc told me he caught the trophy from shore and, not having a net, scrambled into the water after having brought it almost to his feet.

I asked him if he had any photos. He had none. I told him I had a camera, would like to photograph what the taxidermist had wrought. He told me the fish had not been mounted. With growing dismay I asked him what he had done with the world's record northern. His answer:

"I ate it."

(Incidentally, I'm still trying to find the mounting, if one was made, of the state record muskellunge caught by Arthur Lawton of the Albany area in 1957 in the St. Lawrence River. That fish ran sixty-nine pounds, fifteen ounces! Hopefully it was not also consumed).

In the realm of the unusual, you have heard of the famous Lake Champlain monster, which several say they have sighted but not photographed as it traveled its undulating way hither and yon in this 110-mile-long lake. There may indeed be basis for the existence of an actual something, although it may not be all monster.

It could have been a sturgeon; these fish once were not uncommon to Champlain. And Samuel Champlain, the armor-plated gentleman who was the first white man to see that lake, did mention a huge fish, calling it "a great long monster, lying in the lake, allowing birds to land on its beak, then snapping them in whole."

What Champlain probably saw was a garpike.

The Champlain monster may have grown from Indian legend.

Paintings created by a member of the Iroquois Confederacy show a giant serpent in a lake. In one picture an Indian girl rides twixt its steer-like horns.

This is a photographic reproduction of a watercolor painted by the late Ernie Smith, a Seneca, and probably represents a legend of the past in Iroquoian culture – or, possibly, the force of good and evil. If it did represent a legend, could that legend have persisted for hundreds of years and possibly have started the story of the Lake Champlain monster called "Champy" by moderns? The painting above was one of many displayed at the New York State Museum. It is owned by the Rochester Museum.

But one cannot discount comparatively modern sightings. A former editor of Vermont Life Magazine, for instance, said he and his wife spotted an eel-like creature in 1962 swimming north of Burlington, Vt. which, he said, "defies any explanation I can think of."

A University of Vermont professor of zoology a few years ago reportedly was unwilling to flatly deny the existence of the creature which, on occasion, was described as "snake-like, twenty to thirty feet in length."

History itself furnishes more reports. One has it that the fish, reptile or whatever was sighted by early residents of Port Henry in 1819, and it is to be emphasized the sighting did not follow a corn husking bee or a barn raising!

The Lake George monster, called George, was of a different kind. He was made by man, was used in a practical joke. The story goes that George was manipu-

lated by ropes and pulleys from shore and on one occasion he popped out of the lake alongside a rowboat containing a young man and his starry-eyed bride who had, up to that point, enjoyed the tranquility and acrobatics of a honeymoon.

Upon the frightful appearance of the apparition, the man shed his knightly veneer and dived overboard, leaving his bride chattering. I do not know how long the marriage endured. I do know George remains revered, and has been loaned as an exhibit to the Lake George Association where, last I saw, it adorned that organization's office, staring at the world which once it convulsed.

(The rope-pulley arrangement apparently is not too unusual. Victor Talbott of Earlton, Greene County, tells me that Silver Lake in Wyoming County, was the scene of a "serpent" which appeared, terrorized, then dis-

Glens Falls photographer Walter Grishkot snapped George, the Lake George "monster" at just the right moment for a moment of drama. This weird creation, manipulated by ropes and pulleys from shore, scared the wits out of scores of vacationists before the hoax was disclosed. George stands above five feet high — or did, in his prime — was painted in bright colors, and possessed glass power insulators for eyes!

appeared. **Later he learned that when a shorefront hotel was demolished, an air pump, valves and a pipe which went into the lake, were found. These fed the "serpent," which was constructed of inflatable rubber).**

Methods of fishing, and not for monsters, show ingenuity. One scuba diver lowered himself into a trout pool with rod and line and fished at his pleasure, ten to fifteen feet below the surface. A puzzled conservation officer questioned the legality of such procedure, but upon inquiring of a superior was told to make no arrest. The superior later told me:

"On what basis? The guy had a rod and reel, was licensed to angle, and that's what he was doing. What the hell could we do, charge him with — fishing underwater?"

Scuba divers do not always meet up with fish, nor ancient relics of an Adirondack past. One, stroking his

way toward his boat in Lake George, collided with a swimming timber rattlesnake. No injuries were reported. Both parties, however, registered increased blood pressure.

The captain of a Lake George cruise boat told me several years ago that during periods of drought rattlers swimming in The Narrows near the Tongue Mountain Ranges were not unusual to see. The reptiles moved from the talus slopes downward, following such prey as thirsty mice. One Schenectady camper spotted three rattlers on an island occupied by himself and his family. They broke camp in record time.

Fishing tales are in such number it is difficult to be representative. In the Cambridge area of Washington County, an otter went on a rampage, practically wiped out a trout population in a hatchery. At the Warrensburg, State Hatchery, the late manager, Erwin Annis, told

14

me he had problems with water snakes, which would rest along the edges of a pool containing fry (small fish) and the reptiles would entice the little ones by flicking their tongues. When near enough, it was curtains for the curious trout.

Kingfishers also were a pest at Warrensburg; these birds are not particular in observance of New York State laws.

For that matter, neither is the snapping turtle, the bald eagle or the gull. I once saw and heard a screaming eagle dive bomb a gull carrying a fish it had caught or found in Lake George. The gull dropped the tid-bit and the eagle, with extraordinary ease plucked it in mid-air with its talons, flying then to a tree on the East side.

The East side of Lake George long has been noted for a hawk flyway. All this, of course, before DDT got busy and cut into the number of these magnificent national symbols. With DDT outlawed, and with "wilderness areas" designated in the Adirondacks, where no machine of any kind is allowed, where primitiveness may return, so may these wonderful birds. Let us hope. Indeed, let us pray.

A noted and incredibly wrinkled Isaac Walton is the snapping turtle. Its strike is lightning fast, and it doesn't always concentrate on fish.

I watched one huge turtle in the Sacandaga Reservoir drag down a mature mallard. Moving my canoe over the spot I saw the reptile, six feet down, tearing the duck to pieces. The kill was an ugly sight. Nature in the raw, but no more ugly than watching a northern pike snap a duckling into oblivion while a desperate mother herds the rest of her tiny paddlers away from the scene.

There remains, in retrospect, one of the most unusual stories of what constitutes a creel. Conservation officers spotted a mixed group on the West side of Lake George and there was suspicion members were fishing for bass out of season.

A "visit" was paid the group. No fish were seen. But the officers did watch, with total fascination, the bosom of one of the ladies in the party; that portion of her anatomy heaved and twitched in astonishing fashion. Since The Law frowns upon a male officer searching any female suspect, a matron was called to do the frisk.

She found the lady with the nervous bosom was using her bra as a creel; the somewhat spacious cups contained several small but lively bass!

And lastly: Not all who seek fish come across what they expect. A man named Sampson Paul, who lived at Lake George many a moon ago, took to his boat to spear a meal. He returned with a panther, which he impaled as it swam the lake.

And so the yarns go. In the mountains' earlier years when tourists began to move in, there were plenty of fish to talk about and catch. Old hotel registers often bear notations of guests having caught a hundred or more brook trout in a day's efforts.

Ted Aber, a historian of note in the Indian Lake section, had this item in his column, "The Way Things Were," published in the Hamilton County News:

"The fishermen were out. On Sunday, Jan. 6, 1901, George Burton of Lake Pleasant and his young son, Wilbur, went fishing for pickerel at Indian Lake. They landed 893 pounds in nine hours, the largest fish weighing 28 pounds, six ounces. It was said to have been the greatest catch made there in a long length of time."

In days even before the above, supplying "the market" could be done — and was — by dynamiting ponds and lakes. Other times "suppliers" would compete with the otter, mink, fisher, snapping turtles and loons and fish hawks such as the osprey by netting.

Those days, like the ones where "sportsmen" would drive a frantic, dog-chased deer into a lake and kill it from a boat by clubbing it to death, have gone. Today some of the best fishing lakes in the North Country at elevations from 1,500 feet and above, are barren from acid rains and that situation is growing more crucial by the year; well over 200 spots are now dead.

The procedure of killing game today also is far different from that of days long past when settlers began to move into Adirondack areas such as Washington County. For instance, killing deer today is known euphemistically as "harvesting." There are strict laws to observe. There are licenses to obtain. Survival of Man in the wilderness is no longer the question. Survival of wildlife is.

I give you an example of a type of hunt in the 1800's:

It could have been termed the Circle of Death, and was used by Washington County farmers to exterminate timber wolves and any other predator which preyed upon livestock. This method of eradication was unknowingly patterned after the same type of deadly envelopment perfected by the Asiatic conqueror, Ghengis Khan, when that worthy found his hordes idle and in need of action, food and fun.

Essentially the Khan formed his scores of thousands of mounted troops into a giant circle with a diameter of miles. As it gradually closed inward, animals within became more concentrated until at times they were literally massed. And then the savage, pitiless destruction began. Thousands of animals were slaughtered.

The Washington County settlers moved with equal precision but on a vastly smaller scale. Obviously the maneuver proved successful, since few predators escaped, and such hunts were periodically staged. And, one might imagine, not only predators were killed. The whitetails must have suffered as well.

Thus another phase of life vanished with the times. But while such times may disappear, the plentiful yarns live on and will for generations to come, embellished, I am sure, to the extent where some of them may even become unrecognizable!

THE PHENOMENAL FLOATING ISLANDS OF HIGLEY FLOW

**Thousands of Tons of Floating Islands
Plagued Not Only Campers But
the Power Company Until They
Were Sliced and Hurled Into
Watery Oblivion**

First reports weren't believed. Which was understandable; there was no precedent. The Adirondacks had never seen anything quite like it.

A tousled haired, pajama-clad camper at Higley Flow, groggy from more than jousting with abundant sleep, arose, blinked in disbelief as he gazed through his window. The day before his dock was a structure surrounded on three sides by water.

That day it rested on what appeared to be an acre of solid earth, landscaped by Nature with deadened grasses and shrubs. Red-winged blackbirds trilled from several trees. The mass undulated like an electrically driven therapeutic bed. The stench of rotting vegetation corrupted the air.

A day later the mass floated away, a tangible Flying Dutchman of plant growth shifted into gear by high winds and current.

This was in 1914.

A year later the waters of Higley Flow swirled, emitted a gargantuan belch and another acre rose sluggishly into view.

The phenomenon continued for almost thirty years. Where once there was open water, land masses suddenly were born. The Pandora's Box seemed inexhaustible in content. The explanation was a simple one, once head scratching evolved into academic analysis.

Higley Flow was turning topsy turvy! A portion of the bottom was rising to the top!

In some cases the islands, born in the depths, crested in sizeable chunks. In other instances literally acres struggled to the surface, hoving into view in sections like some giant scuttled barge whose belly had become filled with air.

The domain known as Higley Flow is a man-made reservoir, created in 1912 when a hydro-electric power plant was constructed on the Raquette River, thus creating Higley Falls. The dam also created the upstream area known as The Flow, a spot which eventually became a favorite recreational area.

Camps and summer homes bloomed along the shores. Once free of their murky womb, the floating islands presented unusual problems. They were as unwanted as

16

next year's tax bills. In some instances, boats were literally landlocked at docks until the islands released their firm clutch and shifted. Campers found little comfort in the masses and the power company, Central New York Power, now part of Niagara Mohawk Power Corporation, found even less happiness; pieces of the islands on occasion broke loose and, carried by the winds and current toward the gulping mouth of the power plant's intake, plugged that aperture as effectively as a truck load of sodden rags. The intake found the mass indigestible and the man hours spent in cleaning the tunnel zoomed.

Over a period of years, while the islands floated willy-nilly, trees took root, and grew. Some went skyward high enough to serve as sails. Thus islands became rafts without rudders save the winds. Periodically the power company sent crews to trim the trees down to size. But the winds still whistled shrilly through the growth and the islands still moved in erratic fashion.

The problem literally got its beginning untold centuries ago when a huge swamp developed along the borders of the channel of the Raquette. Perhaps at one time the swamp was an adjoining pond or a small lake, entered and fed by the river; a body of water which over intervening centuries became the victim of a geriatrical process known as eutrophication, the filling in and throttling of a body of water by vegetation. Thus a swamp is born where waters once flowed with freedom. The Adirondacks are sprinkled with such bogs.

It is known that the swamp did indeed exist, and when the waters of Higley Flow backed up because of the new dam, the swamp became covered.

Nature did not take this scheduled dunking without striking back. She knew she had the makings of a problem which would perplex and frustrate many.

Physically, before the waters of The Flow covered the area, the swamp appeared as any other. But the thick mat of dead and living plant life, which included not only grasses but shrubbery and trees, had no solid anchoring base; the swamp rested upon a bed of loose glacial sand so lacking in texture and nutrients that root growth was unable to remain stable, exist and grab.

What is described as a "tender" of the Niagara Mohawk "Navy" is seen on its way toward the swampy "mother ship," an island cruising the waters of Higley Flow. Sections of this island averaged six feet in thickness. Others went deeper.

Gripping the sand was like clutching a ball of warm grease; nothing save gravity held the bog's growth to the sand below. The swamp, in effect, was a frosting to a cake; the tangled mass was nothing more than a huge, thick carpet, as much as fifteen feet thick in spots, resting on unresisting, uncaring sand.

Thus when the reservoir waters backed up, the swamp mass reacted in normal fashion; lighter than water, it began to rise slowly from its ancient bed. And in rising, it split into floating islands. One could duplicate the process in miniature by placing a sponge in a pan of water, then filling the pan completely.

Higley Flow, eight miles south of Potsdam in St. Lawrence County, thus became an astonishing novelty in the North Country. Also it became a dinosaur-sized headache to many.

Disposal of some of the islands, which continued to pop up like midget Loch Ness monsters at unexpected intervals, was an easy task; they were merely towed or pushed by boat into the current on quiet days and sent over the dam into a splintered, ruptured future. But there were several too large to handle in this fashion.

One, considered the last of many to appear, ran about 600 by 800 feet in size, which meant a surface area of 480,000 square feet, or eleven acres. Its estimated weight was 172,000 pounds, or eighty-six tons! This magnificent monster ran fifteen feet in thickness at its deepest portion. And it remained afloat for several years.

It was on this island that botanically minded observers learned of a curious fact, that the mass was covered with pitcher plants, considered the only carnivorous plants which grow that far north. Pitcher plants snare and eat bugs.

Records show the power company tried many ways of ridding The Flow of the larger nuisances. The company found (and this was in the day before such unecological procedures were frowned upon) that they would not burn, even when soaked in oil or gasoline. They were also too stubborn to be sunk. They couldn't be weighted with heavy rocks; the boulders would slowly sink through the confusing mass. Dynamite had no effect; the explosive force was easily absorbed and dissipated into a million tiny labyrinths. A blast merely frightened fish.

Eventually through the years, an interesting struggle developed between the power company and campers. A series of stone-filled crib piers was built across the mouth of what is known as the bay area, and a heavy log chain was strung from crib to crib. This kept the islands in the bay, but that is exactly where campers didn't want them. The latter had little sympathy with Lost Worlds suddenly appearing at their lakeshore doorsteps.

What has been somewhat delicately described as a "duel" came into existence; the chain would be cut at night and power company crews would repair the linkage during the day. And meanwhile another portion

The map above shows the general plan of operations in the assault upon the floating islands. Islands were sawed into sections; these were pushed by boat into the Raquette River channel of The Flow. The next step was destruction over the dam.

of the islands would break off and float languidly, inexorably away, and once again throttle the plant's overworked gullet.

The company found in the 1940's that campers had decided themselves upon the ultimate solution. This was not to cut the chain only to see it replaced, but to steal the whole thing. This was done one gloomy night. It has never been found.

Big Business, in warfare with Recreational Forces, had to find another solution.

It did.

Executive sessions were held; ideas advanced; strategies perfected. The eventual solution came from pooling ideas from outsiders with ideas of the men who had been in charge of most of the work of keeping the islands corraled. This included Elmer Fadden and also Fred "Big Moose" Gabbert of the St. Lawrence area maintenance crews, as well as Bob Powell, operating superintendent, and Walter Fielder, then central division hydraulic engineer, whose academic background, I am sure, never included a course on how to assault floating islands.

Trying to pull the islands apart didn't work either. They were as tightly entangled as fishlines in streamside brush, as lovers who faced separation. It was a brain cracker until somebody came up with the idea of cutting the islands into sections while they were Winter frozen. In this way, it was felt, they could be sliced neatly into sections and sent into oblivion over the dam.

Charles E. Waggamen, a Glens Falls contractor, had been called into consulations. He got the job. I contacted Mr. Waggaman at the time of this writing; found him to be in Florida. I also found his recollections vivid about the project. His first thought, if the islands were to be sliced, was that a saw big enough to do the job had to be found. His quest for such ended with the late Howard Mason, widely known in the Glens Falls-Lake George area as a contractor, collector and writer.

"Howard showed me a drag saw he had in his barn," said Mr. Waggaman. "It was old and rusty, was powered by a one cylinder engine, but it was workable. I bought it for $125."

(A drag saw can be likened somewhat to a cross-cut saw and was manipulated back and forth by two "arms").

Mr. Waggaman's first move was to clean the apparatus and then weld two lengths of saw together. This gave him about twelve feet of cutting edge, good enough, he thought, to do the island slicing. He gave the finished product to Bill Howard to transport to the Higley Flow battleground. On the way, Bill stopped off at a restaurant at Tupper Lake, the huge saw parked in his truck. In Tupper Lake any saw will draw the quick attention of wandering lumberjacks. This one did. And when Howard came out of the restaurant, he was accosted by a 'jack with a French accent.

"We've been making bets," said the man, "on just what kind of a saw this is. So what kind is it?"

Howard looked at the logger and his group. His reply: "It's an island saw!"

And with that bit of informaton dispensed, he got into his truck and drove away. He never did discover who won the bet — if anyone.

Over at The Flow, the saw was turned over to the expert usage of Sherry Bolton of Glens Falls. Mr. Waggaman's firm, incidentally, is now known as Waggaman and Collyer Contractors, Inc., and is located at 178 Dix Avenue, Glens Falls.

Over at The Flow, things got moving. According to one report, "the winter of 1942-43 saw strange procedures on Higley Flow."

Crews were seen on the islands; they were men representing both the company and the Waggaman firm. The Waggaman men handled the sawing; the power company men handled the rest.

A one cyclinder gasoline engine, purchased second hand for $125, drove two saw blades, welded together, through the frozen islands.

To anchor the islands, holes were cut into the ice and six-foot timbers, attached to cables, were inserted. When these flattened against the islands' undersides, the cables were drawn tight by truck winches on shore. In this fashion the islands were held immobilized. One aspect of the procedure is pictured.

Here outboards can be seen pushing a section of an island out of the bay on the west side of Higley Flow, into the main current. Trucks on shore, winch-equipped, reeled in cables attached to the island to provide additional power.

The islands were cut into squares. In the center of each a hole was cut through the tangle and a six-foot timber, with a steel cable tied around the middle, was inserted. Once under the mass, the timber floated snugly and flatly against the underside and the cable was drawn tight. It proved to be a method of installing an "anchor" by which the islands could be towed. Towing power came from winches on shore-based trucks.

The big island cut-up climaxed the activities when it was sliced into sixteen sections to meet its scheduled doom over the dam.

The sawing process took nearly four months, from December, 1942, until the end of March, 1943. Operations were then suspended until Spring floods on the Raquette.

Thus it was in May that the problem of almost thirty years in the making saw the beginning of the end. The waters of Higley Flow were moving at 10,500 cubic feet per second past a given point. This represented 79,000 gallons per second, or about seven times the natural flow. Not since the great floods of 1913 had such volume been noted. The water spilling over the dam's top was five feet deep. The time was ideal for destruction.

Piece by piece, the islands were hauled out of their sanctuaries where they had been anchored, some by winches, some nudged by outboard motor boats. The eleven-acre mass, now merely cut-up sections, approached the dam. There the thick sections hung until irresistible water pressures were built up behind. Then over they went. The Raquette turned chocolate brown for miles below the falls. The debris was not only mud, but mosses, other plants and swamp materials. There was no harm to fish or other marine life and the streambed was not damaged. But the spillage kept mills and communities downstream busy for days cleaning out water intakes. They had, however, been notified of the scheduled onslaught and were prepared.

The debris laden waters, according to Jack Mowers, Supervisor of Photography for Niagara Mohawk, who shot pictures of the entire demolition period, gave rise to a typical North Country tale.

The late Bernard J. (Bun) Scanlon was Chief Operator on the lower Raquette, living at Yaleville, a small mill town just north of Norwood. Bun, says Mowers, claimed that on one morning after the main section of the big island had gone by, he saw a couple of northern pike in a backwater near his home.

They were taking a bath!

The destruction of the islands proved a feat which captured the imagination of the industrial world. It was mentioned in the pages of Scientific American, in Popular Mechanics and Popular Science magazines. A movie of the job was made; was shown thousands of times throughout the state and elsewhere, until it was worn out. A Portugese translation was made for a showing of the film to an engineering convention in Rio de Janiero.

Today only still photos, taken by Mowers, tell the story of an event never undertaken before 1942 and never undertaken in the Adirondacks since. But the legend still lives on. As it always will.

Pictured above is the center section of the largest island, some 80 tons of it, as it appeared starting its slow descent over Higley Dam. In other photo the mighty mass is shown breaking up into huge chunks as the waters of Raquette River begin their giant swallowing job.

This is "Moose's Gang" of hardy individuals who helped in the giant project. From left to right: Fred Halford, Matt Stowe, Armond Alford, Howard Smith, foreman Fred (Moose) Gabbert, Ralph Gilmore, Francis Robar, Roy Barney and Bernard Howard.

The man who witnessed the entire slicing operations at Higley Flow, and who put them on film, is Jack L. Mowers, Syracuse, Supervisor, Photography, for Niagara Mohawk Power Corporation. The author is highly indebted to Jack for his cooperation in furnishing prints of the remarkable project.

THE SKULL

**Gen. Montcalm Was Called "The Little Fellow"
By Indian Allies, But He Became One Of
The Greatest Threats To British
Conquest In The Adirondacks**

Compulsion is a strange experience. In a history buff it can be touched off by a sentence or spoken word.

In the "History of Frederick the Great," by Thomas Carlyle, for instance, published in 1897, Carlyle wrote one sentence which struck a spark in my mind; that the skull of Montcalm, the French military genius, "is in the Ursulines Convent at Quebec, shown to the idly curious to this day."

This, remember, was penned in 1897.

Was it still there? I found it indeed still remains. And behind it is one of the most unusual stories of its kind I have ever covered.

Montcalm, after his forays into the Adirondack wilderness, was killed in the Battle of Quebec in 1759. But from that year on, until 1833, seventy-four long years, the burial place of this remarkable warrior remained a total mystery.

During the Winter of 1975-76 I felt compelled to see and photograph the relic. The compulsion, I suppose, was based upon the fact that this was not the usual kind of metallic artifact of the French and Indian War of the mid 1700's, but was an actual relic of a human who functioned during those days of conquest, of a soldier of rare capability who almost upset the British lion's applecart in North America.

My arrangements were made with Sister Sainte Croix, O.S.U., a most gracious lady who, I learned later, spent her younger years in the Nantucket area of Massachusetts.

Writing from the 17th century convent, located in the Old City section of Quebec, the good Sister said:

"By all means visit and take as many photographs as you wish." Later she wrote: "You know, of course, we have had the skull only since 1833."

"But," I replied in a followup letter, "Montcalm was killed in 1759. What happened in the intervening years?"

And that led to the full, fascinating story of this legendary man, remarkably unpublicized in America, a man who shortly before he died, predicted the American Revolution if he were defeated! Does history hold similar parallels? I doubt it.

The emotional impact upon first view of The Skull, and I have no hesitation in admitting it, is profound. It is encased in a glass case, and that case is in turn enclosed within clear plastic walls, for reasons to be described.

The eyeless caverns stare with brooding sightlessness; they once witnessed what no living person has ever seen, the total destruction of one empire and the building of another in the North Country of New York State.

They once were brilliantly alive windows through which a man almost unequalled in military history saw the magnificence of the virgin forest of this state; saw and directed, with masterly skill and against tremendous odds, early fighters, some in uniform, some only in paint and buckskin clouts, in battles noted for total ferocity and bloodiness; battles fought against the gloomy backdrop of a primitive Adirondack wilderness inhabited by animal species long since gone; a wilderness so vast, so rugged, it remained uncharted for more than two centuries after it was first viewed.

The brain is long lost, its genius disintegrated, now part of the earth upon which it once directed armies in quest of empire. The hearing abilities which once recorded the shrieks of the wounded, the hoarse shouts of victory, the shrill war cries of warriors painted like demons and whose performance equalled the painted image, have vanished with the flesh of the body.

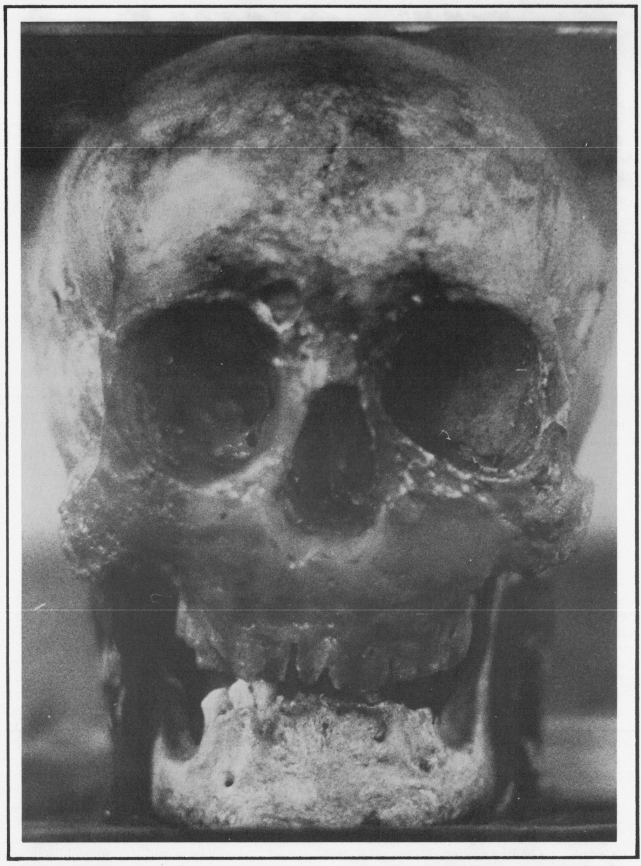

This, plus a small portion of arm bone, is all that remains in tangible form of Gen. Montcalm — a somber skull at the Ursuline Convent in Old Quebec City. Because the skull was stolen (and returned) a few years ago, the relic is now behind glass which, in turn, is protected by unbreakable plastic. The skull faintly shows the effect of a saber wound suffered by Montcalm at the top of his head.

A portrait of the man the Indians fondly called "The Little Fellow," Gen. Montcalm, one of the greatest European generals to lead armies of conquests during the French and Indian War period. Photo is from a painting in a Fort Ticonderoga publication.

But The Skull remains, truly the only tangible evidence of the most famous French general who ever ordered European and aboriginal troops into action in the Corridor of Death known as the Lake Champlain and Lake George valleys.

It is an encasement of fragile bone; represents an exhibit of outstanding interest to those who visit the Ursuline Convent, a building so old it still contains a chapel in which Christianized Indians once prayed, then departed for bloody raids and a harvest of scalps. One can lose one's self in reverie quickly within its massively thick, quiet walls.

Alongside the relic is a small and equally fragile bone, a few inches in length. It is dark brown from age and exposure. It is part of an arm.

This, then, is all that exists of the mortal remains of Louis-Joseph de Gozon Marquis de Montcalm, the fiery tempered commander of Fort Ticonderoga; the ultimate conqueror of the British outpost known as Fort William Henry at Lake George, in August, 1757.

History is controversial. It may define Montcalm as villain or hero in the massacre at Fort William Henry, but history can be certain of one thing. Montcalm did make an attempt to stop his Indian and Canadian allies from perpetrating the greatest massacre ever to cloud the Adirondack region, a savagery which resulted in the butchery of hundreds of the helpless.

Of this tragic episode, Louis Antoine de Bougainville, Montcalm's trusted (and Boswellian aide) wrote:

"The French officers were blameless for the massacre. Officers risked their lives. But England will reproach us for a long time to come."

He was quite correct and England did more than reproach.

That country, thunderstruck, made furious by the wolfish brutality produced in the American wilderness, declared grimly that henceforth in any battle won by British forces, there would be "two capitulations."

One would be for regular French troops and officers. The other would be for Canadians and Indians. One can easily imagine what the grim British mind of the times conjured for captured Canadians and Indians fighting with the French. Death by flogging would have been merciful by comparison.

The British lion had good reason for this decision. A brief description of the Indian allies of the French, for instance, might substantiate the division in surrender.

Listed among the many tribal allies were the Shawnees and Delawares. History records that at one time warriors devoured an English officer "whose pallor and plumpness tempted them!" The Canadian fighter of the time, incidentally, was little better in savagery; life was harsh, survival in many cases was from day to day, even under normal circumstances. As for Montcalm, how does one govern wolfishness ingrained by environment and the almost Neanderthalic conditions under which many of these people lived?

French royalty offered little in the way of material help to stem British thrusts. Corrupt politicians bled their own troop supplies; stole and sold food destined for soldiers of the line; sickness was rampant; corruption the great evil.

Of the Marquis de Vaudreuil, the last governor of Canada, Bougainville wrote:

"He, Montcalm, is under the orders of a man, limited, without talent, perhaps free from vice, but having all the faults of a petty spirit, filled with Canadian prejudices, which are all the most foolish, jealous, glorious, wishing to take all credit to themselves. He no more confides in Montcalm than in the lowest lieutenant."

This Bougainville inscribed in June, 1757, unaware that a mere two years later his idol would fall on the Plains of Abraham in Quebec during a British attack; unaware that from the day he died on September 14, 1759, until the year 1833, that Montcalm's grave would be a place of mystery, not to be found until a girl, nine years old, who witnessed the hasty burial, would recall the exact spot when she reached the age of eighty-three!

Gen. Montcalm arrived in North America in May, 1756, as France and England were reaching for each

This dramatic painting shows Montcalm congratulating his troops following victory over the British general Abercrombie and 16,000 British and Colonial fighters in 1758. Abercrombie assembled the largest army ever assembled in the Adirondack region at that time for an assault on Fort Ticonderoga but his plans turned into disaster. Photo of painting used courtesy of Fort Ticonderoga.

other's throats to control the northeastern United States continental empire. Under his command were regular French forces, highly trained, disciplined with strictness inconceivable to the modern day soldier. But, of course, there were others. On June 30, 1757, he wrote his brother:

"We have 8,000 men, 1,800 of whom are Indians, naked, painted black, red, howling, bellowing, dancing, singing the war song, getting drunk, yelling for 'broth,'' that is to say, blood. They are drawn from 500 leagues by the smell of fresh human flesh and the chance to teach their young men how one carves up a human being destined for the pot."

(Assuming the French league was about two-and-one-half-miles, this means Indians came from distances more than 1,000 miles.)

Again, from Bougainville, about the Indians:

"These men were naked save for a piece of cloth in front and behind, faces and body painted, feather on their heads, symbol and sign of war, tomahawk and spear in hand. In general, these are brawny men, large of good appearance, almost all are very fat."

Described specifically were the Menominees, or "Wild Oats People," who once gave a six-year-old boy an

Englishman to kill for a reason which developed horror — to stop the child from crying. The victim w survivor of a defeat suffered by Lt. Col. J Bradstreet.

In this wild array of primitives also were the Otta Chippewas, Abnakis, Algonquins, French-conve Iroquois, Nipissings, Michilimackinacs, as well as Shawnees and Delawares mentioned. Some histor feel there were Sioux from the eastern fringe of S territory.

The Indians were fascinated by Montcalm, evide it on June 14, 1757, when the Michilimacki complimented him personally on the French captur the British fort at Oswego, thus restoring French cor to the Lake Ontario region, and control meant riches of furs.

"We wished to see," said an Indian orator, ' **famous man who on putting his feet on the ground destroyed the English ramparts. From his reputa and exploits we thought that his head would be lo the clouds. But behold, you are a little fellow, Fa and it is in your eyes that we find the grandeur of loftiest pine trees and the spirit of the eagle."**

This old print is seldom seen; shows Montcalm trying desperately to call off killing of the surrendered garrison during the Massacre at Fort William Henry, now a reconstructed frontier outpost at Lake George. Montcalm's efforts, as did those of his officers, proved futile; even women and children fell before the tomahawks.

Montcalm was a small man indeed; his skull reflects his physical stature. But these facts must be remembered:

This was the man who, born near Nimes, France, in 1711, received a military commission at age fifteen at Hainut, and who first saw action on the Rhine in the War of the Polish Succession. This was the man, who, small though in size, was tall in courage; wounded five times in the Battle of Piacenza during the War of the Austrian Succession. The Skull in the Ursuline Convent shows visible evidence of a saber wound on the top of the head.

This was the man who was honest, courtly, loyal to his own troops, hot tempered and impetuous and whose "hasty speech gained him many enemies." Enemies, one might add, among the jealous.

This was the man who married Angelique Louise Talon du Boulay and who fathered ten children. And this was the soldier of France who became a captain at age seventeen and who by 1756, when he arrived in North America to knot the crumbling French empire together, was a Brigadier General at age forty-four.

His first victory was scored on August 14, 1756, when he struck Oswego and captured 1,700 prisoners and considerable armament, thus infusing plasma into shrunken French military veins.

His defense of Fort Ticonderoga (then called Carillon) was a superb accomplishment against a British army of 16,000, commanded by Gen. Abercrombie, whose brains did not match his desires on July 8, 1758. Although commanding the largest army ever assembled in the Adirondack region at that time, Abercrombie was routed.

The British lion, however, proved a restless carnivore.

A year later, Gen. Amherst, with 11,000 men, better organized, under tighter discipline and under far more capable leadership, went after Ticonderoga, and Montcalm, knowing the inevitable, retired to Quebec, leaving Col. Bourlamarque in command of a small force of 2,300 men. Montcalm's decision was not based upon cowardice, but common sense. He knew by this time, Quebec was the key. Bourlamarque ordered his men to blow the fort to bits and debris landed on the skeletal remains of men who had fallen during the Abercrombie assault.

According to Carroll Vincent Lonergan of Ticonderoga, owner of Historic Fort Mt. Hope, and author of "Ticonderoga, Historic Portage," one of Amherst's men, helping to bring up artillery, was "able to identify the remains of a close relative by the markings and shape of his teeth."

Thus the dead had been left unattended on the field, furnishing food for wolves and other carnivores.

Now shift the scene to Quebec.

Here in this city which borders the St. Lawrence River, Montcalm prepared to hold the French empire, or what remained of it. Here the harassed man was at bay. Here his final days approached. Here belongs the eerie story of his death and the aftermath.

The British, under Gen. James Wolfe, made their first attack and were repulsed. Meanwhile, they had brought the full force of their Navy up the St. Lawrence and began a steady, relentless, grinding bombardment of the city. For sixty-eight days destruction rained upon the area. Twenty-two warships, eight thousand men, including six companies of American Colonials, went after Quebec with predatory precision and anticipation.

On September 12, 1759, a British force managed to land and captured French cannon. British commandos climbed the steep cliffs to the Plains of Abraham. Other troops followed. The army was ready for battle at 8 a.m.

As was the custom in those more orderly days of war, Gen. Wolfe waited for Montcalm to appear. Courtesy, even with death the ultimate objective, was the order of the day. War was a chess game. Men were the pawns. The date was now September 13.

The French marched into position about 10 a.m., and the battle was joined and closed; Wolfe, age thirty-three, was wounded three times and lived only long enough to learn of victory. The battle itself lasted only a few minutes; some say ten, some say not more than twenty.

Montcalm led his forces in person but was wounded by a musket ball and died the next day, September 14, being spared the shame of knowing full defeat and witnessing the shattering of French dreams. His nightmare was over. He was forty-eight.

He died at 5 a.m. The Cathedral in Quebec was in ruins. He could not be buried there, I was told by Sister Sainte Croix. His remains were carried to the Ursuline Chapel. No carpenter could be found in the vast confusion to construct a casket. Finally an old convent workman known as Bohhomme Michel, "weeping bitterly," made a crude box of pine, and near the grating of the Chapel within the Convent, Montcalm was placed in a hole torn into the floor by a British cannon ball.

The hole was enlarged only slightly to hold the casket. Hastily flung dirt closed it over. It was patted down; no mound was left visible. No marker was put into place. Father Resche and eight Ursuline nuns remaining to guard the Convent sang the Libera.

And during this time, a little girl, age nine years, Amable Dube, was an awed spectator. She was a little girl possessed of, as it later developed, phenomenal memory. She eventually became an Ursuline Sister and in the year 1833, at age eighty-three, she happened to be included in a discussion as to the exact location where Montcalm's body had been buried, a mystery up to that very day.

The famous French fighter is memorialized in many spots on the historic grounds which contain Fort Ticonderoga. This is one of them; it commemorates the defeat of the British in 1758.

She walked to a spot on the convent floor, pointed, and said:

"He rests here."

The drama can be imagined. Workmen excavated and the grave was opened. But found was only The Skull and part of the arm. The earth had devoured all else.

"Everything," Sister Sainte Croix told me, "was in dust."

Everything, that is, save the skeletal remains mentioned. And these have remained in the Ursuline Convent ever since and have been disturbed only once, during the Spring of 1975, when The Skull was stolen. The Quebec police were tipped off to the theft by an unknown tipster and they called the Convent. The nun who answered refused to discuss the matter until a uniformed police officer appeared and identified himself. One did.

Within twenty-four hours The Skull was returned. Who stole it, or why, is not known. A prank perhaps. But The Skull is now back in place, under glass, protected by a plastic shield, and the extraordinary museum in which it is located, bearing antiques of priceless quality, is visited daily by as many as 500 persons during the tourist season. The museum is open every day from two to five p.m., Sundays included, and during all seasons. This, as of this writing.

One must most assuredly be impressed by this simple relic. One must be impressed by the prediction the brain once within it made.

You gaze upon The Skull and you learn that Montcalm, on August 24, 1759, wrote that "M. Wolfe, if he understands his trade, will take to beat and ruin me if we meet in fight."

In the same letter, Montcalm wrote:

"If he beat me here, France has lost America utterly; yes, and one's only conclusion is, in ten years farther, America will be in revolt against England!"

Consider this letter, written in 1759, and then consider the start of the American Revolution in May, 1775, when Ethan Allen and his Green Mountain Boys captured British-held Fort Ticonderoga.

Montcalm, on the eve of his death, was wrong by only six years!

The story of Gen. Montcalm and Gen. Wolfe has special significance for these two gentlemen. Gerald Wolfe, left, an insurance man who has Emil K. Zaenglein, right, as a client, lives in Harlemville, a hamlet in Columbia County near Ghent. Mr. Zaenglein lives a few miles distant at R.D. 1, Chatham, also in Columbia County.

The significance of their relationship is not in the business field but in historical background. Mr. Wolfe's ancestry can be traced to the British general, James Wolfe, who defeated Montcalm in the Battle of Quebec. Mr. Zaenglein can trace his ancestry to Gen. Montcalm!

Their historical relationship, insofar as the author is concerned, came to light during festivities in Columbia County during the reenactment of the transfer of Revolutionary War cannon from Fort Ticonderoga over the famous Knox Trail, part of which wound its way through Columbia County. A portion of this trail still exists in original form, as may be seen in photos which follow. Both men, incidentally, are looking at a mounted photo of Gen. Montcalm's skull, taken by the author.

While the transfer of cannon from Fort Ticonderoga to General Washington in the Boston area in 1775 has no connection with the chapter which you have completed, the thought is that you might be interested in what part of the reenactment of the trek by Col. Knox and his men may have looked like. The scenes above were snapped on a portion of the trail still in its original form near Nolan's Corners in Columbia County. In the lower photo, the lone figure is that of Fuller Walker, who played the part of Col. Knox during part of the trek. Photo shows beginning of long climb to the top of a ridge.

THE REMINGTON HEIST

**While Strolling Through the
Woods One Day, Leo Hickey
Found Not the Honey Tree
He Sought, But an
Astonishing Treasure**

On August 24, 1968, Leo J. Hickey of Keene Valley, a retired carpenter, took off into a quiet portion of the Adirondack wilderness near his home.

His quest: A honey bee tree with its treasure of sticky sweetness, which he had spotted a year before while instructing some young people in safe use of a rifle.

Mr. Hickey was roaming an area in the vicinity of Old Route 73, some four hundred yards from the present Route 73, and about twenty feet from the shoulder of the old highway, now a pathway moving into the past.

He anticipated an interesting day.

As events developed, that is exactly what it turned out to be.

At 8:15 a.m. his keen eyes spotted disturbed earth at the base of a tree. He investigated. And what he found put the honey bee tree completely out of mind and purpose.

At his feet, half buried, was an old ten-gallon lard can, upside down. Inside, wrapped loosely in a portion of a blanket, was a statue of bronze, twenty-four inches in height, mounted on a bronze base about eleven by sixteen inches in size.

The statue was of a cowboy astride a rearing horse. In front of the animal's lifted forelegs was a coiled rattlesnake.

Mr. Hickey became understandably curious. He found the statue somewhat heavy, encrusted here and there with earth from its burial. He inspected the area more fully; found no signs of ownership; no note, no metal plate; nothing which would give any indication whatsoever where the statue had come from, or who the individual was who had interred it.

Mr. Hickey, sensing his find was hardly a casual one, promptly notified Trooper R.H. Mapes of SP Wilmington, a station in the shadow of Whiteface Mountain. After examination and closer inspection, an inscription was found at the top of the base, near the horse's rear legs. It read:

"Copyright by Frederic Remington."

Inscribed at a lower level on the base was: "Roman Bronze Works, N.Y." The number "29" was found inscribed under the base itself.

Thus in this novel, rather casual fashion Mr. Hickey hit an artistic jackpot, and opened another unusual story of the North Country, a story which eventually involved not only the New York, but the Massachusetts State Police, the FBI, several museums and art galleries and a host of private art collectors; a story which pursued its normal finish to the Berkshire School for Boys in Sheffield, Mass.

It is also a story involving one of the most remarkable artists and sculptors ever to come out of the Adirondack region; Canton-born Frederic Remington, world famous in his hey-day; a man of vast appetite and the ability to satisfy it; a man who painted what he saw in the Adirondacks, particularly in the Cranberry Lake section, and who gained equal fame in his dramatic Far West scenes and sculptures.

Remington was born Oct. 4, 1861, in Canton and after a vigorous, somewhat gusty, lusty life which took him into faraway places, died in 1909, at the age of forty-eight. The signs of genius he left behind are many; his was a prolific lifetime and his fame was international. The largest collection of his works reportedly is located in the Whitney Museum, Cody, Wyoming, but it is a matter of record that the blossoming of his genius began in the Adirondack Mountains.

On the day Mr. Hickey excavated his find, it was taken to an area antique dealer who, after dutiful appraisal, said its worth probably would be about $750.

Later, a Lake Placid dealer said the statue, if an authentic Remington, would be worth about $10,000. Both were quite wrong.

By this time it had become obvious this was no ordinary creation; it was removed to the State Police at Malone for safe keeping, and the hunt for the owner, as well as the person who buried the statue was begun.

Meantime, a visit to the scene of the find revealed footprints near the discovery tree, footprints neither of Mr. Hickey's nor the investigating officers' making. It can reasonably be established that the individual who did the burying did indeed return to the scene but, upon finding his cache gone, took off. He has not been found.

As the investigation continued, the statue was transported to the Remington Museum in Ogdensburg on September 9, by Inv. E.H. Van Schaick, and there it was examined by Coy Ludwig, museum director, and others.

The statue was declared authentic. It was entitled "The Rattlesnake," one of Remington's favorites. It was the twenty-ninth casting from an original created by the noted artist.

Further, it was found, it was cast about 1905 by one Riccardo Bertelli of the Roman Bronze Works in New York City, and was one of a hundred, possibly 125, sold at one time exclusively by the prestigious Tiffany's in New York. The exact number of castings remains unknown. The value of each does not.

More information was to develop as time went on.

In 1968, the year of the Keene Valley find, an authentic Remington sold at a Golman auction in Long Island for $25,000. As the State Police search continued, the value of the Keene Valley statue rose to a similar sum. Then an art gallery in New York estimated that it might, if auctioned, bring as high as $35,000. Two other experts in the Remington field hiked that total to an astonishing $40,000. Today's value may be even higher because of increased interest in Remingtons.

All of which was a far cry from the original $750 set by the first dealer. It pays to shop around.

Police by this time found themselves in somewhat of a quandry. No theft of a Remington had been reported to them and a check throughout the state revealed no results. It seemed incredible that anyone owning a statue valued at $40,000 would remain quiet any length of time about such a loss. The yell of the owner should have been heard throughout the world of art.

While it was first thought that it had been removed from the museum in Ogdensburg, it was found that this was not so. There was, and is, a similar casting there, according to a report by Trooper J.P. Williams of Wilmington, which is numbered "100" and which had been cast for Mrs. Remington, the former Eva Caten of Gloversville. That statue, according to the SP report, was insured for $8,500.

State Police kept doggedly at their task. Scores of art galleries and hundreds of individuals, many of them private collectors, were contacted and the result was always the same: Zero. As time went on it seemed even more incredible that no report of theft had been made.

The search went even into prison. In the Plattsburgh area, for instance, an "antique collector" in custody ($3,000 worth of antiques were found in his possession and there was doubt he owned them) was questioned. He told officers he had nothing to do with the Remington matter; matter of fact, he said, he was not familiar with the artist's works.

Then coincidence began reaching into the scene.

On October 10, less than three months after the statue was found, Alan Thielker, a former art teacher at the Berkshire School for Boys in Sheffield, Mass., visited the Remington Museum at Ogdensburg. While talking to Coy Ludwig, he mentioned casually that his school had

Leo J. Hickey, who discovered the famous Remington statue buried at the base of a tree is pictured seated in his home in Keene Valley as he tells the story of the finding and subsequent events leading to the return of the creation to its owners.

had a similar creation, but that he heard it had been stolen; the theft, he said, had been reported in a newspaper.

Activity then switched into Massachusetts. SP Captain R.S. Charland was notified and the investigation continued with Dr. John Godman, headmaster at the Bay State School.

Here the story, after passing through its labyrinth of calls and personal contacts, finally came out.

Here we see Frederic Remington busy modeling in clay a dramatic sculpture of a buffalo tossing a horse high into the air. The photo, from the Remington Museum in Ogdensburg, was taken in the years after the artist-sculptor created a reputation for his paintings of the Adirondack area – the years when he specialized in paintings and sculptures with a western theme.

The statue, all $40,000 worth of it, had stood on a stone mantel in the Allen House Library for more than a half century. It was a gift of Mr. and Mrs. George H. Clements in 1912, in memory of their son, Brent, who was the first boy to be entered at the school.

The $40,000 creation was such a common sight in the library that it was considered almost as one of the room's fixtures.

School authorities did recall some clues that eventually led to the conclusion that the statue found in Keene Valley by Mr. Hickey was indeed the one which had graced the mantel for more than fifty years. For one thing, one rein was gone and the other was attached to the bit in the horse's mouth with a small piece of wire. And, it was recalled, the rattles on the rattlesnake were missing as well.

The school, police found, had reported the loss to the Massachusetts State Police but the quest obviously had been confined within the borders of that state. Letters and dozens of phone calls finally established the fact that the Remington found by Mr. Hickey while honey bee tree hunting was the Remington stolen from the Berkshire school. Dust from the Allen House mantel was the final proof; it matched dust found in the crevices of the statue.

Police were satisfied, finally, and the sculpture was returned to the school.

But questions still remain.

Who was the thief? And was the heisting of the Remington a prank and if so, why? Any attempt to sell it, even to private collectors would be comparable to selling a stuffed elephant; secretive dealings in the art world are that hard to keep under wraps.

And who made the footprints spotted around the tree where the statue was found, days AFTER Mr. Hickey dug up his extraordinary, lard can-entombed treasure?

There are, of course, suspicions. There always are. But these remain just that. Technically the case is not closed. But will the answer ever be disclosed?

I think not; every year that goes by makes the job harder, the forest thicker.

The Remington Heist will remain one of the mysteries of the Adirondacks.

The total drama that Remington was able to put into his creations in bronze is evidenced in "The Rattlesnake," the sculpture discussed in this chapter. This casting may be seen at the Remington Museum in Ogdensburg, which furnished the photo. Note rattler half coiled on the base, to the left front of the rearing horse. This particular casting reportedly was made for Mrs. Remington, the former Eva Caten of Gloversville.

NIGHTMARE ON THE BOUQUET

What Started as a Routine
Day Turned into One of
Shock and Horror for
a Resident of Keene

For Joseph (Bud) Piserchia, who runs the popular North Country Taxidermy Shop in the pleasant community of Keene, Essex County, the day began in what he considered normal fashion.

You would have thought the same.

He wanted a meal of fresh trout for his family and himself.

So on that memorable day in June, 1976, never to slip from mind or memory, he happily, albeit temporarily, left his bed and board about 5 a.m. and hied himself off to a trout pool he had previously scouted in the South Branch of the Bouquet River, alongside Route 73, at a spot called High Bridge. The stream is also known as the South Fork.

In a small clearing, reachable over a rough, rock-ribbed road, overlooking a likely expanse of open water, he parked his light truck. The area is often used by tenters during vacation weather. Many swim the crystal-clear pools. Many of both sexes do so equipped only with suits which Nature endowed to all.

Here the Bouquet flows with icy coldness and with a happy, lusty enthusiasm, fast and clear from its sources in the high mountains to the south; here it swirls, gushes and falls from pool to pool, passing under Route 73, a two-lane highway which in its own way is as curvaceous and angular as many of the ladies and gentlemen who in bikinis, trunks or in the buff chill themselves in the waters when times are appropriate.

Piserchia began his fishing and ran into luck, hoisting two good-sized brookies, scaleless submersibles which he deposited on a river boulder to reclaim at fishing's end. About 6 a.m. he decided to drop a line downstream. He began walking the rock-strewn shoreline, his fishing rod in his right hand.

Life, it is said by students of our alloted span, is full of surprises. Piserchia was due for one. But it proved more than a surprise.

Without knowing it, he began walking into a nightmare.

Moving along the shoreline of the Bouquet in this locale calls for the balance of an Olympic gymnast; the rocks, some small, some gargantuan, are spaced by Nature in helter-skelter fashion. It is not wheelchair country. A man on crutches would be impaled by his own supports. The area is, in miniature, mountain goat country.

In hopping from one rock to another, in scrambling over others, Piserchia reached his left hand upward, grasping a ledge to steady himself.

Total, immediate pain followed.

Consternation, shock and horror were next in line. As he pulled back, a four-foot-long timber rattlesnake dangled from his flesh about three inches above his wrist; the two needle-sharp fangs had sunk deep into his arm and the writhing reptile, its eyes dark spots of lidless ferocity, clung with English bulldog tenacity.

Piserchia's reaction was instantaneous. He tried to shake the snake loose. He lashed its length repeatedly against rocks. All efforts proved fruitless. Then, desperately, he grasped the reptile behind its pitted head, literally tearing it loose from his arm, then slamming it to the ground with such force that it was stunned. He looked at his arm. The sight of the twin punctures hit his mind a sledgehammer blow.

In this nightmarish scene Piserchia's mind did not become a disaster area. Horror was present, but terror and resulting panic were not. His thoughts raced with Grand Prix speed. The incentive was survival. He ran to his truck, some thirty yards distant, ripped out a length of wire leading to his brake lights, and fashioned a tourniquet.

Thereupon he performed a gesture amazing in view of the reptilian savagery just experienced. He returned to the scene of the encounter, found the snake still inert. With a good-sized sapling the twenty-nine-year-old Adirondacker dispatched it from this life. He then placed the creature in a plastic bag in his truck and the reasoning behind this is self evident; he wanted the snake for positive identification and thus correct treatment.

The rattler pictured, held by Joseph Piserchia, is literally frozen stiff, result of spending time in a freezer. But only a short time before, this reptile was alive and quite well; matter of fact, well enough to sink its fangs into the left wrist of Piserchia, as he fished for trout in a ravine of the South Branch of the Bouquet River.

Minutes were flicking by.

His recollection of those moments is vivid.

"I knew I needed emergency treatment," Piserchia told me later, "and I knew I needed it fast. But I wasn't about to leave the carcass behind. Everything was happening so fast that I guess I was acting almost instinctively by then."

He must have been. He not only recovered the snake, but his fishing equipment as well! He did, however, leave his catch behind.

Put yourself in his position.

It is about 6:15 a.m.; the nearby highway is deserted; there is no friend or other person nearby; loneliness and desperation remain your only companions. The surrounding forest is quiet save for forest noises; these and the gushing waters of the Bouquet are the only sounds. The world in which you stand is awakening from sleep. Yet there is the full, almost unbelievable realization that death, unless checked, is starting to run its slow, inexorable course in your veins.

It is difficult to personalize such a situation unless it has been experienced. Piserchia has no such problem; the drama of that day is there to unreel in memory.

What happened at this point was a race against a competitor already in his body. He drove into Keene at breakneck speed over tortuous Route 73, where he awakened Dr. Tilman Kluwe, and in Dr. Kluwe's office the smitten area, now starting to redden and swell, was lanced. The tourniquet, loosened only momentarily, was re-applied and a call put out for the Keene Ambulance Squad. Members arrived in record time. There are no speed limits in a race for life. Piserchia was removed to Champlain Valley Physicians Hospital in Plattsburgh. (A news report said a call had been placed earlier to the "poison control center" in Albany. This would mean it probably ended up at the Albany Medical Center, probably either in the Emergency Department or in Pediatrics. No control center, as such, existed then.

If the call were indeed placed, it was because poisonous reptile bites are not common in the High Peak re-

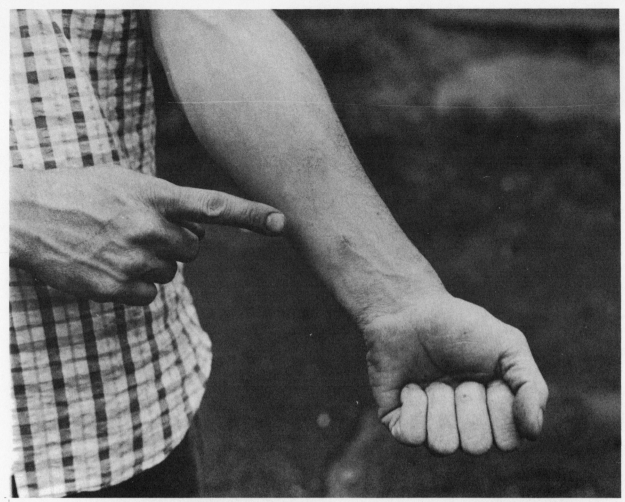

That's the left wrist of Joseph Piserchia you're looking at. Only inches above the palm of his hand note crossed incisions made by a physician on the wound site – incisions made to draw off venom as quickly as possible. The snake clung to the wrist until literally torn from its tenacious hold. Shaking his hand violently did not dislodge it for the victim.

gion of the Adirondacks. As a matter of record, the presence of a timber rattler proved a stunning surprise to those who became acquainted with the incident. Rattlers exist in and around the talus slopes on Tongue Mt. Lake George, far to the east, and in the South Bay area of Lake Champlain; they have denned in these areas long before the white man took over from King George and the Indians.

But the sinuous carriers of venom in the High Peak region have seldom ever been reported as actual fact. Rumors have circulated about sightings of rattlers on such mountains as Pocomoonshine, a precipitous slope highly visible from the northern stretches of Route 9 and, on occasion, on Pitchoff Mountain in the Keene Valley area. But when checked out they have been torpedoed and sunk.

At the Plattsburgh Hospital, Piserchia ran into life regained. Dr. Dean Wheeler, it was found, had practiced medicine in Texas and was familiar with snakebite treatment. He administered shots to ward off tetanus and injected anti-venom serum.

Then came the long wait to see if any signs of shock would develop. But Bud Piserchia, young and vigorous, has a healthy constitution. None did. It was found later that promptness of emergency treatment, which, of course, included his own cut-off of circulation by application of a tourniquet, had allowed only about ten percent of the reptile's poisonous load to spread about the site of the impact of fang and flesh.

The rattler will not be lost to the eyes of posterity. When I, visited Piserchia shortly after the incident, he hauled the creature out of his deep freeze and told me he planned to mount it. Amazingly he viewed the entire episode with almost academic interest.

Interestingly, he found only four rattles on the carcass. The snake had lost two in its losing battle. In describing the length and other physical characteristics of the reptile to Jack Pinto, a Capital Newspapers Photographer who in his own right is an expert in the field of herpetology, I was told a snake with six rattles probably would be about two or three years old. Rattles are added, one by one, as a snake sheds its skin and rattlers raised by Pinto have shed about three times a year.

The rush of Bouquet River branch waters makes a pleasant, never-ending sound in this ravine, jammed with boulders, rimmed with ledges, set amongst trees. The reptilian menace to Piserchia was hidden on one of the ledges; struck when the taxidermist steadied himself as he maneuvered over the rocks. Upstream from this area pictured is a spot oft used by campers and swimmers.

Now, of course, there remains the question unanswered. And it probably never will be in authoritative fashion.

What was a full grown, yellow-phased rattlesnake doing in an area where even the late Raymond Ditmars, world famous herpetologist, once said no poisonous snakes existed? Nothing, however, remains static in Nature. She is as flexible as a belly dancer and, at times, as unpredictable. In the world of wildlife, be it mammal or reptile, it is not logical to make a flat statement on either habit or habitat.

Walter Buckley, New York State Department of Environmental Conservation biologist, who photographed and measured the reptile which attacked Piserchia, said the snake was far removed from areas where others have been hunted or found. He said it was the first confirmed sighting of a rattler within his memory in the region described. But, he reportedly added, where one is found, there probably will be others.

I pursued the matter with William E. Petty, then EnCon's Director of Region Five, with headquarters located in Ray Brook. The confirmed report was also a "first" for him. But he offered a theory that the snake might have been an escapee from a tourist attraction which once existed on Route 9. The "attraction," if such it could be called, was an incongruity insofar as the Adirondacks are concerned; it once held rattlers of several varieties, including timbers and diamondbacks, as well as a pretty good cross section of other snakes, some nonpoisonous such as constrictors, which kill by crushing before devouring.

The possibility exists, it is felt, that a timber rattler slithered through an opening in its enclosure and, following a natural food supply, which would include mice, chipmunks and birds, moved westward. Possibly the reptile was a pregnant female and gave birth to its young alive, as rattlers do, and these, in turn, spread.

It is possible, according to Dr. Edgar Reilly, State Zoologist, to ascertain whether the reptile which attacked Piserchia, was of a northern variety; there is a higher scale count on the timbers living in the Adirondacks because of colder weather.

Whatever the reason for its existence, the snake did indeed inhabit the Bouquet ravine and it did create a sensation among many. Bites can be fatal, although death is not always a direct result. Promptness in treatment should always be considered a "must," and those who hike the ravines and rocky slopes should keep an eye open for snake sign and an ear cocked for the familiar rattle — even though the reptile does not always warn before striking. A surprise attack, as the one made on Piserchia, was done in silence.

The watchword, say experts, is caution, not fear, for the timber rattler wants to tangle with Man about as much as Man wants to tangle with the reptile itself.

Introducing Another Kind of Story

The story you have just completed is based upon fact. It is based upon an actual happening.

But mountains like the Adirondacks are bound, by their very nature, to produce other types of stories of far different character.

Hardly similar in content to the one above, this one is a yarn about a huge reptile which not only reportedly prowled and terrorized the High Peak region at will, but allegedly gobbled up goats and eventually consumed an Adirondack resident except for his boot soles, buttons and camera!

I offer it for total contrast.

It appeared in a magazine circulated nationally. Involved was a twenty-three-foot Royal or reticulated python, a native of the Malay Peninsula, where the air is warm and breezes blow gently on occasion, except during the hurricane season. In the Malayan jungle it kills or immobilizes its prey by constriction, then devours it.

I vouch not one whit for the accuracy of the story, since I did not write it. Had I written it, I still would not vouch. I have tried to locate the author but without success.

The python, of course, is considered the largest snake in the world. Some reputedly have reached thirty feet. When I received a copy of the magazine story from a reader of my Times-Union columns, I read it over once, then once again. It remains fascinating. I mentioned it at one time when stopping at the Spread Eagle Inn in Keene Valley for a snack, and found it had been the topic of many a conversation.

It all started back in the late 1950's when a plane was supposed to have crashed just below the peak of Nipple Top Mt. The plane upon impact disgorged part of its cargo, a consignment of king cobras and several one-year-old pythons, each about five feet long. The aircraft was allegedly enroute from Philadelphia, where it had picked up its cargo from the Philadelphia Zoo. Its destination was Montreal. All snakes aboard were believed to have been exterminated by the crash and fire except one, and this critter certainly proved an exceptionally bright young reptilian sprout. He stayed put in the Adirondacks and grew and grew and grew, and the first thing you know, he reached 300 pounds, and became known as The Strangler, simply because he throttled his victims before passing them into his stomach for recycling.

The sex of The Strangler was determined to be male. How this was ascertained is beyond me, since glimpses of the monster were infrequent and residents became acquainted with his presence mostly through the tracks (or track) he left behind.

The plane crash was reportedly in 1959 or thereabouts. I have not yet been able to find anyone who has heard of such. There was a military plane crash atop Wright's Peak, near Lake Placid, but that hardly carried a reptilian cargo.

The magazine story revealed The Strangler dodged the stomping feet of rescuers sent to the plane, and promptly and wisely vanished into the Adirondack wilderness.

It was drizzling when this occurred, so one must assume the crash occurred during fairly warm weather.

How did the orphaned urchin live? He found himself woodchuck holes or rabbit burrows and feasted on their occupants. A woodchuck swallowed by a five-foot-long snake, only a few inches in diameter? That's what the story said. He must have possessed an extraordinary bulge for a period. With it he could have rocked himself to sleep. Perhaps he did. Can any herpetologist prove snakes do not?

At any rate, one woodchuck led to another; one rabbit led to another, and The Strangler kept growing. One day he found he had outgrown woodchuck and bunny holes and needed roomier quarters. So he located a cave in which the temperature never went below fifty degrees. This was important, because snakes are cold-blooded and in freezing temperatures they do what comes naturally. They freeze. In this cave he spent harsh Winters which, under ordinary circumstances, would have killed any python who is supposed to live in tropical climes and especially one who wasn't equipped with thermal underwear.

One Forest Ranger, whose printed name is unfamiliar to other conservation department workers, supposedly snapped a picture of The Strangler striking at a fawn. Another photo reportedly was taken showing the snake swallowing the whitetail victim.

It was thought The Strangler at one time denned on Mt. Marcy, highest peak in the Adirondacks — southern exposure, of course. He did travel, however. In the Summer of 1969 the monster writhed over into the Newcomb-Minerva area. Some goats were later reported lost. Natives figured bears had gotten to them. Nothing much, says the story, was thought about it, since the natives knew that with the hunting season, hunters would shoot off some bears and thus the balance of nature would thereby be "restored"(!), and, presumably, goats would roam the countryside once again.

One day an Adirondacker who "rented" some land from New York State (a remarkable feat in the "forever wild" area protected by the State Constitution) found snake excrement and a shed skin. Later this gentleman, who shall remain unnamed in this harrowing tale, disappeared, and a friend searched for something besides memories.

Near Henderson Lake he found the vanished man's camera. About 400 yards distant he found some buttons, a pair of boot soles, shoe lace tips and belt buckle. Since the man wasn't wearing any of the mentioned articles, the searcher wisely figured that something had happened to him. The Strangler was blamed.

Search and destroy parties were organized; men from Keene, Keene Valley, St. Hubert's, from Newcomb and Minerva way, men who had suffered losses of domestic stock, were called into the drag net. Tracks of The Strangler were found up on Santanoni Peak; there, also, was found another den of The Strangler, the mouth of the eerie aperture littered with bones, presumably expelled in the digestive process and most assuredly in violation of the anti-litter code of ethics.

To bring this sad tale of high adventure to a merciful conclusion, it can be said, and will be, that The Strangler was finally located, in a tree, naturally. There was a fierce, no-quarter struggle. A knife eventually was used the Strangler accidentally impaled his head. The result was what anybody who knows snakes would expect from a knife in the head: Cessation of life.

After this bit of ferocity, the men descended the mountain to rest and sweat from fear of recent memories. Then they climbed it again. There they found the carcass of The Strangler covered with birds, busily devouring the whole darned thing.

The skeleton, the story goes, is still intact, and is on display at the State University of New York. A most remarkable beast, which survived fifteen tempestous years in New York State!

I find only a few difficulties in this tale. No Forest Ranger or Conservation Officer I contacted remembers a single thing about this extraordinary reptile. I cannot find any record of the plane crash on Nipple Top. I cannot find even the skeleton at State University. But, then, neither can my contacts. I received only peculiar looks in my quest.

Anyway, it's a pretty exciting yarn but it won't keep me out of the Minerva-Newcomb-Marcy-Keene-Keene Valley area, since The Strangler is dead and there are, presumably, no known survivors!

MOUNTAIN GENIUS

What Hath Man Wrought?
In the Adirondacks,
Many Things Which
Have Changed
Your Life!

Most inventions have resulted from necessity, although one must admit the advent of the water bed, the electric back scratcher and toothbrush may leave this assertion open to lively debate. The same may be said of television, that Cyclopean Eye which now cannibalizes the most precious of commodities — time.

Unfortunately, the detailed history of some inventions is lacking.

The wheel, for instance, was conceived by a primitive Edison about 5,000 years ago — or even more — and its inspiration probably resulted from the astute observation that heavy loads could be moved on log rollers; thus, if logs moved objects easily, so would slices cut from them. The unknown genius thereupon hacked off two sections of a log, put a hole in the center of each; found he had to invent an axle on-the-spot, which he did, and thus enabled civilization to cease dragging its heels.

But nobody knows where the wheel was invented and most assuredly, the name of the inventor is buried along with his or her bones. It could have been a woman, you know; they too did some pretty heavy work in those ancient days.

The evolvement of the bow and arrow, which also changed civilization's pattern of life, sometimes in traumatic fashion, follows the same theme. The bow and arrow, as a unit, became the world's sixth successful guided missile, equal in its time to anything of modern day shot into space. It followed in this order: The human canine tooth, the clenched fist, the flung rock, the club and the spear.

This curvaceous creation, today much improved, still hurls its feathered songs of death during the big game season in the Adirondacks, and as a world weapon, it has a history of at least 10,000 years. But again, the toxophilitic cave dweller who bent a stick and tied a string of gut or rawhide to both ends, thus expanding killing power, is unknown and, alas, unhonored.

Inventions actually inspired, created or perfected within the giant Adirondack Park and its fringes are something else. There is proof in time and document that notable ones have changed world-wide patterns of living and enjoyment.

Some illustrations:

• The idea of an electric motor, which most assuredly helped put and keep such Goliaths as the General Electric Company in business, was born at the Penfield-Taft Iron Works at Ironville, up Crown Point way, in Essex County.

• The once ubiquitous milk bottle, a sanitary container which has saved countless lives, originated in Potsdam, in St. Lawrence County, and came about as the result of a little girl dropping a less-than-clean rag doll into a metal can of milk. The milk bottle, which, incredibly, our modern generation has never seen, lasted almost a century, to be replaced by a godsend to those who wish a fast fire starter in their fireplaces — the wax carton.

• The snow tire was not an idle improvisation; the forerunner of this chill weather necessity came from the active brain of an Adirondack builder and inventor, Earl Covey of Big Moose, Herkimer County.

• Marconi did not invent wireless communication, which fact should not infuriate his multitude of devoted followers, for he did indeed improve upon the basic principle of what we now call radio. Wireless communication was invented by a dentist, an Adirondack-born native, raised as a youngster in the Town of Oppenheim, Fulton County, where his genius was nurtured in mountain air, only to blossom elsewhere.

• The pencil as we know it, "lead," bound by wood, came from the historic area of Ticonderoga, where graphite, or "black lead" was found in almost pure form as an earth-bound treasure.

• One of the most famous lures in the world of angling, the Tuttle Devil Bug, was born in the ingenious brain of a man who observed what fish ate, how they ate, and what proved most tasty on the piscatorial menu. Also in the world of fishing, one cannot overlook the equally famous trolling spoon itself, which while created in Vermont, was perfected in the Lake Champlain-Lake George region, and later manufactured at Whitehall, N.Y., and now being produced in Dearborn, Michigan.

• A famous development in old time transportation was the buckboard, a springy buggy capable of carrying

The forge to the left, along with the anvil, might denote the gentleman is a blacksmith. He was indeed. But Thomas Davenport was more than that; he was the inventor of the electric motor, an idea which germinated into reality after a visit to the Penfield-Taft Iron Works in the Crown Point area. Davenport is pictured in this painting by Bruce Mitchell, Keene Valley, with a model of his invention.

—From the First Vermont Bank Collection

humans over rough roads without cracking spines. An Essex County clergyman devised this innovation as he jolted over the type of mountain roads which happily are prehistoric by comparison with modern highways.

And so genius, each evidence of such evaluated in its own way, went from one end of the mountains to the other; agile minds mated with inspiration, created or improved, and society benefited.

If, as said, society benefited from inventions mentioned, the inventor in some cases, did not.

THE ELECTRIC MOTOR

Consider the creator of the electric motor who, according to his physician, died of a broken heart. Deserved recognition did not become his to hold and cherish; poverty was his bleak companion as he created his first motor, using as part of that creation, his wife's silk wedding dress, with which he wrapped the magnet.

Such is the introduction to the story of Thomas Davenport, inventor of the "electro-magnetic machine," now known as the electric motor!

Thomas Davenport was born in 1802 in Williamstown, Vt., and died penniless in Brandon, Vt., at age 49, forgotten by most of the scientific world, and those who did remember this strange, dedicated man, often referred to him as the "Brandon blacksmith," which trade he did follow.

But Davenport was more than a smithy. His fertile mind often leaped from the trade of farriery to what he called "electro-magnetism." He possessed no scientific books on the subject. He possessed no knowledge of what others before him had done in this new field. But despite this vacuum, he devised an electric telegraph, displaying the model to Samuel F.B. Morse, then a portrait painter afflicted with the usual burden of the poor — lack of money.

Morse wore two hats as well, often jumping from painting into the field of electricity. In 1837, he applied for a patent for his own version of the telegraph, evolved, some say, from advice given by Prof. Joseph Henry, a physicist and mathematics professor at Albany Academy in Albany — and, of course, advice from Davenport. The latter received nothing for his aid.

The blacksmith had other things on his mind. Prof. Henry had been working on magnets. The Penfield-Taft Iron Works at Ironville, near Crown Point, now a well known historical area and home of the Penfield Museum, supplied Henry with magnetite iron from which he built his remarkable structures. The professor had succeeded extremely well; had produced a 21-pound horseshoe-shaped magnet that would lift 750 pounds when battery current was applied!

Prof. Henry also was called upon to magnetize or activate magnets in a cylinder at Penfield-Taft which separated iron ore from sands and rock particles.

The magnets fascinated Davenport. He wanted to see one lift a blacksmith's anvil. He felt, even at this time, here indeed was a source of power hithertofore untapped. Travel was not easy in 1833 when he made his first 25-30 mile trip to the Penfield-Taft works in summer, and saw nothing, since Allen Penfield and Timothy Taft were absent. So he returned in December of the same year, witnessed a magnet in operation, purchased it at what was termed an "exorbitant" price and went back to his own forge. The "exorbitant" price was $75!

Power to the magnet was supplied by what was then known as the "crown of cups," created by the Italian physicist, Allessandro Volta, consisting of a series of cups, each filled with brine, into which silver and zinc plates were dipped and then connected externally.

Henry's electro-magnet, with attached battery, was put into operation at the Penfield-Taft operation and many historians consider this the first industrial application of electricity in the United States.

Davenport found that by breaking the circuit, magnetism was destroyed; by reconnecting wires again, the magnet became activated; thus one could create surges of power. In his own words:

"Like a flash of lightning, the thought occurred to me that here was an available power that was within the reach of man!"

The blacksmith had help. Ransom Cook of Saratoga Springs, a machinist, helped him build a number of electro-magnetic machines, and among them was the one carried to Washington, D. C., resulting in U.S. Patent No. 132, dated Feb. 25, 1837. This patent, it is said, gives Davenport "undisputed priority in the matter of innovation and construction of the first electric direct current electric motor."

The New York Herald labeled the motor "the most extraordinary discovery, probably the greatest of ancient and modern times, the greatest the world has ever seen, the greatest the world will ever see."

Tragically, Davenport found the world not interested; he returned to his forge in 1842, died nine years later,

carrying with him his dream — a dream born as the result of a visit to an Adirondack iron works.

An ironic note: It was nearly a century before the electric motor replaced steam as a major power source for both industry and transportation.

THE MILK BOTTLE

In another field, another man, Dr. Hervey D. Thatcher of Potsdam, St. Lawrence County, a druggist by profession, had quite a time — even though not as difficult as Davenport — in obtaining recognition for his invention. And this despite the fact it would prove a life saver.

Dr. Thatcher invented the milk bottle, a receptacle which has been discontinued in favor of the wax cartons of today. As stated, there are those in our modern generation who have never seen the container, yet at one time they were manufactured by the millions in various sizes and shapes.

The invention, and the troubles Dr. Thatcher had in getting milk dealers and the public itself to accept this sanitary container, is outlined in "An Early History of Potsdam," by Marguerite Gurley Chapman which, I am told, can be found in the Potsdam Public Museum.

Like many inventions, this one materialized into reality by chance. Dr. Thatcher on a summery day in 1884 was idly watching a milk delivery to a home when a small girl dropped a filthy rag doll into a 40-quart metal milk can, from which the fluid was dipped during deliveries. Families furnished their own containers. And milk was not the most expensive of commodities in those days. It cost three cents a quart.

Dr. Thatcher was startled when he noted the delivery man shrug off the incident; that worthy merely fished the rag doll out of the milk and returned it to the girl. Whether he used his hand or the ladle is not known.

Long an advocate of sanitation in the handling of milk, because of the always present dangers of bacterial contamination, Dr. Thatcher resolved to do something about changing delivery procedures. He made a wooden form of a bottle, contacted a wood carver, Henry Batchelder, who carved thereon a person milking a cow and using a type of sanitary pail developed by Dr. Thatcher a year previously.

Above this was inscribed: "Absolutely Pure Milk." Beneath read this slogan: "Milk Protector."

The model was submitted to the Whitall-Tatum Company in New York City, which manufactured ink bottles, demijohns and glass insulators. The company was impressed; had a blower create the model in glass. And succeeding bottles had to be blown by hand; a machine to mass produce the receptacle was not even a dream at the time.

If Davenport had difficulties with the acceptance of his motor, Dr. Thatcher had the same kind of hurdles in getting Potsdam people interested. They were not. So he

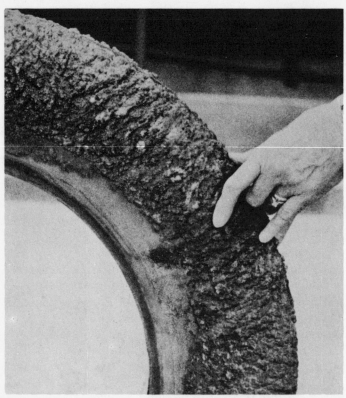

Above, left, is a side view of the famous Covey Snow Tire, showing its rough crepe rubber tread. At right is a head-on view of the surface which made the tire so successful in deep snows. The tire is on exhibit at the Adirondack Museum at Blue Mt. Lake and is one of the originals.

went to Ogdensburg, and his brother-in-law, Harvey Barnhart, and he sunk a reported $7,000 into the project.

The first sunrise on the horizon came when a milk dealer agreed to buy 400 bottles at ten cents each, and pay a royalty of $50 for their use.

On Aug. 8, 1884, Dr. Thatcher bedded a quantity of bottles on a straw bed in a wagon for the dealer and that gentleman set off for Ogdensburg. Bottles were capped with wood plugs carved by Batchelder. But during the journey over rough roads, the bottles were jostled and most of the milk spilled. The dealer found himself forced to return to his farm and start his two-miles of rounds all over, this time using the traditional milk can and ladle. That night he wrote to Dr. Thatcher:

"My Dear Doctor: You must think a man is a fool to be driving around the streets with milk in glass bottles. It is a failure and will never amount to anything."

That's what the dealer said, and one gathers he had about as much imagination as the individual who told the inventor of the zipper it would never replace buttons. He was, of course, totally incorrect. The idea of putting milk into sanitized bottles finally caught on, and the bottle led to the eventual opening of the first Thatcher plant in Pennsylvania in 1902. From then on, the bottle wrote its own history — in the millions upon millions manufactured up to the time the wax carton moved into the picture.

THE SNOW TIRE

There are many plaques in and around the Adirondacks which honor individuals and events. One is of exceptional interest. It reads:

"In memory of Earl W. Covey, 1876-1952, a master builder who lived so much in tune with the life of nature that he was able to duplicate and enhance its beauty in the creation of beautiful buildings from Adirondack trees and rocks."

Earl Covey indeed was a master of his craft; his touch was that of a genius in that he saw, in trees and rocks, the materials which would serve not only useful purposes but literally add to the North Country motif. In no way did his creations detract from the naturalness of scenes about them. (Which, if the author may add, is not the case of some types of construction which have sprung up in the Adirondacks in more recent years).

Covey had a touch of artistry and he combined this with a practical approach. The ability to apply an idea to actual reality is illustrated in the Covey snow tire.

Earl Covey was born at Glenfield, Lewis County, and during his life served not only as a builder, but a woodsman, guide, innkeeper and inventor.

While at Covewood, at Big Moose, which consisted of a main lodge and several cottages, he had difficulty in getting his Ford over a hill in winter — even though the road was plowed out. It was then he began to think about a tire which would consider snow no problem.

Why not, he reasoned, apply the roughened surface of crepe rubber to tires?

At that time, J. E. Hale, manager of the development department for Firestone Tire and Rubber Company, had been a guest at Covewood a number of times. In 1928 Covey discussed the tire with him. Hale's suggestion was that he write Firestone. He did.

The company was interested. A number of tires were made for him and put to use in his area of the Adirondacks. The company followed this up by sending three of its personnel to see how things were shaping up.

In the words of Frances Alden Covey Earl's wife in her book, "The Earl Covey Story," published in 1964, it is stated:

"When the Firestone men saw for themselves what the Covey tires would do, they were convinced that the crepe rubber had better traction than that of ordinary tires."

Reportedly, one of the threesome said that in respect to traction, Covey's tires were better than the ones then produced; the Covey tire, as a photo in this chapter shows, possessed a surface of total roughness, which dug into snow and held its grip.

Covey received his first tires from the Akron, Ohio company in 1929. More tires were manufactured and shipped to accomodate about 40 automobiles in the area. It was found that a truck, with six crepe rubber tires, (dual in the rear), crunched its way through snow 45 inches in depth with ease!

Covey applied for patents both in the United States and Canada. His Canadian patent came through in two years. It took four years to obtain one from the United States. The tire, although working well, had what was called a "limited" life of wear, understandable because of its composition.

But the economic shadow over America, the result of the stock market crash of 1929, had deepened. And the tire, although it bore the Firestone name, was made only on special order for Covey. The complaint was its wearing qualities. And Covey himself recognized that his tire did need toughening.

Along with the deepening depression, came improvements in road clearing machines. More roads were paved. The day when Adirondack roads were so choked with snow that clearing crews literally tunneled their way through some drifts, was gone.

After 1938, according to Mrs. Covey, her husband gave up in his efforts, spending his winters in Florida, far from North Country blizzards.

The tire never reached large scale production, but major tire companies did not drop the idea of manufacturing tires which would master winter. The Covey tire, in its own way, served its purpose. In the words of a friend of Covey's, a former car dealer:

"Do you realize that until Earl invented his tire no one had ever heard of a winter tire?" The friend is quoted in Mrs. Covey's delightful book, a pleasure to read, a story of a man who left his mark on the Adirondack scene in many different ways.

ON WIRELESS COMMUNICATION

If, perchance, conversation languishes in any group meeting in Fulton County, a good share of which is in the southern central Adirondacks, casually mention you do not believe a Fulton County native invented radio. Radio? Right!

Reaction will prove swift from those who know; you'll be figuratively lanced, clubbed and battle-axed with an avalanche of proof that Dr. Mahlon Loomis, a dentist born on July 21, 1826, in the Town of Oppenheim, not only invented wireless telegraphy, but had it patented in the United States in 1872, two years before Guglielmo Marconi was born in Bologna, Italy!

Astonishing? Yes indeed. But, I think, indisputable.

Marconi, you will be told, developed, or perfected what Dr. Loomis began and this, in a way, parallels development of other great inventions. One instance: While Alexander Graham Bell is credited with the invention of the telephone, that much used, much abused instrument would not be what it is today without fur-

Here's the Fulton County native who started it all. While Marconi is sometimes credited with the invention of radio, Dr. Mahlon Loomis, above, actually pioneered the extraordinary invention. Marconi in later years perfected it.

45

ther development, or improvement, if you will, by Thomas Alva Edison.

Relatively unheralded save by staunch believers in his genius, Dr. Mahlon Loomis was the precocious son of Nathan and Waitie Jane Barber Loomis; Mahlon's dad was the son of a Baptist minister who came to the Town of Oppenheim from Massachusetts, and this branch of the Loomis family lived in Oppenheim Town for approximately two generations.

In his early days, Mahlon Loomis moved with his family to Virginia, and later studied dentistry in Ohio; family records indicate he practiced dentistry in Ohio, Virginia and several other areas before moving to Washington, D.C.

He was married to Achsah Ashley on May 28, 1856, when communication was technologically limited. The Morse telegraph came into general use in America in 1851, with private companies using the inventor's patent, and private companies were in the picture because the United States government had decided, after a demonstration in 1844, that the telegraph had no future and withdrew its support!

Bell received his patent for the telephone on March 7, 1876. That was about the extent of fast communication in those days.

Loomis, by the time of his marriage, had demonstrated he was no ordinary dentist; two years before his marriage, at age 28, he patented a kaolin process for making false teeth. (Kaolin is a pure white clay used in the manufacture of chinaware).

In 1858, at age 32, Loomis' thoughts were other than on gaping mouths and abscessed teeth; they were roaming the atmosphere. He said:

"I believe as soon as something can be found to bear the same relation to the earth that a wire does, a tele-graphic communication can be without wire. What relation does a wire bear to the earth? That is a question to be settled, and one which I must write about at some other time."

Back to drilling and extractions he went for a time.

According to Marion C. Mang, Town of Oppenheim historian, Loomis was convinced that static electricity in the atmosphere could be harnessed as a source of never ending power, making it possible to dispense with costly batteries in telegraphy, and he proved successful in experimenting with such electricity.

It was in October, 1866, that the former Adirondack native deserted his dentist's chair temporarily, that he established two stations on separate mountains some 20 miles apart, in Virginia. The tragedy to New York State history is that if he had remained in this state, the Adirondacks might have been the scene of that important happenstance.

His experiment without wires worked. It was performed a full eight years before the birth of Marconi, and it was done before such witnesses as U.S. Senator Samuel Pomeroy of Kansas and Rep. John A. Bingham of Ohio, both of whom later supported Loomis in futile efforts to obtain federal monies to commercialize his discovery.

In a notebook on file in the Library of Congress, Dr. Loomis describes his venture in this fashion:

"From two mountain peaks of the Blue Ridge in Virginia, which are only about 2,000 feet above tide water, two kites were let up, one from each summit.

"These kites had each a small piece of fine copper wire gauze about 14 inches square attached to their undersides and connected also with the wire 600 feet in length which held the kites when they were up.

This is a sketch made by Dr. Mahlon Loomis of his assistant waiting for the wireless signals from Bear's Den, in 1866, at a station atop Furnace Mountain, Virginia, during one of his early experiments. The original sketch is in the Mahlon Loomis collection; this one has been reproduced through courtesy of the Library of Congress in Washington, D.C. The kite is not visible in the sketch, but wire from it is visible, attached to instrument known as a galvanometer, alongside assistant, which registered wireless signals.

"The day was clear and cool, with a breeze strong enough to hold the kites firmly at anchor when they were flown. The equipment and apparatus at both stations were exactly alike. The time pieces — (watches) — of both parties having been set exactly alike — a message was sent from the first station to the opposite station at the time decided upon, and was received clear and distinct.

"Then the opposite station sent the same message back to the first station, a perfect duplicate of those sent from it. Although no 'transmitting' key was made use of, nor any 'sounder' key to voice the message, yet they were just as clear and precise as any sped over a wire."

At predetermined intervals, individuals helping Dr. Loomis grounded a wire which ran through the galvanometer to the kite, causing the other instrument at the other mountain to register. Each time the experiment was repeated, the needles on the galvanometers reflected the impulses every time the circuit was completed.

One could visualize this as a scene duplicating Franklin's famous foray with a kite — with, of course, major variations!

In 1870, Loomis successfully transmitted signals between two U.S. Navy ships in Chesapeake Bay. That was one success in the middle of two failures. In 1868, a group of Boston promoters agreed to finance his work, but they were ruined in the Black Friday financial panic and Loomis remained fundless. In 1871, a Chicago group offered $20,000 for the establishment of "radio stations" in the Rocky Mountain region, but the Chicago fire which roasted Mrs. O'Leary's cow also burned out these financial hopes.

It was in 1872, on July 30, that the United States got around to issuing its first patent on radio, No. 129,971, entitled "Improvements on Telegraphing."

In 1873, Congress chartered the Loomis Aerial Telegraph Company, authorizing capital stock of $200,000, with the privilege of increasing it to $2 million. President U.S. Grant signed the bill after passage by the Senate, but the money was never forthcoming! Was there suspicion of the "future" of radio, as there had been in Davenport's electric motor and Morse's telegraph? Perhaps. But one congressman, pleading in behalf of Loomis, said:

"He entertains a dream and it may be only a dream, a wild dream, that when his proposition comes to be fully applied, it may light and warm your houses."

Dr. Loomis died on Oct. 13, 1886, at age 60, at the home of his brother, George, at Terra Alta, West Vir-

Admiration, and rightfully so, is expressed by Marion C. Mang, Town of Oppenheim Historian, and Lewis Decker of Gloversville, at the site of the Mahlon Loomis marker in front of the Town of Oppenheim garage. Decker served as Coordinator of the Fulton County BiCentennial Committee, and the marker was unveiled with ceremony as part of the county's observance of the anniversary. The marker bluntly credits Dr. Loomis with the invention of wireless communication — or radio.

ginia, and is buried in the Terra Alta Cemetery. Eight months before his passing, he remained persistent in his experimentations; he installed two "radio" stations in Terra Alta and transmitted messages two miles between them.

Otis B. Young, Director of Cooperative Atomic and Capacitor Research, University of Southern Illinois, long interested in Loomis, prepared an affidavit in later years, stating:

"**I am convinced that Doctor Mahlon Loomis, an American dentist of Washington, D.C., did in 1864 discover and invent radio or aerial wireless communication.**"

Young thus gives credit to Loomis two years before the famous witnessed experiment in Virginia.

Nearer to home, in Fulton County, and far more recently, the Fulton County BiCentennial Committee, under direction of its coordinator, Lewis Decker of Gloversville, plus other Loomis believers, took matters into their own hands and transmitted their own message of belief by unveiling an historical marker eulogizing the Fulton County native.

This ceremony, which I attended, took place at the Town of Oppenheim garage, and the enthusiasm displayed was tremendous; Fulton County, on this day, had come into its own.

The "Mahlon Loomis" park, as the spot is sometimes known, is located off Route 29, and during the ceremonies, Rep. Donald J. Mitchell and County Legislator Charles Dolge were among those who spoke. On April 5, 1978, State Senator Hugh Farley introduced a resolution giving Loomis his fair recognition in New York State. It was adopted. The resolution, among other many things, said:

"...his proper recognition has been denied him all too long.

THE COVERED PENCIL

In 1858, Hyman Lipman of Philadelphia had a bright idea. He had made a mistake as he wrote a letter in pencil. So he used an eraser. But it wasn't attached to the pencil. Lipman allowed that it should be. So he patented his idea, and thus we have the pencil of today, workable at both ends.

But Lipman would have had no opportunity to patent his novel idea if he hadn't had the pencil in the first place, and that brings us to the Ticonderoga area, where Lake George, in its own inexorable way, flows into a stream called LaChute, and thereby descends, over a distance, 200 feet down into Lake Champlain.

About 1815, graphite, sometimes called "black lead" or "plumbago," was discovered in the Ti area. Its first general use was for the polishing of iron stoves. In the 1830's another use for this form of carbon was found — steel makers began to line their crucibles with this mineral.

There was still another use. Pencils were made from it. Pencils not as we know them today, but sticks of graphite.

In the interesting volume, "Ticonderoga — Patches and Patterns From Its Past," published in 1969 by The Ticonderoga Historical Society, there is discussion of the evolution of a slim rod of graphite into the pencil as we know it today. The manuscript for the volume, incidentally, was prepared by Jane M. Lape, who also headed editorial supervision. With her worked three others from the historical society, Marguerite Balding, Stephanie DeChame and Arthur Carr.

Graphite was found in veins; one, for instance, was opened which contained the mineral four to 18 inches in width, six to eight feet in depth, and more than 100 feet in length. It didn't take long for Guy C. Baldwin, a partner of Nathan DeLano in processing and marketing of the material, to improve upon the "graphite stick."

In 1839, a patent was issued to Baldwin for the first solid pencil, that is, graphite bound with wood. These pencils were about five inches long, round, and a bit on the rough side. They were made in two parts and glued together. The wood used was either poplar or basswood. (The grandson of Nathan DeLano [the latter Baldwin's brother-in-law] wrote the above description in 1931 as part of his recollections of the product).

The famous "Ticonderoga" pencil was manufactured for a number of years, with an annual sale of up to $3,000 dollars!

So once again we are offered evidence of Adirondack ingenuity — this time a development of an instrument which is used throughout the world.

THE TROLLING SPOON AND THE TUTTLE DEVIL BUG

Let's take the trolling spoon first. Again we come to an invention which, although conceived out of state was fully developed in the waters of Lake Champlain and in Lake George to the south.

Chance, always present in the field of innovation figured in this creation.

Julio T. Buel, born in 1812, near Lake Bomoseen Vt., north of Fair Haven and only a few miles inland from the east shore of Lake Champlain, was quite a trout fisherman. When only a youngster he noted trout would rise when he tossed bits of bright material into the waters. One day he soldered a hook to a piece of tin and twisted it so it would revolve when drawn through the water. He caught himself a mess of fish, became the wonder of his neighborhood.

But his big moment arrived when he was 18, and was eating lunch in a boat. A soup spoon was accidentally dropped overboard and as it spiraled downward, it was struck by a large fish before it hit bottom. That incident led to another, his next step. He obtained a tablespoon and soldered a hook to that bit of tableware.

As long as the trolling spoon exists in the world of fishing, nobody can forget Julio T. Buel, who invented the lure, and later manufactured a wide variety at Whitehall.

The report of use of this new spoon:

"His first efforts in Lake Bomoseen with this remarkable crude construction was a revelation to all the fishermen in the area; the size and quantity of the fish he took from the depths of the lake had never before been approached."

Buel moved to Whitehall in 1844, at age 32, with the original intent of entering the fur business. However, with Champlain at his doorstep, fishing took up considerable of his time. So did the making of lures.

Lake George was the scene of many of his efforts as well. His devices were tested not only in these waters, but in the many Adirondack streams and ponds in the region. Lake George proved a particularly fine testing spot, since he could witness both lure and fish actions deep in its clear waters. It was in Lake George that Buel first caught fish by deep trolling.

His lures proved so successful he began manufacturing them. One of the trolling spoons was named "The Old Reliable" and "The Original Trolling Spoon," because that's exactly what it was patterned after.

In later years these lures and other of comparable results were manufactured by Northern Specialty, headed by Ruth Jackson; the Jackson family ran the business for about 15 years in Whitehall, and in 1976 sold it to the Lou J. Eppinger Manufacturing Company, Dearborn, Michigan, headed by Edward A. Eppinger, president. His company has continued the fine quality and skill which went into the famous lures.

In the course of writing this chapter, I contacted Mr. Eppinger to pursue certain bits of information, and to request permission to utilize background material embodied in a booklet put out by the Eppinger Company called "The Spooners." That permission was granted and in the course of that granting, I learned his

organization had purchased the assets of still another famous fishing lure maker — the O.C. Tuttle Devil Bug Company of Old Forge in the Central Adirondacks.

Therein is another tremendously interesting story of another bit of fishing equipment, this one originating in the North Country and one whose fame has spread far and wide.

The mechanics of observing and putting that observation into practical use is a rare quality. Earl Covey had it with his snow tire; Thomas Davenport had it with his electric motor; most assuredly others mentioned in this chapter possessed the same ability.

There is no question but that Orley C. Tuttle had that gift.

This gentleman, in years gone by, had fished lakes in the Old Forge region and like Julio Buel he was an observer of fish tastes. In the 1930's he told a writer for National Geographic Magazine of the time and circumstances when the idea for the famous Tuttle Bug hit him.

He saw the floating carcass of a dead deer during a trip in 1919. To him the carcass seemed to be "all atremble." There was reason for the whitetail to have the shakes. The water under the deer was literally alive with trout, tearing away at both hide and hair. He caught two of them, cut them open, found their stomachs were "full of deer hair."

Tuttle mulled over the situation. And he came to the conclusion there was a salt and alum taste in the hair that fish liked, "and that's the taste of all insects, nearly."

The attack on the deer was not the only action witnessed. Noted was a hatch of a large beetle of a type he said he had never before seen, and whenever these insects hit the water, bass went at them with violent lunges.

A closeup of one of the Tuttle Devil Bugs, this one patterned after a mouse, has gained fame as a bass lure.

Orley C. Tuttle and his wife, Lottie, pose with understandable pride, with two fine Adirondack bucks. It was Tuttle, also a devoted fisherman, who devised the famous Tuttle Devil Bug, and it was his wife, a licensed guide and an accomplished artist, who colored the lures and also created art work for advertising brochures and other advertisements.

Tuttle that night fashioned an insect similar to the ones he had seen, and he made his model of deer hair.

His wife, when asked her opinion, told her spouse she thought it "looked like the devil," and thus was born the name Devil Bug. The following morning Tuttle went fishing and caught 25 bass, 24 of them on his new lure. There was no question that he had devised an extraordinary tid-bit for a hungry fish prowling for a menu. The fame of the bug spread rapidly; is now international in scope.

Manufacture of the Devil Bug began and Lottie, his wife, an artist, and a licensed guide as well, helped by hand-painting the lures. She also did art work for brochures and advertisements. Sales grew. So did the variety of bugs. Fame came to the Tuttle family; Robert Page Lincoln, in "Black Bass Fishing," credited Tuttle with being the first to make bugs and mice counterparts out of deer hair.

In 1922, only three years after the bug was conceived, sales went to 50,000; work was farmed out to Old Forge residents to keep up with the demand.

In 1935 the Tuttles turned the business over to their daughter and son-in-law, Edith and Clarence Morcy, and the Morcys continued the business through selected retail outlets and mail order. Certainly a compliment to their skill was that one of the outlets was the prestigious Abercrombie & Fitch Co., in New York City.

Mrs. Clarence Morcy, pictured at her home at Fourth Lake a few years ago, as she worked on the creation of one of the famous Tuttle Devil Bugs.

Here is Bruce Mitchell's conception of Julio Buel, inventor of the trolling spoon, as he used his lure. Buel later perfected his innovation in Lake Champlain and Lake George, and began manufacturing his product in Whitehall. His original spoon was a piece of tin to which he soldered a hook; after tin, came a hook soldered to a tablespoon.

O.C. Tuttle died in 1943; his wife passed away in 1936.

After the death of Clarence Morcy, Mrs. Morcy continued the manufacture, but on a vastly diminished scale. I visited the charming craftslady at her home at Fourth Lake a few winters ago, was her guest for several hours, found she still made an occasional lure, possessed a fairly good supply, and had lost none of the precise skill that went into their making.

Mrs. Morcy sold her business in 1974 to Al Stripp, an art teacher in Old Forge, later repurchased it, and sold it to the Lou J. Eppinger Manufacturing Company. According to Mr. Eppinger, Mrs. Morcy was most helpful in transmitting her own methods of tying the Devil Bugs to the Eppinger family; the Tuttle touch, therefore, is not lost.

Bruce Mitchell, Keene Valley, at work on one of his many paintings for the First Vermont Bank Collection. Two of his paintings are reproduced in this chapter.

The aches and pains experienced by Rev. Cyrus Comstock of Essex County before the turn of the century proved a blessing to those who rode behind a horse over rough mountain roads. Rev. Comstock used a long, springy platform of wood to connect the front and rear axles of his new buggy, called it the "buckboard," and by 1900 his invention had spread throughout the nation. The buckboard pictured may be seen at the Adirondack Museum at Blue Mt. Lake.

THE BUCKBOARD

Toward the end of the 19th century, Rev. Cyrus Comstock of Essex County, often rode the unbelievably rough roads of his heavily wooded area in a buggy, and equally often he was not happy about the effect on his posterior. He was not only a man of God, but of invention as well, and after considering the bruises a ride administered to his anatomy, he decided to improve the riding qualities of his mode of transporation. All very understandable if joints creaked during a sermon.

Earlier in the century logging wagons possessed a rack, called a buckboard, at the front, to prevent logs from skipping forward and "bucking" the horses in their rear ends, thus spooking them into unexpected, violent maneuverings. Eventually such a contrivance became known as a buckboard wagon.

Rev. Comstock had observed empty wagons of this type; had also observed drivers riding comfortably on the long, springy board that connected the front and rear axles. And he reasoned, with logic that was proved, the same principle could be applied to smaller wagons carrying human cargoes.

He adopted the idea to his buggy, called his creation a buckboard, even though it had nothing to do with the log rack that originated the name.

By 1900, Rev. Comstock's Adirondack marvel — which some called a "gift to the sanctity of the spine," — had spread throughout the entire country. It had the flexibility of a circus net; gentled impact of highway rocks, and unquestionably cut widely into the use of ointments and salves sold to relieve assaulted muscles.

There is a buckboard on display at the Adirondack Museum at Blue Mt. Lake, and its description reads in this fashion:

"Essentially a buckboard consists of a pair of axles connected by a long, flexible plank platform carrying one or more seats. The natural spring of the plank provides a relatively easy ride even over bad roads. More elaborate buckboard construction included steel helper springs and further refinements."

The displayed article called the Glens Falls Buckboard, was made by the Joubert & White factory in Glens Falls, which organization claimed it had originated and patented its own type. It was also known as the Joubert & White Buckboard. The company sold throughout the world; made them from their own, or customer's designs.

Apparently there was controversy surrounding the origin of the Glens Falls product, since this statement is attributed to the company:

"We now have numerous imitators, our designs are speedily copied, and the plagiarist boldly seeks to divert business meant for us by using our trade marks and titles. We wish to emphasize the fact that we are, and always have been, Joubert & White, and are not otherwise connected. World trade is conducted mostly by mail, with a catalogue of some 50 models." End quote.

52

The Floating Kitchen? An Adirondack innovation if ever there was one! I am indebted to Fern McKee of the Schroon Lake area for use of this old-time pictorial classic. Such a craft was built of logs, contained a stove and tables, upon which that most respected (and sometimes not respected) of personages, the cook, prepared the daily fare. Note novel stance of the gentleman second from right. As lumbering operations ceased in one spot, the floating beanery was either dismantled or towed to a new working location.

The author freely admits there are other inventions which might have been noted herein, but the thought in writing this chapter was to choose a comparatively representative few and to describe them in as much detail as possible in space unquestionably limited.

The Adirondack guide boat has been bypassed simply because hundreds of pages of type have been printed on this novel craft and to pursue it further would only mean repetition of facts already widely known. The same can be said of many innovations in the field of mining in the North Country, particularly in the tapping of garnet resources in the North Creek-North River area.

Adirondack furniture has not been discussed because while much of it has been unusual, some forms have been copies of that found in lodges in Europe. However, I would like to call attention to the famous Westport chair, designed by Thomas Lee about 1900; this rugged but restful article was patented in 1905 and proved popular throughout the region. One can be seen at the Adirondack Museum.

In the field of lumbering, I have used only one photo to illustrate the unique floating kitchen, practical because of the many lakes and ponds in the tracts scheduled for scalping. The kitchen may or may not have been Adirondack born, but I believe it was, since the park area was among the first of regions tapped, particularly for white pine and oak.

The kitchen is now an object of the past. Perhaps scores of other innovations have appeared on the scene in similar fashion, then vanished because of changing times. Who can really say?

What can be said of those discussed is that although one could view the Adirondacks as rugged, wild and primitive country, where living once upon a time called for the greatest of physical effort and stamina, genius did not take a back seat to muscle, even in the early days.

The Adirondack area has produced inventive minds and there is no question in my own that it will continue to do so. Can better be said of any region in New York State?

THE OLDEST PERSON IN THE WORLD

"Three Score and Ten" is the Biblical
Description of a Life Span,
But a Herkimer County
Native Proved Otherwise

It's been said — and often — that women outlive men.

This was proved in extraordinary fashion in the case of a Herkimer County woman who, according to the Guinness Book of World Records, attained the greatest authenticated age in the world.

She was Mrs. Delina (Grandma) Filkins, who was born on May 4, 1815, and who died at age 113 years, 214 days!

She outlived a gentleman named Pierre Joubert, Canada, who died at age 113 years, 124 days. Joubert was born July 15, 1701, died Nov. 16, 1814.

The process of aging is glacial in concept. It never ceases its slow, sometimes chilling advance. It is as remorseless as a falling tree downed by wind, and how one survives the twilight years is pretty much up to muscle, mind and security.

Methuselah, one of the Biblical patriarchs, clung tenaciously, sturdily, to life until the age of 969. That assertion to some is open to argument; is based on the Book of Genesis.

Belief is up to the individual. I have no quarrel with the Bible, but on the basis of the current definition of a generation being thirty years, I find it a bit difficult to believe that a man could, in one lifetime, live through a total of more than thirty-two modern generations. One can leave that subject to speculative theologians to ponder upon.

In Russia, in 1978, the official Tass News Agency, which at times leaves much to be desired in the way of total accuracy, said that Medjid Agayev observed his 143rd birthday in the Village of Tikyaband in the Republic of Azerbaijan, and during the same year, Tass also reported the 115th birthday of one Deletkhan Khekilaveva in the North Caucaus Village of Chikola.

She, incidentally, reportedly had 150 grandchildren, great grandchildren and great-great grandchildren, which leads one to believe that neither she nor her descendants had to undergo any degree of fertility rites.

In a study of documented centenarians, it has been learned that out of every two billion, one hundred million individuals in the world, only one may attain the doubtful Valhalla of 115 years before departing favorite haunts and taking up spiritual residence elsewhere.

I do have a suspicion that Russian reports on longevity might be a bit exaggerated and not exactly based upon authenticated birth records.

Then, too, there is a gentleman named Charlie Smith, who resides in Florida, and who, at this writing, is reportedly 136 years old, but a geriatric psychiatrist is reported to have said:

"It can be demonstrated that he is definitely 120 and in all probability, it appears that is close to 136."

I would like to see Charlie Smith's birth record. And that goes for Medjid Agayev and Deletkhan Khekilaveva. Obviously, Methuselah's, if one exists, is buried in the ages.

All of which brings us back to Herkimer County, considered by the Adirondack Association as one of the thirteen counties representative of the North Country.

This highly scenic county, which is split by the Mohawk River, has been distinguished by many things other than Revolutionary War happenstances.

It was, for instance, the residence of Mrs. Amos Eddy who, in 1852, died at age seventy-seven and who, following an autopsy widely reported in Utica, N.Y., newspapers, was found to have been pregnant for fifty years! Her attending physician, Dr. William H.H. Parkhurst, also a Herkimer County resident, attended her needs during the final ten years of her life and participated in the post mortem examination.

The detailed story of Mrs. Eddy and her lithopedian, or "stone baby," is contained in this writer's first book, "Adirondack Album, No. 1."

Now one finds Herkimer County can claim still another record in the field of human tenacity.

That record, as divulged earlier, is held by Mrs. Filkins, who died Dec. 4, 1928, in Richfield Springs, Otsego County.

Above is the portrait painted of Mrs. Delina (Grandma) Filkins, "oldest person in the world," according to the Guinness Book of Records. The Portrait was painted when Mrs. Filkins was 113, by the famous artist, Leonebel Jacobs of New York City, on commission by Bartlett Arkell, Canajoharie benefactor. The painting is the property of the Canajoharie Library and Art Gallery.

Thus she was six when Abraham Lincoln was born, and fifty when he became the victim of John Wilkes Booth. The entire Lincolnian period was there for her to see and hear about.

She was twenty-two when the famous naturalist and geologist, Ebenezer Emmons, who conducted the first natural history of New York, applied the name "Adirondacks" to the North Country, known to the Iroquois as Ho-de-no-sau-nee-ga. She was the same age when the first recorded ascent of Mt. Marcy was made by the white man.

She was thirty-three when John Brown, the abolitionist, purchased two farms near Lake Placid; his former residence exists as a historical landmark even today.

She lived, during her youth, when the Adirondacks could point to a population of mountain lions, timber wolves, elk, moose, and the Canada lynx and wolverine, now officially extinct.

During the earlier years of her life she read that the Prospect Hotel at Blue Mt. Lake became the first hotel in the world to install electric lights.

She was alive and well when iron ore for the Union ironclad, the Monitor, was dug from the Adirondack crust. And she read of its entombment off Cape Hatteras.

When I point out she was an amazing person, it is backed by facts. When she was 106 years old, for instance, she underwent surgery of an unspecified nature, considered serious. She bounced back. The operation was termed "one of the most remarkable surgical operations known to medical history."

While today cataracts and glaucoma plague so many of our elderly citizens, Grandma Filkins never wore eye glasses until later years. Up to her final illness, she did her own housework and dressed herself in neat fashion. She also sewed and read a great deal.

Although in her twilight years she had no teeth, artificial or otherwise, she managed to eat well and enjoyed everything placed on the table, including meat, of which she was particularly fond. Her gums must have had the hardness of an Eskimo's.

During her final illness, attributable to the time-honored condition described as "infirmities of old age," she refused to stay in bed, but sat propped up in her favorite chair.

She bore six children and the oldest at the time of her death was a mere ninety-one!

Truly, as one studies her life, the conclusion is inescapable; she saw America grow. On August 6, 1836, she witnessed the first railroad train pass through the Mohawk Valley between Utica and Schenectady. (The first train to join Hudson's River and the Mohawk ran between Albany and Schenectady Aug. 9, 1831). What she saw was the extension of railroad facilities, still in a most primitive stage.

While during her lifetime she saw many trains thereafter, she never rode one!

Nor did she ever ride a trolley car. On the occasion of her 100th birthday, Mrs. Filkins did consent to her first automobile ride. This was on May 14, 1915. One can imagine this was hardly Utopian in comfort, since roads were poor and the cars of that long past day were not exactly waterbeds in riding qualities.

When Clinton's Ditch, otherwise known as the Erie Canal, was opened in 1825, and thus created an agricultural and industrial upheaval in the Mohawk Valley, her father, William Eaker, took her and the rest of his family to Little Falls, there to see the passing of the patron saint of the Erie, New York State Governor DeWitt Clinton. He rode by in the packet boat, Seneca Chief, which craft officially opened the Big Ditch.

At the age of 112 she was considered the oldest woman in the United States, and on her birthday, May 4, 1927, she refused an offer of a ride in an "aeroplane" only because of "cold and stormy weather."

On that day she arose as usual at 5 a.m., made her bed, ate a hearty breakfast, then watched her granddaughter-in-law, Mrs. Bert Filkins, bake the festive cake. After that, she leaned back in her chair, read newspapers and prepared to receive visitors. Among those who honored her was the late Owen D. Young, sage of Van Hornesville and chairman of the board of the General Electric Company.

The cake, incidentally, contained 112 candles, which gives one an idea of its size. It is not recorded whether Grandma Filkins blew the flames into oblivion with one blast, but it would not have been astonishing if she did.

Among letters of congratulations was one from then President Calvin Coolidge. By then she had lived through twenty-six presidential administrations. As a concession to the occasion, she didn't go to bed at her usual hour, 7 p.m.

Her birthday that year was widely publicized in several newspapers, including the Fort Plain Standard, and I am indebted to Frank Chamberlain, formerly of that newspaper, and, as of this writing, foreman and part owner of the Fort Plain Printing Company, for copies of stories of the event. The Standard no longer exists under that name; is now the Courier-Standard-Express.

Another year rolled by and at age 113 this gracious lady became the subject of a portrait, painted by Leonebel Jacobs of New York City; Mrs. Jacobs was commissioned by Bartlett Arkell of Canajoharie and New York, a well known benefactor of Canajoharie, and whose name is carried by the library and famous art gallery of that community.

Upon completion of the portrait, made on the farm where Mrs. Filkins lived, the elderly woman expressed her pleasure in a delightful way. She kissed the hand of the artist.

The portrait, shown in this chapter, is in the collection of the art gallery and I am indebted to its Curator, Edward Lipowicz, for permission to reproduce it.

The ancestral background of Grandma Filkins had roots in another area of northeastern New York; her grandparents' names were Eaker and Harwick, and were descendants of pioneers who came from Holland and settled on a portion of the huge land holdings of the Dutch patroon, Van Rensselaer, below Albany.

When the English defeated the Dutch in 1664, the Eaker family moved to Albany, then later traveled westward into the Herkimer County area, described then as "the unbroken wilderness on the northern slopes of the Mohawk-Susquehanna Divide."

Age is like money. The more of each attained, the greater the fame. As increased prestige came to Mrs. Filkins local newspapers not only consistently carried stories about her, but so did a New York City sheet. That newspaper remains unnamed and perhaps fortunately so, because a story printed therein was the result of wild imagination and, I have no doubt, that imagination was fired by liberal doses of Big City dew, a liquid often used as a mental crutch by newsmen of that day.

There was, the newspaper said, an "Indian uprising in the Mohawk Valley," when Mrs. Filkins was four years old, which would have been in 1819, long after Revolutionary War revenge had scattered valley Indians northward, some into the Adirondacks, some into Canada. When the alarm was "sounded," read the fanciful report, her parents rushed their children, including Delina, into a hideout arranged for such such a surprise visit.

The same newspaper, still putting fiction before fact, said her father, "fearing the child's sobbing might be their death warrant, took a homespun handkerchief of flax and tied it gently over the little girl's mouth." A gentle way of saying he gagged her.

Grandma Filkins, as time moved on, did give in to one punishment by Nature. She became deaf during her late years. But her interest in the passing scene remained high and her observations pertinent to the times. James Madison was President of the United States when she came into the world, and she had many observations on those who succeeded him.

Aside from political comment, she considered the "present times of 1928" were far better than the "good old days." This she said despite the fact that 1928 was her last.

With the memory of past and present, she made many observations on such things as women's apparel. In the main, it was reported, she approved of short skirts, bobbed hair and "modern feminine ways," although what her opinion would be on present day moral structures of society, and such wisps as bikinis, has to be guessed at. At one time she qualified her remark about short skirts. She said she did not approve of "extremely short skirts."

On the Volstead, or prohibition law, she thought it a good thing to have around. Once again, one can only wonder what she would think of today's Booze and Drug Subculture.

On the international front, her comment on China, made in 1927, was that "this nation with its many peoples, is just waking up and modernizing." This, remember, in 1927; she was far ahead of world politicians on that score. Can we imagine her comments today not only on China, but the Soviet Union, the rise of Arab nations and the mid East situation?

Unknown to this writer, at least, was her opinion on slavery. One can assume, and safely so, that based upon her philosophy, she was against it. Obviously she was fiercely independent and possessed a do-it-yourself determination.

The one inexorable advance she could not stop was age. In reporting the death of this remarkable woman, the Fort Plain Standard said she "retained marvelous health and vitality up until a few weeks ago when she began to fail."

Grandma Filkins passed away quietly and buried with her in the Van Hornesville Cemetery, are all the recollections of a life well lived, of upheavals in the American way of life; of wars; of periods of peace; of family and friends, and of an existence utterly amazing in the span of time covered.

Even in death she is to be given everlasting tribute.

MOUNTAIN MAILDOG

**He Never Carried Mail But He Traveled 143,000 Miles
With It, And Much of His Meanderings
Were Through Mountain Territory**

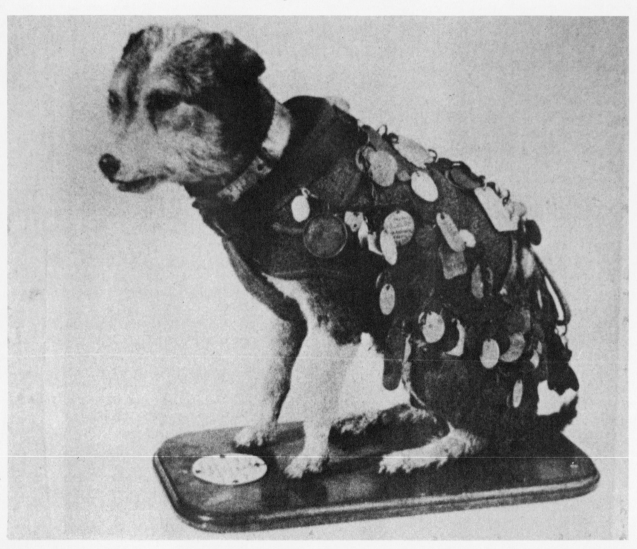

Owney is now a muted mutt memorialized by a taxidermist's skill and compassion.

His carcass, draped with bestowed medals and tags of honor and affection, is mounted in the Hall of Stamps and Mails in the Smithsonian Institution's National Museum of History and Technology, Washington, D.C.

He has been on display since 1964. Untold thousands who never saw this remarkable canine alive, have thus had a chance to not only to see, but to photograph his preserved hide, structure and materialistic accolades.

Today he remains one of the most famous dogs in history, and during his extraordinary career of riding the rails put more mileage through the Adirondacks than any other pooch in existence, then or now. Because times have changed so radically, no other dog will ever

have Owney's opportunity to fame, food and richness in memory; the railroad mail car is, to all intent and purpose, a dead juggernaut.

Owney's background was, to put it mildly, shrouded and even in dog circles, debatable. If ever he had required a birth certificate, certain spaces would have been as blank as a void, including the name, origin and breed of his mother, the background of his father and the date of his birth.

The fact remains, however, that he was born, probably in some backyard, under-the-porch maternity ward and thus came whimperingly into existence, a friendless pooch who was, within a comparatively short time, about to find that his entire world would be filled with two-legged friends until the very last; he was a dog about to find that a wag of a tail, the lick on the hand, was the Open Sesame to thousands upon thousands of miles of free travel, plenty of food and free lodgings, albeit unusual ones.

He had no Alladin's lamp to rub. But he did, in his own way, rub thousands of postal workers of the past just the right way. His story is a fascinating one; will always remain in a category all its very own.

Owney made his appearance for the first time at the Albany, N.Y. Post Office in 1888, ninety-two years ago as of this writing. The circumstances surrounding his debut as the world's greatest four-legged Marco Polo are not known; what is, is that he saw an open door, sniffed, liked and digested the odors just beyond, wandered in, wagged his tail and was immediately befriended by postal clerks.

Once inside and fed a few times, Owney adopted the place. Eventually he was to adopt the entire United States Mail system. He liked the smell of mail pouches and used them as bedding spots. In no time at all, he was soon riding the sacks placed on hand-drawn wagons, which transported them to awaiting trains. And it was only a natural procedure that finally he was formally introduced to the interior of a mail car, now a mobile post office of the past.

Here he felt completely at home. Here were the letters and packages inscribed in a writing he could not understand, nor did he care to. Here was a huge car, heated, peopled with active workers, and here was his home, beloved despite its jerky movements, stops, and the constant, grinding noise of iron wheels on iron tracks.

The lonely, eerie wail of the whistle of the steam locomotive hauling the car soon became a soothing sound, particularly at night, as the trains roared their way through the quietness of an Adirondack night, through small communities, through long stretches of wilderness, along the picturesque shores of Lake Champlain.

There was comfort in these sounds; they became familiar friends; there was comfort in the frequent petting he received from the men with whom he rode; there was pleasure in the fuss and bother they made over his small stature, his bright eyes, his perky stance.

How and when he got the name of Owney is not known. One version is that postal workers kept repeating the question:

"Owney, Owney, who is your owner?"

The name stuck. It became official. His name became as well known as any whistle stop.

He was petted in Albany, petted in Fort Edward; was known in Lake George; was at home when the train pulled into Whitehall, Port Henry, Plattsburgh and points in between.

In his day mail moved up and down Lake George and Lake Champlain by boat, after discharge from trains. He unquestionably got his sea legs while riding some of these vessels; he really got them when in later years, just

before his violent demise, he traveled around the world by steam train and ship.

His travels through the Adirondacks were made as train traffic and construction increased. It was in 1876, for instance, according to Harold K. Hochschild, a benefactor of the Adirondack Museum at Blue Mountain Lake, and the author of several North Country oriented publications, that the Delaware and Hudson completed the last link in its line from Albany to Montreal.

And, according to Mr. Hochschild in his book, "Adirondack Railroads, Real and Phantom," it was in 1889 that the D&H purchased the Adirondack Railroad which was built in 1865-71 by Dr. Thomas Clark Durant, running from Saratoga Springs to North Creek.

By 1892 a line from Herkimer in the Mohawk Valley had reached the Fulton Chain and a line aimed south from Malone had reached Childwold. Within a few months the lines met near Big Moose and trains were moving along its trackage within a matter of days.

There are no records that this writer has come across that Owney rode all these lines but most assuredly he did ride the train to Montreal, since postal workers in that city knew the dog well. Thus Owney became international.

To me, at least, it is not debatable conjecture that wherever a mail train ran in the Adirondacks, so ran Owney.

What eventually occurred was a natural happenstance. Postal workers in many areas started keeping a record of the dog's travels. This was done in simple fashion; a card was fastened to Owney's collar, asking that his journeys through various areas be properly recorded in some form or fashion by members of the Railway Mail Service.

Tracking Owney took unusual turns. Some workers fastened trinkets to his collar. Some fastened metal tags; others attached medals and still others varied the theme by tying messages. Eventually the collection became a figurative stone collar around Owney's neck and a "jacket," or harness was purchased and installed on the mutt by the then Postmaster General John Wanamaker.

That allowed more room for the gadgets, but even then, so many were attached that they became too heavy a burden and on occasion several were removed and sent on to Albany for safe keeping. A portion of the more than one thousand tags, medals, tokens and trinkets is on display at the Smithsonian. Where others have disappeared is a matter unknown.

One writer in 1894 said when Owney moved, the rattle of tags and other trinkets sounded "like bells on a junk wagon."

Actually, when the weight was reduced, the situation didn't bother the dog too much. As a matter of act, when anyone tried "tampering" with his assorted armor plate, he displayed unmistakable displeasure and voiced it. As a mild mannered kind of animal, he did not make a practice of nipping.

Because his home base was Albany, his trips into the North Country were frequent. But the Adirondacks were not the only area visited by this waif of the rails. He dropped in not only to Washington, D.C., but Philadelphia as well. He arrived in style at Detroit, Denver, Atlanta, El Paso, Winnipeg in Canada. He visited Mexico and even Alaska, but probably his most notable trip was abroad.

The noted Adirondack traveler was shipped to Tacoma, Washington, by way of Alaska, in 1895. On August 19, that year, he pranced up the gangplank of the steamship Victoria, collar rattling, and his traveling companions happened to be his favorite forms of bedding, twenty-four sacks of mail.

The ship carried Owney to Hong Kong. But here something misfired; there was no ship to carry him farther on his journey, so Owney backtracked to Yokohama on the same ship, a distance of some 1,500 miles.

Japan proved quite an experience for the Albany-based mongrel. He was issued a passport and the astonishing document contained some rather unusual instructions.

One was that Owney was to avoid driving too fast on narrow roadways. He was also informed he was not to attend fires while on horseback. And, to cap it off, he was specifically ordered not to write graffiti on the walls of any public building, not even a dog print. I do not know, nor does history record, if fire hydrants existed in the Japanese city of that time, but I would assume that the Japanese also cautioned Owney about performing certain necessities of life on valuable plant life.

At any rate, from Japan he went on finally to Shanghai, then down the coastline to Foochow, and in that city was entertained by sailors aboard the United States cruiser, Detroit. Ship's officers gave the dog a ribbon during a brief ceremony and had the name of the vessel inscribed thereon.

Owney's travels took him on to Singapore, across the Indian Ocean, even through the Suez Canal. He eventually landed in New York City aboard the steamship Port Philip and from this area was dispatched by rail to Tacoma, his starting point. He arrived Dec. 29, 1895 and was properly wined and dined.

Honors continued. Owney received the silver medal of the Mascoutah Kennel Club in Chicago in March, 1897, and then moved westward for the last time.

San Francisco was his destination and here he attended the convention of the National Association of Railway Postal Clerks. Owney was brought on stage and in this climax of his career, received a fifteen minute ovation. He remained mute, wondering what it was all about.

Time, however, was taking its toll. Owney had lost the sight of his right eye and in 1897 was on a diet of milk and soft foods. His life was coming to an end. And tragically, it was to prove an end of violence. In the late Spring of 1897 the lovable mutt boarded a train and traveled to Toledo, Ohio.

Here — and what it was has not been determined — "something" happened.

On June 11 Owney was shot and killed.

One story has it that he bit a clerk, quite an accomplishment for a small dog on a milk and soft food diet and quite a commentary upon the individual with the gun, even if Owney did nip.

In Toledo he was taken to a taxidermist and thus in death preserved. His mounting was sent to the Post Office Department's Museum in Washington, D.C. It was in 1911 that he was given to the Smithsonian, and he made at least one more public appearance outside Washington before going on permanent display. He was exhibited at the Chicago Century of Progress Exposition in 1933.

It was in 1964 that it was determined that this mutt, beloved and pampered by so many; a dog which in his own way did more traveling through the Adirondacks than most guides, would be given the international recognition he so richly deserved.

THE McCREA "INCIDENT"

**The Murder of Jane McCrea Was the Silent
Voice of Doom for British General
Burgoyne, But Who Actually
Killed the Girl?**

Portent of ultimate disaster may appear in many disguised forms.

On July 27, 1777, a Sunday, the ominous portent to British General John (Gentleman Johnny) Burgoyne, was a piece of human skin, a scalp from which dangled a luxurious growth of dark hair, reportedly more than a yard in length.

The scalp was that of Jane McCrea (sometimes referred to as Jeannie) and it had been ripped off the top of her head that day at noon near Fort Edward on the Upper Hudson River, a frontier bastion both during the French and Indian War in the mid-1700's, and the Revolution, two decades later.

Jane McCrea was, as it came to be proved, no ordinary murder victim.

She possessed considerable beauty and charm; was well liked by area settlers, and was an American sympathizer who had fallen in love in earlier days with a young man who eventually went over to the British side of hostilities.

Her killing occurred as she was on her way to join her lover. She supposedly had received safe conduct privileges for that purpose. She reportedly was dressed in her wedding clothes at the time of her death.

While others, favorable to the American cause, were fleeing the Fort Edward area, she chose to remain, even in the face of an advancing British army and its Indian allies. It is entirely possible to believe that she did receive assurances that she would not be molested; that she would reach and rejoin her betrothed, that marriage would follow.

What kind of married life would have ensued between a wife bound by oath to a husband, both on opposing sides of the fence of war, could only be conjecture. But the marriage never occurred.

She was murdered and the removal of the ghastly trophy and the reported stripping and mutilation of her body by Burgoyne's Indians did indeed portend a disaster. It helped lead to one of major proportions.

It is entirely possible, also, that this act of impromptu and violent surgery changed world history because in the Battle of Saratoga, some months later, the Ameri-

cans were the victors and the victory convinced France to intervene on the side of the colonists. The point may be argumentative but many events in history fall into a similar category. That is one reason why the study of history becomes a fascinating one.

The point is that Jane's death aroused American fury and fear and solidified those emotions. In time to come an American army, swollen with volunteers, who figured their own families might well meet the McCrea fate despite British promises, defeated Burgoyne and forced his surrender in October, 1777. The basic aim of the British invasion down Lake Champlain and through the Hudson Valley was part of an overall plan to split the colonies; once split, subjugation could come at leisure. Burgoyne was only one phase of the strategy, but his part was vital.

His defeat was a shot in the arm to American dreams. But it was a permanent tranquilizer to British aims.

All stories have a beginning and continuity. It is this beginning and resulting actions which are of major interest to me; the defeat was the aftermath; Jane's dealer of death was the unknown individual who pulled the trigger of the starting gun that led to the defeat. Not only defeat, but it helped eventually to relieve Burgoyne of his command. And, of course, there came an American victory when it was most needed.

There are those who believe the McCrea killing has been over emphasized as a major cause of the downfall of the British and their allies. I do not think so. For instance, one can ask the question: Did British politicians feel the McCrea death had any impact on the fortunes of war at this point?

One only has to review testimony given in the British Parliament two years later, as the Burgoyne campaign was analyzed. Part of the testimony will be given later in this chapter.

But first there is background needed in some detail for the opening of the McCrea story. For one thing, what exactly did the Americans face in the British forces opposing and advancing southward upon them?

Burgoyne, the illegitimate son of a British nobleman, was forty-seven, experienced on European battlefields;

This painting, the reproduction of which is used courtesy of the Glens Falls Insurance Company, a member of the Continental Insurance Companies, represents one artist's version of the capture of Jane McCrea. There are several concepts of the scene; this is one of the best known, and purportedly shows the argument between two Indians on what her ultimate fate should be.

energetic, and fond of good living, as a matter of fact, so fond of it that he took as his mistress the wife of a commissary in his army. How that worthy felt about the arrangement history leaves untold. But apparently such gonadal combines were not overly frowned upon in those somewhat primitive days.

In Burgoyne's army were five thousand British and more than three thousand Germans, called generally Hessians, but beside detachments from Hesse-Cassel and Hesse-Hanau, there was a full regiment of Brunswick infantry and a detachment of dismounted Brunswick dragoons. Using the general term Hessians, it can be said that many were literally sold into British military service by their German masters.

For instance, on Feb. 16, 1776, in London, Lord Weymouth laid before the British House of Commons three treaties. The first was one with the hereditary prince of Hesse-Darmstadt, the second was between King George III and the Duke of Brunswick, and the third was a treaty with the Landgrave of Hesse-Cassel. The three all-powerful and brutal German masters agreed to furnish a total of approximately 17,000 men

to face British army discipline and American gunpower; it should be remembered this manpower was ruthlessly commandeered; the German mercenaries were literally in some cases taken from the fields in which they worked, from their homes and, in some cases, dragged out from church services. There was a smack of Hitlerism in the procedure since the rulers possessed, as did Hitler, the power of life or death.

The Duke of Brunswick, who supplied 4,084 men, got an "annual subsidy" of 15,519 pounds so long as his troops continued to serve, and double that sum for each of the two years following their dismissal. If a mercenary died in battle, his master received additional monies for his venture into barbarism. The soldier's family, one gathers, received notice and that is about all.

The Landgrave of Hesse-Cassel, noted for his madness for money, furnished 12,000 men; received 10,281 pounds during service of the soldiers, which payment also was to be continued until the end of the twelve months notice of dismissal.

He drove a hard bargain in human flesh, bone and soul, but the British were willing to pay in solid pounds.

The prince of Hesse-Darmstadt furnished 688 men and his annual subsidy was 6,000 pounds, and also along with this sum, King George guaranteed the prince's dominions against foreign attack. Another hard bargain.

Now along with the Hessians, of course, there were the Indian allies of the British. The latter had their Mohawks but also possessed an astonishing array of other aboriginal talent. When Burgoyne reached Skenesboro, now Whitehall, on Lake Champlain, in his southbound campaign, he had a number of Indians in his Pandora's Box of warfare, but was joined by about five hundred more, including Sioux, Sacs, Foxes, Menomonees, Winnegagoes, Ottawas and Chippewas, from Canada, from the straits of Michilimackinac, from the shores of Lake Michigan, even from the distant Mississippi area.

They were under command of the noted, forceful partisan, St. Luc la Corne de St. Luc, who had terrorized the eastern Adirondack region during the French and Indian War two decades before.

He, remarkably, could qualify today for senior citizen status and Social Security. He was sixty-six!

The British commanders were well aware of the dangers of employing Indians against American rebels. Some actually did not favor it and there was corresponding political and humanitarian dissent in England as well. Memories remained ever present of savage atrocities.

Burgoyne was also well aware of such. For instance, a few months before his defeat, on June 17, 1777, he camped with his army at the mouth of the Bouquet River, Lake Champlain. On June 21, he called a council of those Indians present and forcefully pointed out that in this particular campaign, the Indians should use caution in their killing, for mixed with the "enemy," that is, the Americans, were Tories, or those still faithful to King George. The Indians were advised to stay away from subjects of the crown; to keep their tomahawks in their belts, their knives in their sheaths.

Said Burgoyne:

"I positively forbid bloodshed when you are not opposed in arms.

"Aged men, women and children and prisoners of war must be held sacred from the knife or hatchet, even in the time of actual conflict.

"You shall receive compensation for the prisoners you take, but you shall be called to account for scalps.

"In conformity and indulgence of your customs, which have affixed an idea of honor to such badges of victory, you shall be allowed to take scalps of the dead when killed by your fire and in fair opposition; but on no account or pretense, or sublety or prevarication, are they to be taken from the wounded or even the dying; and still less pardonable if possible, will be held to kill men in that condition on purpose, and upon a supposition that this protection of the wounded would thereby be evaded."

"Gentleman Johnny" Burgoyne, British commander, who warned his Indian allies against undue violence, pictured above, in this reproduction of a Fort Ticonderoga painting.

An Iroquois chief said his Indians would live up to such directions.

Burgoyne at this time never knew as he spoke that possibly within his audience were those who would help catapault him from his leadership through murder. He had not the slightest knowledge of the existence of Jane McCrea nor her family. And if he did, never in his wildest dreams would he ever have connected this girl, described of "middling stature, finely formed, distinguished for the profuseness of her dark and shining hair and celebrated for her more than common beauty" with his approaching catastrophe.

About 1768 two Scotch families, the McCreas and the Joneses came from New Jersey and settled in the wilderness along the western bank of the Hudson River, near and below Fort Edward.

The widow Jones had six sons, Jonathan, John, Dunham, Daniel, David and Solomon. The family ran a ferry near the old fort, a structure now regrettably no longer in existence.

Another version of the killing is this painting owned by the New York State Historical Association. Howsoever the scene appeared, the murder helped doom Gen. Burgoyne.

The McCreas settled a few miles farther downstream. Jeannie was the daughter of a Presbyterian minister who, upon the death of Jane's mother, remarried. Jane then went to live with a brother, John, also on the bank of the Hudson. The McCrea brothers were strongly in favor of the American cause; the Joneses adhered to British aims.

Tradition has it, and there is little reason to doubt, that there had sprung up the mentioned deep love between Jane and David Jones before the two families left New Jersey, and that the relationship continued, even though David, as did his family, favored the British side. David not only favored, but joined British forces and was in the army advancing southward with Burgoyne.

Communication between the two had been maintained, but just how and when they managed to formulate plans for marriage—is untold by history in its specifics. Mail did move, but one must assume the system was not overly loaded with perfection. But Jane did know that David was in the advancing force and, obviously, David knew of her location.

It was a waiting game for the McCrea girl, for there was no way that Burgoyne's army could plan a time table it could keep. Its travel was slow, beset by difficulties.

The final drama for Jane begins to unfold at this point.

As the British and Hessians advanced toward Saratoga with their Indian allies, Jane's brother, John, proposed that she go down river with other refugees fleeing the slow-crawling English juggernaut.

But Jane obviously had a mind of her own. She decided to "linger," waiting for David. As a matter of record, on the day before her death, she proceeded up Hudson's River and crossed at the Jones ferry. The old ferryman, after the war, often spoke of how well she looked, dressed as he expressed it, "in her wedding clothes."

Whatever she did do, it took courage.

After the river crossing Jane went to the home of Peter Freel, near Fort Edward, where she stayed the night. After breakfast she went to the home of a Mrs.

McNeil, also near the fort. Mrs. McNeil, history tells us, was related to Brig. Gen. Fraser of the British army.

On the fateful day, the Americans sent out a scouting party under leadership of a Lt. Palmer. The party was ambushed by about 200 Indians. The Americans retreated; the Indians ran them down like rabbits, scalped eighteen, including Lt. Palmer.

Blood was running hot in Indian veins. They rushed into the home of Mrs. McNeil, found both women. Jane was placed on horseback for the ride to Gen. Fraser's camp. Mrs. McNeil, however, was a corpulent woman, too heavy to mount by herself and the Indians had no patience nor desire to help.

She walked.

It is at this point that historical reports again begin to differ.

The invasion of the McNeil home had been witnessed from the fort.

Shots were heard. Jane fell from her horse. Says one old account:

"It was but the work of a moment for the scalping knife and the dark, flowing locks of poor Jeannie were dangling all bloodstained at the belt of an Indian chief." Her body was stripped and dragged out of sight of the fort and the Indians proceeded their way to the Fraser encampment.

(Fraser, incidentally, was shot from his horse during the Burgoyne defeat and killed. The reported marksman was Timothy Murphy, a tough, rugged frontier scout who hailed from the Schoharie County frontier.)

The next morning the Americans evacuated the fort, found the body of Jane resting near Lt. Palmer; both were hastily buried in rude graves below Fort Edward.

Where accounts differ is in the actual manner of Jane's death. One version has it that after the Indians had taken the two women, they were pursued by soldiers from the fort and Jane was struck by musket balls from American, not Indian guns.

Mrs. McNeil did not learn of Jane's demise until she reached the British camp. But she did charge the Indians with the murder and they, according to one report, denied it. But in another version, it was said the Indians stopped at a spot owned by a William Griffins, and showed the scalps not only of the eighteen soldiers, but Jeannie's, and admitted they did the killing.

Burgoyne, aghast, believed the Indians were responsible. He believed that after Jane had been made captive by one band, another claimed her and in the heat of the ensuing dispute, one of the savages killed her on the spot.

The British general demanded the Indians furnish the murderer for the hangman's noose. But officers, including the Earl of Harrington, feared that a hanging, a method of death most feared, most abhorred by the Indians, would cause them to desert. Some, as a matter of fact, already had.

Burgoyne's mind was thus changed.

At any rate, retribution followed at Saratoga; more specifically, I imagine, it could be called the Battle of Bemis Heights. The catastrophe figured in a discussion in the British Parliament in 1779 when the House of Commons conducted an inquiry into the failure of the campaign. This, one would imagine, would attest to the importance of the McCrea "incident." Testimony was offered by the Earl of Harrington, already mentioned above, and a portion of the discussion went as follows:

Question: Does your lordship remember Gen. Burgoyne's' receiving at Fort Anne (north of Fort Edward) the news of the murder of Miss McCrea?

Answer: I do.

Q: Did Gen. Burgoyne repair immediately to the Indian camp and call them to council, assisted by Brig. Gen. Fraser?

A: He did.

Q: What passed at that council?

A: Gen. Burgoyne threatened the culprit with death, insisted that he should be delivered up and there were many gentlemen of the army, and I own I was one of the number, who feared that he would put that threat in execution. Motives of policy, I believe, alone prevented him from it; and if he had not pardoned the man, which he did, I believe the total desertion of the Indians would have ensured, and the consequences, on their return through Canada, might have been dreadful, not to speak of the weight they would have thrown into the opposite scale had they gone over to the enemy, which I rather imagine would have been the case.

Along Route 4, in the general area of Fort Edward, is this marble marker, near the spot where rests the body of Lt. Van Veghten, killed on the day Jane McCrea was murdered. He was an officer in Col. McCrea's regiment.

Q: Do you remember Gen. Burgoyne's restraining the Indian parties from going out without a British officer or proper conductor, who would be responsible for their behavior?

A: I do.

Q: Do you remember Mr. St. Luc's reporting discontent among the Indians soon after our arrival at Fort Edward?

A: I do.

Q: How long was that after enforcing the restraints above mentioned?

A: I cannot exactly say; I should imagine about three weeks or a month.

Q: Does your lordship recollect Gen. Burgoyne's telling Mr. St. Luc that he had rather lose every Indian than connive at their enormities, or using language to that effect?

A: I do.

Q: Does your lordship remember what passed in council with the Indians at Fort Edward?

A: To the best of my recollection much the same exhortation to act with humanity, and much the same rewards were offered for saving their prisoners.

Q: Do you recollect the circumstances of the Indians desiring to return home at that time?

A: I do, perfectly well.

Q: Do you remember that many quitted the army without leave?

A: I do, immediately after the council and the next morning.

Q: Was it not the general opinion that the deserti of the Indians then, and afterwards, were caused by restraint upon their cruelties and habits of plunder?

A: It was.

Thus, overseas, the echoes of the death of a g whose age, oddly enough, has long been in questi Was she seventeen, as it appears on her tombstone, twenty, or twenty-three as some others maintain?

No matter. She had been murdered "most foul" and events had followed their irresistable, gloo course for the invaders.

In 1826, Jane McCrea's remains were disinterred a placed in what was described as the "village cemeter They rest today, in fact, in Union Cemetery, betwe Fort Edward and Hudson Falls.

A novel point should be revealed as this story proaches its end. For several years an old pine tree sto near the spot where Jane's body was found.

It was chopped down in 1853 by an enterprising torian-businessman and converted into souvenirs. T chop-up-and-bring-home syndrome was evident even those days.

And even today, in Union Cemetery, where Jan buried alongside Duncan Campbell, a member of Black Watch killed in a British assault against F Ticonderoga during the earlier French and Indian war has been found necessary to place an iron fence arou both tombstones.

Souvenir fever had not died out during the advanc years. It was found that hunters of mementoes were s busy at work, this time with chisels and hammers!

HERE REST THE REMAINS
OF
JANE McCREA.
AGED 17
MADE CAPTIVE AND MURDERED
BY A BAND OF INDIANS,
WHILE ON A VISIT TO A RELATIVE IN
THIS NEIGHBORHOOD,
A.D. 1777.

TO COMMEMORATE
ONE OF THE MOST THRILLING INCIDENTS
IN THE ANNALS OF THE AMERICAN REVOLUTION
TO DO JUSTICE TO THE FAME OF THE GALLANT
BRITISH OFFICER TO WHOM SHE WAS AFFIANCED
AND AS A SIMPLE TRIBUTE
TO THE MEMORY OF THE DEPARTED,
THIS STONE IS ERECTED
BY HER NEIGHBOR
SARAH HANNA PAYN
A.D. 1852.

Her final resting place. The tombstone over Jane McCrea's grave rests behind an iron fence in Union Cemetery between Fort Edward and Hudson Falls; within the same area is the stone marking the grave of Duncan Campbell, killed in the assault against Fort Ticonderoga.

CHAOS ON THE NORTHWAY

Interstate 87, called most commonly the Adirondack Northway, is a streak of concrete which snakes its way from Albany to the Canadian border, often passing through mountain scenes of unsurpassed beauty and placidity.

It is a godsend to the Driver-in-a-Hurry; not a single blinker or red, yellow and green traffic light mars its 176-mile length. Generally on balmy days it is a highway of ease in traveling except, on occasion, when cars dart rabbit-like into the main stream at points of entry.

It is a super highway with 123 miles of connecting and access roads and ramps. Its construction was made possible only through a constitutional amendment, since a portion travels through the Forest Preserve, that is, land set aside as "forever wild," untouchable by axe or chain saw and, in some instances accessible only by foot travel.

Some call the 2,350,000-acre Adirondack preserve a "decaying forest," since management is impossible, but such application is open to argument.

Whether the Northway runs a "proper" course northward is also open to debate. There was discussion before construction began that it should be channeled through the Champlain Valley region. Local political pressures, however, exerted by counties which now enjoy its benefits, forced it through its present route — so say some. In retrospect, the Champlain route may have proved the most productive, since communities such as Ticonderoga, Crown Point, Essex, Port Henry, Westport and others northward could easily use more transient traffic and the additional income such would bring.

But that is the past. The Northway is now a permanent bit of construction: In the opinion of Raymond T. Schuler, former commissioner of the New York State Department of Transportation, and now president of the Business Council of New York State, it is a highway designed to withstand decades of heavy use.

It is getting just that.

This highway does have its moods. Sometimes in summer's heat, sections will heave a big sigh and transportation department crews will dutifully erect "bump ahead" signs or, if the highway splits in jagged fashion, State Police will route motorists around the spots. Winter at times has the same effect. Such occurrences, however, are comparatively rare.

The first sections of this strip were laid in 1957; the final segments were laid to rest and opened to traffic in 1967; the entire highway was financed with ninety percent federal monies and ten percent state. Ostensibly it can be used for military purposes if something other than Japanese beetles invade.

Construction workers were happy in the knowledge that in building the Northway they would not encounter one difficulty met in construction of the portion of Route 9-N which runs from Bolton Landing, on Lake George's west shore, up and over Tongue Mt., descending into the Silver Bay-Hague area.

That difficulty rested upon the fact that Tongue Mt. was, and is, noted for its population of timber rattlesnakes. In building the road it was not unusual for the big shovels to disrupt reptilian dens and there were times when the scoop dripped writhing snakes!

Beauty along the Northway, which is quite a distance west of Tongue Mt., is not unknown. In 1966 a 23-mile stretch between Lake George and Pottersville in Warren County was adjudged "America's Most Scenic New Highway" in a contest sponsored by Parade Magazine. Earlier, in 1960, the highway's twin steel-arch center span bridges crossing the Mohawk River twixt Albany and Saratoga Counties were cited in a "Most Beautiful Bridge" competition held by the American Institute of Steel Construction. The highway since has been awarded more blue ribbons than a prize poodle of unquestioned legitimate ancestry.

No blue ribbon would be in keeping with one aspect of the system, which developed over a period of a few years. While the Northway today contains many rest areas, one in the Clifton Park region, southbound lane, has been closed during night hours.

The reason? It had developed into a pow-wow area for homosexuals, a pick-up area for those who found traveling alone was too much to bear, and needed selective companionship. Preceding the closing off of the area, home owners living near it had made many complaints about the noise and rowdiness and the dress — or lack of it — seen on many of the merry-makers.

It is a highway which pioneered a system of emergency telephones every half mile, in both south and northbound lanes, each connected directly to State Police substations. Thus no stranded driver remains long isolated in the mountains. I ran out of gas just once, and that was in the Warrensburg area about 2:30 a.m. The response was almost immediate and, I might add, thoroughly appreciated.

It is a man-made trail alongside which "mountains" have grown by the hand of Man. One such is frequently referred to as "Mount Trashmore"; is beside the northbound lane in the Glens Falls vicinity, and is the result of municipal trash deposited not in a ravine but in a growing pile, with layers of trash covered by layers of bulldozed earth.

This may be the coming thing in trash disposal, this building of small mountains, along with the ultimate landscaping and possible use as recreational sites. Other states have so done. Mount Trashmore, however, has seen no growth in several months; Glens Falls has ceased building it heavenwards.

Interstate 87 is a road of pleasure, happiness, of death and injury. Hundreds of humans since its birth have been killed or injured. To many forms of animal life it has become a morgue, a morgue of concrete, rather than marble slabs.

Deer, bear, foxes, opposums, squirrels, rabbits, skunks, raccoons, owls and hawks and even ducks waddling in their absurd manner across the lanes have seen their final glimpse of life on its slabs.

This writer has often referred to the Northway as the "Smorgasbord for Crows," and for good reason. Scores of these highly articulate birds can be seen in early morning hours over a length of many miles, busily pecking away at carcasses. I will presume the turkey buzzards of the North Country do not ignore the welfare program.

There are caution signs denoting deer crossings, but while drivers, or most of them anyway, can read, the whitetails have not yet received the benefits of a New York State education. Thus some of them, using old game trails which criss-crossed the highway route for hundreds of years, meet death before the onrush of Man's most ferocious highway predator, the automobile.

Horses have met death, but in far different form. For a period of a few years many members of humane society chapters called the Northway the "Torture Trail," and this was bestowed because of the cruelty

This is the famous "Mount Trashmore" along the northbound lane of the Northway, which grew from a mole hill of trash hauled in from Glens Falls. The mountain will not grow another inch since Glens Falls has ceased and desisted dumping and disposes its collections elsewhere. A bit on the sorrowful side, because the Adirondacks could use another hill or two.

The motorist didn't expect this and neither did the bear which was crossing the northbound lane of the Northway in the Chestertown section. This accident can be termed unusual, since bruin was jay walking in broad daylight, about 5 p.m. when he joined his ancestors.

shown to the animals while they were being transported to Canadian slaughter houses, for product sale overseas. Horse meat is a big thing in Europe, and America's East furnishes millions of pounds. To get to slaughter houses, the horses must be transported by truck. And herein was the torture, for the animals were jammed so tightly they were unable to move; in some instances, they were never fed nor given water during the long haul to oblivion.

In other instances the weight of the horses broke sections of the trailer floor, and horse legs crashed through, dangling, as the truck moved at 60 or more miles per hour. The situation aroused such fury when it became known, that State Police cracked down, many times ordering trucks to pull over into an area and calling for veterinarians to inspect the piteous cargoes. In one case I know of, horses were temporarily released while the driver was held, and another truck ordered so the load could be split. It was not uncommon to find dead animals in transit. All of which is a sad commentary even though the animals were destined for death.

The Northway can be termed, and has been, as a boon by some, a bust by others. The highway is thrice blessed by motorists interested in reaching their camps, cottages or favorite recreational areas in quickest possible times. And it has been called a bust by those who view the additional hordes of travelers it has attracted with total dismay, particularly city dwellers who give not one damn for preservation, peace or tranquility, and who leave sections of the mountains turned into garbage and junk heaps.

This highway, this marvel of construction, has, putting it bluntly, brought in not only the desirables but the undesirables. It has proved its worth and non-worth in easy access for those traveling from major population centers. Nobody in their right mind today and now can call the Adirondacks an isolated region.

Like any highway, the Northway has seen rough times. None has ever equalled the chaotic happenstance which struck on March 14, 1972.

That was a day to remember.

Snow began that day slowly, at 3:18 a.m., and for hours thereafter continued its inexorable blanketing. Within a few hours the highway surface became eel-slick.

At about 7:30 a.m., a tractor-trailer, performing an acrobatic feat not unusual with such behemoths, jack-knifed in the south bound lane, about a mile north of the Vischer Ferry exit.

The time of 7:30 a.m. is a busy one; thousands ride the highway's backbone on their way to work.

If it was a bad time for the truck accident, it was worse for those unsuspecting drivers who followed, and whose vision was somewhat limited by the falling snow.

The first motorist to spot the immobilized truck saw it too late to pull off to one side, and thus safety. He skidded to a stop on the highway itself. He was the first. Then came another and his stop was more spectacular. He hit the first car not only with a feeling of total helplessness, but with a resounding whomp.

From that time on, skids and crashes were the order of the morning. One car after another piled into the growing heap; fenders were smashed and torn, radiators were knocked inwards, drivers shaken, cut and bruised.

Trooper B. C. Masterpolo said at the start of the Big Pile-up that there were twenty to thirty cars "compressed into one huge pile." And that was only the beginning. It began to look like the Jersey Turnpike in a heavy fog.

People found themselves trapped. Some smashed windows to get out and avoid oncoming cars. Gasoline spilled. Fumes hovered. State Police said if the fumes or gasoline had ignited there would have been a catastrophe of major proportions. Trooper Masterpolo, with Trooper D. R. Nolan were among the first to attempt the nearly impossible mission of investigation and mop-up.

The pile of banged-up cars began to resemble a roadside junk yard. It continued to grow as driver after driver, confronted suddenly by the mounting mass, hit the brakes. One driver who staggered weakly into an area diner several hours later, reported his car had been struck, in rapid succession, by three others trying to slither to a total stop. After the third impact, there was even less peace. So, said he:

"I got out and ran like hell!"

State Police sealed off entry ramps and diverted vehicles still capable of moving off into exits at Vischer Ferry and Clifton Park. Ambulances were summoned. So were tow trucks, owners of which had a field day. The Halfmoon Rescue Squad sent two ambulances and called for a third from Malta. The Clifton Park Fire Department sent apparatus. Rescue vehicles had to travel north of the Instant Junk Yard, then double back to the south. Ambulance crews were kept busy dispensing first aid on the spot for cuts, bruises and the shakes.

One vehicle, caught in the mighty crunch, represented a catering service and the driver calmly opened the tailgate and served hot coffee to chilled, bedeviled and bewildered motorists many of them wandering aimlessly about, wondering, as do all motorists involved in accidents, why this had happened to them.

At least 100 cars became involved in this unbelievable scene.

One man said he was glad he hadn't been the last man to smash into the massive pile-up because "that guy practically hit everybody else and he can't sue anybody!"

The scene was nightmarish in the soft gloom of falling snow, the silence punctuated by the sound of approaching cars, then the inevitable sound of crashes. Yet miraculously, and this is a term which can be aptly used in this instance, there were no serious injuries reported at the time. Area hospitals did, however, treat several for minor ones.

Traffic was backed up for several miles and even in that back-up minor chain reaction collisions occurred.

It was a day to remember, all right. And as one driver remarked as he gazed sorrowfully at the smashed fenders and front end of his vehicle:

"How the hell will I ever be able to forget it?"

He had good reason to say just that. The vehicle he drove was his wife's new car!

On succeeding pages, scenes of the worst pile-up of cars in the Northway's history may be seen. These excellent photographs were taken by the late Bob Paley of Capital Newspapers for the Knickerbocker News, and Paul D. Kniskern, also of Capital Newspapers, for The Times-Union.

Rear ends, front ends, sides – all were points of impact. . .

Narrow squeeze, and the driver in the middle didn't fit!. . .

Fender benders, bumper benders, hood benders. You name it. It was all there. . .

No licensed junk yard this; another scene of the carnage. . .

What would you be thinking if your car were in the center?. . .

Freddy's Snack Bar truck dispensed coffee during the Big Wait. . .

How much gas was used in waiting for the untanglement will never be known!. . .

The weather reflected the gloom of backed up drivers. . .

MAN IN CHAINS

Haunted By His Past, Tormented By His
Present, The Man Sought Salvation
In The Woods. One Of The Most
Unusual And Little Known
Stories In The Adirondacks

What happened that wild night in the forest could have represented frames from a horror movie in the making. But there were no cameras. There were no lights. It was a sight unseen.

The utter ferocity with which the man attacked the chains binding him to a tree was understandable.

He was without food.

He was without water.

His throat was as parched as a dried mudbank. Body wastes lay near him. His mind was a howling wilderness of deeds past done, unforgiven, deeds to be atoned.

Exposed portions of his body were pin-pointed with punctures and ugly red swellings. For three days and three nights, blackflies, mosquitoes and punkies, hellions in miniature which he had never before experienced in such numbers, added to his misery. The hordes and their savage bites were ceaseless. Purgatory would have been a paradise.

The purity of soul which he had sought had turned into a nightmare. The sudden, astonishing prospect of shackled death became no solace but an incentive to escape the Adirondack wilderness into which he had voluntarily committed himself. What began as an adventure into the known had reversed into a misadventure into terror.

The weapon in his hand was a rock, bloodied by his own frantic efforts to use it as a hammer. Under incessant, furious pounding, the linkage finally split. He was free at last. With chains dragging, padlocks scuffing the pine-needled floor, he staggered out of the forest, away from the torment that hummed on a million wings.

The date was May 24, 1975.

At 1:30 a.m., State Police at the Westport station on Route 9N received a call that an "unknown subject with a handgun" had been sighted on that highway near the New York State Department of Transportation garage complex. At 1:35 a.m., Troopers J.C. McAuliffe and Richard A. Bunning spotted an apparition walking the shoulders of the highway.

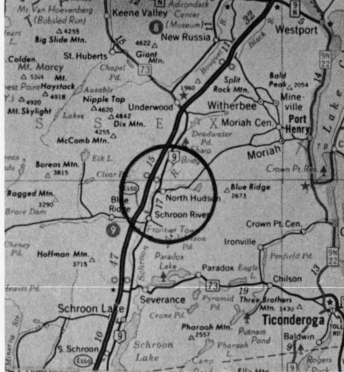

What they saw registered with difficulty, even to men who in the course of their duties had seen the unbelievable in human behavior. The six-foot, three-inch, 175-pound man blinking in the glare of the patrol car headlights was literally entwined in steel. He was bearded and his hair was long. His clothing was shabby and a pungent odor was his mantle. Unkempt would have been a description of kindness.

A heavy duty, galvanized chain was padlocked around both feet. More chains were wound around his neck. One hand was held by handcuffs of Spanish origin. A padlock hung from linkage over his shoulder. The caller to the Westport SP had mistaken the lock for a gun. It was an understandable error in view of the hour, the dimness of the light.

More bands of steel ran from his neck, under his shirt, under two pairs of trousers and under three sets of long underwear. His walk was the listless shuffle of a prisoner solidly trussed for chain gang duty. His voice was hoarsened from his ordeal; his screams had remained unheard, absorbed by the imperturbable forest about him. The woods had heard worse in days of Adirondack warfare long gone by.

Thus, in this most unusual manner, The Man in Chains came to dramatic attention in the North Country of New York State as a New York City native who traveled into the Adirondacks to "fast for forty days and forty nights," for the purpose, he told police, "to discover himself and purify his body and soul."

He was twenty-seven years old. He was in good health. His wish, as his bizarre story unraveled its erratic course, was to "unlive," among other things, a charge of incest, recorded on New York City Police Department and Family Court records five tragic years before.

He was, at the same time, no stranger to North Country law. May of 1975 was not a gentle month. Before Troopers McAuliffe and Bunning saw him, he had been arrested in the Town of Elizabethtown one early morning for soliciting a ride; earlier he had been stopped by Trooper R.J. Savage, SP Plattsburgh, on a similar charge, in the Town of Peru, Clinton County. During the same month Trooper J.P. Weisbeck, also of SP Plattsburgh, checked him out near Keeseville, Essex County. His record also disclosed he had been involved in an assault charge in Malone, Franklin County.

In the course of his brushes with the law, he had been given a ticket to New York City by the Clinton County Social Services Department. Ostensibly he made the trip to "collect his welfare money," but the Adirondacks drew him northward once again. The urge was not resistable.

It might be assumed, however, that the Bible played a part in his decision. Verse 1, Chapter 4, Book of Matthew, describes the temptation of Jesus alone in the desert. This portion, quoted from the New Testament, says:

"Then Jesus was led by the Spirit up into the desert to be tempted by the devil. After a fast of forty days and nights he was very hungry.

" 'If you really are the Son of God,' said the tempter, 'tell these stones to turn into loaves.' "

There is more to the chapter, but Verse 11 ends in this fashion:

"Then the devil let him alone, and angels came to him and took care of him."

What thoughts ran through the labyrinth of the man's mind as he fastened the padlocks, one by one, in the Westport area, can only be imagined. They must remain conjecture only, for he spoke to no one of his projected fast, nor did he notify anyone of his excursion into possible oblivion — or hoped for salvation.

He did, and this is important to note, choose a location where loose rocks were abundant and within reach.

Did he think of the Biblical phraseology as he made his choice? Who can tell?

A last, lingering look, then a moment of decision, and he tossed the padlock keys into budding underbrush, beyond reach. Perhaps he felt the conscience he was trying to appease would become a tangible locksmith to set him free upon purification. Perhaps he thought the chains would drop their inexorable clutch upon completion of his fast.

He settled back for his ordeal, a man now caught in a boa constrictor of steel.

Hell was the result.

The three days and three nights were all he could endure. One agony piled upon another. His smashing of the linkage with a rock followed. When he met Troopers McAuliffe and Bunning he told them he knew there was a State Police station nearby and he "wanted to feel safe." He said his fast was based on the conclusion that it would "enable him to know what it was all about and where he was going the rest of his life." He told troopers he "liked chains and locks;" had developed this novel fondness for these articles of bondage since early childhood.

More ideas poured forth; they spun dizzily; they ran with the galloping unevenness of a football player practicing broken field running. In his appearance before a Town Justice, for instance, he voiced this unusual thought:

If Man, he said, demonstrated the perfection of spacial technology by going to the moon, nonetheless Man had failed to perfect a method of manufacture which comes naturally to a cow, the making of milk from grass. A simple thing. Why had not it been discovered? Grass was an inexhaustible source. He also spoke of starry skies, of open spaces, of running waters.

Then he spoke of the future.

He promised to return to the "desert" of the Adirondack wilderness, vowing this time to ignore one portion of the Biblical verse mentioned. This time, he said, there would be no loose rocks where he would begin his fast.

Thus tragedy continued in creation. He was examined by mental health authorities. Symptoms noted included indifference, withdrawal, delusions of persecution and omnipotence and hallucinations. He was not considered dangerous. He was released. He was not considered violent. No one had been harmed. His promise had not yet been born in fact. He was, indeed, a man of strange idiosyncracies, but the world is filled with wanderers who live in hellish strange worlds all their own.

So far, what he had accomplished was a mere prelude to the ultimate drama in which he was the lonely, silent, and desperate participant.

For a comparatively short time he became, in essence, a temporary memory.

He remained such until Oct. 26, 1975, five months after his Westport experience, when at 8:45 a.m., a deer hunter from Croton-on-Hudson, scouting an area about a half mile west of the Adirondack Northway, in the

Hunters, moving in the Town of North Hudson came across this tragedy. Note chains looped and locked around hemlock trunk at left and at right. The chains were loose enough to allow the man to move, but even so he was restricted to an area beyond the reach of keys he had thrown away. The body was found about a half mile west of the Adirondack Northway. These are photos used in the investigation.

Town of North Hudson, Essex County, stumbled over what he thought was a skull of a deer.

According to a report made later by Inv. M.E. Hunt, Troop B, Westport, "after picking up the skull and noticing it seemed more human than animals, he (the hunter) started looking around and found what appeared to be shoes chained to a tree; he further saw clothes, canteens, and plastic bags in the vicinity. He realized he had discovered the remains of a human body."

State Police records, which I examined, described the body as having been found in a prone position, fully clothed and with a three-quarter length coat. There was a chain looped around a large hemlock tree and each end was fastened to the man's ankles by padlocks. His left wrist was shackled with handcuffs to another length of chain and this linkage in turn was wound around still another hemlock, and also was anchored by padlocks. In effect, he had spread-eagled himself into a position which allowed him only limited freedom of movement.

The investigation was conducted by Capt. R.V. DePuy and Lt. J.H. Lawliss, Malone; Lt. A.E. Smith, Saranac Lake; Inv. Hunt, and Troopers D.E. Hanchett and R.E. Carlson of Schroon Lake.

Lawmen found several packs of Pall Mall cigarettes near the body, as well as two cans of smoking tobacco; cigarette papers; eighty booklets of matches; a writing tablet of eight-by-ten inch paper, all pages blank; three ball point pens; a green duffle bag; two brown plastic capsules, or pill vials, and several large, empty green plastic bags.

There was no sign of violence.

The body was in what was described as an "advanced stage of decomposition." There was no way to learn how long it had been exposed.

The man wore work clothing and his feet were encased in Spanish made canvas shoes, size thirteen. The feet were chained with 5/16 inch thick linkage, 116 inches long. The left hand was shackled with linkage of similar dimension, 70 inches in length.

No identification was present in any form.

Subsequently, Inv. Charles O'Connell of SP Plattsburgh, accompanied by Sgt. Rex Blanchard and Airman First Class Mark Holley, from the Plattsburgh Air Force Base, went over the scene with a metal detector borrowed from the installation.

Found were six nickel-plated keys and what appeared to be a version of a house, apartment or padlock key. The keys were found eleven feet from the body, buried in leaves into which they had been flung.

If identity was not immediately available to police, the memory of the Westport incident was still vivid. Recalled was the "man in chains" of the previous May, whose identity had been established. The connection was inescapable.

Contact was made with SP Manhattan and investigation there revealed that the subject had not been seen for "several months" at his New York City hotel. A dental chart and X-rays were obtained and forwarded to SP Westport, where a comparative examination of the upper and lower jaws of the skull was made by Dr. Paul J. Kullman of Elizabethtown.

Identification was conclusive. The dead man was the one seen on May 24. An autopsy was performed by Dr. Walter Frederick, Lake Placid pathologist, at Moses Ludington Hospital, Ticonderoga. The coroner, Dr. Wilfred Cohen, Keeseville, determined death was accidental; that is no one else was involved.

His body remained unclaimed, unwanted. A relative, determined to be next of kin by police search, wanted nothing to do with the remains. Thus, still as lonely in death, as in life, The Man in Chains was buried by the Marvin Funeral Home, Elizabethtown, at Essex County expense.

Little was ever learned of his background; he had a mental history; was born out of wedlock and his father was unknown. Examples of poetry he had written of "starry skies, open spaces and running waters," were found, pathetic reminders of a young man's quest for an outlet to release, to some extent at least, internal turmoil.

Also found were additional details of a police record: A 1969 charge of possession of a weapon; a 1970 charge of incest, already mentioned, with no further details; and a 1974 charge of assault, second, in New York City, with disposition of the case unknown.

In his second attempt to purify his body and soul the tragic victim indeed was tempted by the devil. But the demon which filled his mind also remained at his wide. No angels appeared to save or care for him.

Furthermore, true to his vow following his attempted fast at Westport, he unquestionably had chosen his spot with care.

He had selected a location with no loose rocks within sight or reach.

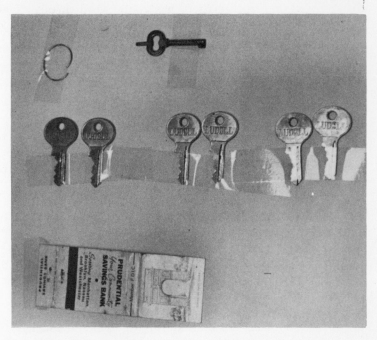

This was the sad scene (left) which met the eyes of those investigating the man who died in chains. Above are keys and a match folder found in nearby underbrush, several feet distant, where the victim had tossed them, thus sealing his fate.

BUG-TIME STORIES

**The Blackfly Not Only
"Takes the Cake" in The
Adirondacks, but
bites it!**

To become thoroughly innoculated with the fever of Adirondack Park adventure, the traveler therein should make it a point of honor to be punctured by the ubiquitous, infamous, much-maligned blackfly.

For this you receive no Purple Heart. But you do get the Order of the Red Welt. No man, woman, child, beast or bird is a true Adirondacker without this accolade.

To adequately discuss this hump-backed scourge of the mountains one must go into its background and find out why such a mighty mite was created in the first place.

Since nothing documentary has come down through the ages we must rely somewhat on legend.

Thus one may trace its origin back to one calm night in Hell, when singed wolves bayed at a full lava moon; when fires were banked for the day, and the devil, hereinafter known as Lucifer or Smokey Bare because he usually wore only a suit of soot, decided to come topside for a bit of despicable action.

So he left off boiling up some fresh rocks for a new volcano he had in mind, and horned his way through the earth's crust, appearing, it is reported, in the general vicinity of Paradox Lake.

Here he crawled from beneath a rock, looked about, neither saw nor heard anyone or anything scratching an itch, and thereupon invented the blackfly.

He made two sexes because that was the Nature of Things as they should be, according to the word spread around by the best known Adirondack guide boat builder of that ancient day, J. Noah, who years before, just before a big shower, built the biggest guide boat the world has ever seen, for all things, both great and small.

You will not find this remarkable accomplishment listed in the Guinness Book of Records.

Now there may be some spirited debate about all this from completely reliable entomologists and historians, but that is the way the blackfly, sometimes also known as the Buffalo gnat because of its large, humped thorax, came into existence. As a reflex action, Lucifer also invented the gypsy moth. He already had, in previous visitations to the Northeast, invented the punkies or "no-see-ums," the stable and deer flies and, of course, the mosquito.

After his more recent invention, he curled his tail and disappeared downward to warm his feet in more familiar surroundings.

The Adirondack blackfly from a metric standpoint is, milligram for milligram, the most powerful stealth weapon of all times. Released in hordes it would have kept Attila the Hun helpless; sent Hannibal's elephants into frenzy and would have turned Alexander the Great into a jumping jack. All skilled historians know that the reason Napoleon is often pictured with a troubled face and his hand inside his shirt is because he was scratching an itch caused by some blackflies picked up during one of his campaigns.

Well, so much for the invention on how and why the bug was invented, and the reader may judge for him or herself its veracity. If disbelief is to be evidenced, can the agnostic present a more sensible version?

From a factual standpoint, the bug is now with us and in great numbers, trillions, I would imagine, and to all intent and purpose it will continue to be during its seasonal explosions, and the best the Mountain Adventurer can do is to coat his or her exposed portions with a modern day repellent, or remain locked in the cellar.

In the golden days of yore, before a button could be pressed on a small container, and a magic stream of relief would pour forth, other repellents were used.

These mixtures in many instances were home-made. Some were quite simple. Bear grease, preferably rancid, with an odor bad enough to force a skunk to put a clothespin on his nose, was applied. In the western area of the state a blackish, gooey substance, which oozed into pools of water and which was scooped from the surface with flat paddles by Indians, was used.

This substance was petroleum, and Peter Kalm, the Swedish naturalist who traveled this area in 1750, observed that to encourage an added release of oil, Indians drove long poles into shallow pools of water, puncturing the bottoms, and oil flowed from these apertures with suitable force and in suitable quantity. This oil was used not only as a repellent, or a base in which herbs were mixed, but for medicinal purposes as well.

In much later days Citronella oil, made from an Asiatic grass, was used. Coal tar mixtures were not un-

When Nature decides to create another pest, she probably will pattern her new product after the Adirondack blackfly, which considers no man a friend. This remarkable drawing was made by Robin D. Rothman.

Blackfly assaults have been portrayed by artists for well over a century. Here's a sketch of 1859 vintage printed in Harper's New Monthly Magazine, showing two sports and how they defeated attacks!

common; some of these were applied with bacon grease as a base. Anything which smelled to high heaven was thought to be efficient. All of which offered some degree of protection, but not much.

Henry David Thoreau, one-time hermit, a wildlife observer and author, in "Allegash and East Branch," had this comment on the insect under discussion:

"I now first began to be seriously molested by the blackfly...which I first felt and then saw, in swarms about me...the hunters will tell bloody stories about them, how they settle in a ring about your neck, before you know it, and are wiped off in great numbers with your blood."

The Rev. W.H.H. Murray in the late 1800's took a softer view, saying newspaper and magazine writers had given an "erroneous impression" about the flies. He called some of the anecdotes and experiences described as "the merest balderdash imaginable." Said Mr. Murray, whose book, "Adventures in the Wilderness" led thousands of city folk to move in and "enjoy" the Adirondacks:

"I regard it (the fly) as one of the most harmless and least vexatious of the insect family."

Mr. Murray said he and his wife camped the mountains for five years and were never to any great extent worth mentioning "disturbed by its presence."

That same gentleman, however, in describing adequate wilderness outfits for the ladies, did suggest wearing a net of fine Swiss mull to cover the face and neck; buckskin gloves with armlets buttoned tightly at elbow

height, and a short walking dress, with Turkish drawers fastened tightly at the ankle. A bit of salve might come in handy as well, said he.

Early prisoners at Clinton Prison at Dannemora in Clinton County might have disagreed with Mr. Murray. When convicts managed to escape this prison, once described as the "Siberia of the North," they fell victims to blackfly assaults. Many returned voluntarily, savaged with bites from the mites.

Dr. Hugo Jamnback, an internationally known entomologist, in a publication "Bloodsucking Flies and Other Outdoor Nuisance Arthropods of New York State," included this quote made by an author in 1914:

"When numerous they crawl into openings in the clothing, up the trousers-legs and sleeves, under loose collars and hat-bands, inflicting their bites in unexpected places remote from the point of entry."

The author of that quote has been proved quite correct. The flies, entering a crevice in clothing, will crawl with enthusiasm and stealth over portions of the body more modestly protected and with disregard for anatomical tenderness will delightedly bite.

Dr. Jamnback wrote extensively of the pest in the publication mentioned, which was issued by the University of the State of New York, State Museum and Science Service, State Education Department.

Dr. Jamnback does differ with Rev. Murray; says most people suffer more from blackfly bites than from mosquito punctures. There will be general agreement with this; the Man of the Cloth was trying to sell a book. Dr. Jamnback is acquainting the public with a fact of life and his is the approach of a scientist.

Says he:

"Blackflies are annoying in the spring and early summer in the Catskill Mountains, the Hudson Highlands and the Allegany Hills but they reach peak numbers in the Adirondack Mountains where they are an important factor in the economy because they drive away tourists and interfere with lumbering, mining and building."

Dr. Jamnback presents some facts which may startle. He points out that only two of the 29 species so far recorded from New York State are serious pests of man. Three, he says, do not suck blood at all. Seventeen are primarily mammal feeders (mammalophilic) and the remaining nine species prefer birds (ornithophilic). "Thus," he says, "blackflies are more discriminating in their choice of victims than mosquitoes."

In the world of biting flies, where the insects seek blood as the main source of protein food needed for egg production, the females are the acupuncturists; the stable fly is considered the only biting fly where both male and female bite. Males of other species, which would include mosquitoes, blackflies, punkies, horse flies and deer flies, suck plant juices and nectars. This from a Cornell Extension bulletin, New York State College of Agriculture.

In New York State the blackflies transmit no known disease to man but some, called the Turkey gnat, can carry disease organisms to the gobblers. Ducks also may receive their own form of harmful innoculations. And other forms of birdlife can be affected by transmission.

This state, however, is lucky in that animal life is little affected; the flies specialize mostly in annoying. To escape, even temporarily, larger animals such as deer will seek relief in ponds and lakes. The twitch of a whitetail's flag is not necessarily an indication of danger. Smaller animals are equally bothered. Anyone who has walked a dog on a hiking or camping trip in the wilderness has seen the effect upon pets. The flies are not discriminatory in bodily areas or apertures pestered!

Prosimulium mixtum is considered the first of the pest species to attack man in the spring. Simulium venustum is the second. The former emerges as larvae from eggs in swiftly flowing streams during the fall, winter or early spring; the larvae develop until late April or early May in the Adirondacks; they pupate in early or mid-May and the adults, ready to wreak vengeance on a world never seen, are able to fly instantly upon emergence. These midget gangsters seek man from mid-May into early June.

Simulium venustum has two or more generations in warm streams a year but only one in cold waters. Eggs deposited during late summer hatch the following spring when water temperatures rise to about 45 degrees F. And the adults are most bothersome from the end of May into early July, which many consider the welcome "end" of the season of flying Draculas.

Some Adirondackers and others believe blackflies grow gray with age. Not so, and the reason for the mistake is easily explained. As the population of the first species mentioned declines, second species members grow in numbers. The legs of P. mixtum are brownish. S. venustum have white bands. Thus as the season progresses, the "gray bands" appear and that, to some, signifies the aging process and the end of assaults for the year.

Blackflies are active even during bright sunlight, do not bite at night but that void, of course, is cheerfully filled by other biting bugs. Blackflies inadvertently caught indoors during the day, when they will bite, will not exercise that privilege in confinement, but will seek release, usually at a window, upon which, if closed, they will crawl until they die.

The blackflies show a difference in biting habits from punkies. Some species of the latter are most annoying on nights when there is a full moon. There may be significance to this but it has not been documented. It may be a romantic one.

As for control methods, spraying blackfly larvae has proved the most effective, but extreme care must be used in selection of chemicals dispersed, since like it or not, the larvae is an important part of the food chain of trout. Spraying is best done from air. There have been carefully done experiments with attempts to introduce a parasitic worm which attacks larvae, but results have not diminished the fly to any noticeable extent.

The general feeling is that Lucifer's invention is here to stay and fly and draw blood, and since periods of annoyance are seasonal, most users of the wilderness accept that fact and shrug it off, or fight it all to the advantage of spray and ointment manufacturers. A good mosquito repellent, it's said, will cause equal consternation to a hungry blackfly. There is one consolation among resort owners in the Adirondacks, however.

Skiers are not affected; the bugs won't and can't move in winter's chill.

ANOTHER PEST

I call your attention to the gypsy moth, a European introduction and vitally important to our mountain areas because of the extraordinary skill of the ugly caterpillars of this moth to defoliate trees. Such defoliation is not uncommon; foresters point out that one stripping will not necessarily kill a tree because of food reserves in the tree itself. Second or third attacks will often kill.

The gypsy moth was imported into the United States from Europe deliberately by a scientist who in 1868 thought he might use them to make silk. Why and how he figured that theory out is not known. The imported moths escaped from their confinement in a Massachusetts laboratory and since that time this pest has become the major insect threat to the hardwood forests of the Northeastern United States!

The favorite food seems to be oak, but the voracious, chomping caterpillars will attack the leaves of maples, birch and cherry.

The eggs are deposited by the female moth, whitish in color, on the bark of trees, sometimes in the case of rough bark slabs which overlap, under the slabs. These egg clusters, slightly orange in color when they first appear, can vary in size to an inch or longer; contain hundreds of eggs; 400 or more to a cluster is not uncommon. Ten clusters on one tree therefore, if all goes well in the hatching will produce 4,000 caterpillars, tiny at birth, ranging from one-and-one-half to two inches in length when full grown and marked with orange-reddish spots on their back. They are hairy enough to repel most birds, although the scarlet tanager, downy woodpecker, the nuthatch and both the black-billed and yellow-billed cuckoo will go after the young.

Spiders may eat larvae which become entangled in webs; ants may prey upon newly hatched larvae. Only one parasite, the wasp called Apanteles melanocelus is known to parasitize the young. A ground beetle, Calosoma frigidum, will attack a grown caterpillar; another, Calosoma sycophanta will also eat the hairy apparitions. The white-footed mouse will attack not only larvae but pupae as well. This mouse usually bites off the head, "skins" the worm and eats what is left, or a portion of it.

Eggs began hatching about the first of May at a time when a tree has begun to produce sizeable foliage. The

Photo at left shows two female gypsy moths in process of laying egg clusters; clusters are dark masses under the insects. Each will contain hundreds of eggs. The host tree is birch.

Two more adult female gypsy moths are shown with egg clusters, also on a birch tree. Pupal shells from which they emerged are shown directly to the right of the moths. Adult female gypsy moths cannot fly.

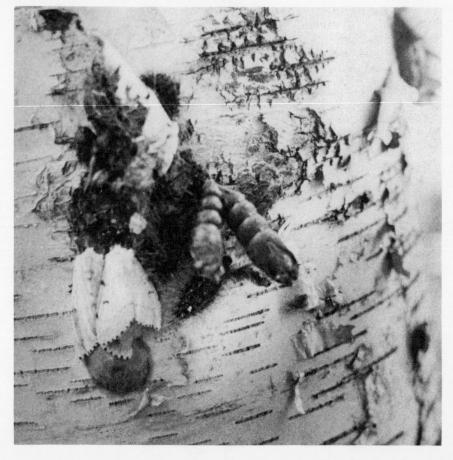

There are no voracious predators of the gypsy moth caterpillar who kill in such numbers as to diminish the threat, but the field mouse on occasion will eat the hairy tid-bit. Above is reproduction of painting by Wayne Trimm of the NYS Department of Environmental Conservation.

larvae move into the foliated areas and many will spin downward on a silken thread, to be picked up by the wind and dispersed to other and sometimes more productive areas of food. Such is Nature's unappreciated way.

Once established, caterpillars grow fast. At one point in growth they rest during daylight hours and continue to do so for the balance of their caterpillar existence. They eat at night, descending the host tree to find hiding spots during daylight. This is why in so many instances, people will find these furry pests crawling across lawns in great numbers, crawling up building foundations, crawling under leaves, even under picnic tables and into window blinds. If a resting spot can be found on trees, they will remain there.

Some owners who prize their trees will place burlap around the trunk a few feet above the ground, and the caterpillars have been known to crawl into the folds of such for daylight rest. If they do, their disposal is simple. At dusk, they move upward once again, into the realm of leaves. Those which have left the host tree will find their way back by following a silken thread trail which they have laid. This, in effect, is the same principle used by spelunkers who unwind balls of cord as they move into underground labyrinths; when exploration is done they merely follow the cord to cave's entrance.

Eventually the caterpillars will enter the pupa stage and about two weeks will be spent as pupae. The small cocoon is dark brown; can be found almost anywhere, even in lawn furniture. The moth will emerge but the adult female cannot fly; she remains in one spot, emitting an odor of sexual attractant, and the males respond vigorously. Eggs are laid in a single mass and the clusters are covered with hair from the female's abdomen.

If clusters are seen — and they are plainly visible to any determined searcher, from ground level upwards to ten or twelve feet — brushing them off, with eggs landing on the ground, is not the answer. Some of the eggs, if undamaged, will live through winter and hatch. The cluster must be destroyed by pressure or fire. Many people will use a puttying knife on reachable egg masses. It might be a wise move to search them out before next spring's hatching; a general massacre of eggs may save several trees.

The individual, therefore, can actually do something about the gypsy moth in a very limited way. But insofar as the blackfly and other biting insects are concerned, that's another kind of story.

The Mountain Adventurer will simply have to bear it. But he doesn't have to grin in so doing, and that's one bit of relief!

STORIES IN STONE AND STATUARY

Not Only Man, But Nature Herself, Has Sculpted Monuments In the North Country

You move over the Gilmantown Road, part dirt, part paved, from Wells to Speculator, which some consider a shortcut twixt the two communities, and you find the road has been rerouted in certain short portions. Thus "Bidwell's Hotel Rock" can be seen only by leaving the current highway route.

The "Hotel Rock," pictured in this chapter, is a huge boulder split by the forces of Nature, and it got its name in unusual fashion. The driver of a buggy, obviously named Bidwell, drove the road many years ago during a blizzard. The weather became too rough for the horse and its load. Bidwell led the animal into the boulder cleft for shelter, then took off on foot for his hearth and possibly a pewter mug of hot buttered rum. He must have made it, since there is no record of his perishing in the storm.

The following day he returned for his horse. He found it dead; the animal, to escape wintery blasts, had wedged itself farther into the aperture and in its struggles to free itself, broke its neck. So the story goes.

Now travel through another Adirondack area, Crown Point, and there is a monument of stone with a plaque which has not yet been vandalized, calling your attention to the fact that Israel Putnam, a noted New York State French and Indian War fighter, was once captured by Indians near this spot.

Move to the Crown Point picnic area, near the site of Fort St. Frederic, where the giant stone monument to Samuel Champlain stands, looking over the expanse of the lake. Here you will find, if you inspect closely enough, a bronze sculpture by Auguste Rodin, the famous French sculptor who created the masterpiece known as "The Thinker."

Look, then, over the ruins of Fort St. Frederic, once a vital outpost of French conquest, built in 1730; it is now rubble; the fort and citadel were blown to Hades by the French themselves in the face of an advancing British army.

Look then to nearby Fort Amherst, built by the British, now only a skeletal remain, but still preserving memories of the past.

In the Lake George Battleground Park, adjacent to Lake George village, visitors often stop and gape at magnificent examples of sculpture; statues of Father

"Bidwell's Hotel Rock" along the Gilmantown Rd., between Speculator and Wells, gets a sniff-over from the author's dog. But the animal finds the scent of the horse which died at this spot long gone!

Isaac Jogues, discoverer of the lake; of Sir William Johnson and an Indian ally, harking back to the Battle of Lake George in 1755, in which King Hendrick, the Mohawk chief, was killed by a French bayonet. Nearby is the bronze figure of a thirsty Indian warrior, bending over small pool, a scene now surrounded by fencing, since vandals with no concept of the honor of history, broke the bow which once he held.

Then, too, in this same park, is a more modern bit of memory in stone and bronze, this one to a gifted woman, Winifred S. La Rose erected in August, 1980; it is the only monument I know of erected to the memory of a woman for services performed for the Adirondacks, a region she profoundly loved. It is well deserved.

But stories in stone or bronze are contained not only in specific, deliberately created pieces of art and craftsmanship. There are other kinds.

The caverns of soft twilight, which are the old horizontal shafts of iron mines, are tangible mementos in themselves, representative of the efforts of those sturdy souls who in early years hacked their way into Adirondack crust for ore and riches. And, too, there are still pits and shafts where ambitious men tried to reach suspected riches of gold and silver — riches which did not exist in any notable quantity.

Forms of the past take many shapes and sizes. I consider, for instance, Lock 12 of the original Champlain Canal, which can be seen from Route 4, south of Fort Edward, as a monument to the area's past; it is as solidly built, as well preserved as are the locks of the original Erie Canal which can be found on the Vischer Ferry Nature Preserve in Saratoga County. The men who cut, sized and measured stone, built well in those days.

The greatest and most majestic monuments of all, I suppose, are the mountains themselves. Nature heaved them out of the earth. Man merely made his works here and there amongst natural wonders.

It is artistically tragic that New York State, with all its avowed interest upon the arts, has not publicized its past and present along such major highways as the Thruway and the Adirondack Northway. I speak of the state itself, not private agencies, not small communities which have done their very best.

I consider still that the concrete statue called "the Wheel," or something like that, (Doughnut is the better term), in the southbound lane of the Northway, Schroon Lake rest area, as grotesque and hardly representative of what the state has to offer. It represents nothing of the state's past nor present. It is totally unlike the heroic statue of Nick Stoner, famous Adirondack fighter and guide of past wars, which can be seen on the Nick Stoner Golf Course in Fulton County. **(Both the "Doughnut" and the Stoner figure were pictured in Adirondack Album, Volume 1.)**

At this point, it is useless to believe that the state will ever act to place in points often seen by the traveler, examples of statuary which denote famous humans, now long gone, but vitally important to our past. It is useless to believe the state or any organization backed by the state will ever furnish what I call educational statuary, symbolizing realistic forms of animal life in stone or bronze along the Northway, the most logical superhighway for such.

The placing of this kind of art work would create an open air museum for untold scores of thousands to see. There have been millions of dollars spent in modernistic "art" in Albany's South Mall, in itself a giant monument to the late Gov. Rockefeller's casual attitude toward state expenditures. Many who roam the Mall pass them by with hardly a glance. I recall in one instance, a painting of solid color, was mistaken for a tarpaulin covering a doorway. Can this be construed as art? The point is debatable.

Seeing today what something was, is something to be enjoyed immensely. Welded steel bars and flats may be considered a form of art and this is well and good for those who so consider, but what do they represent except what was in the mind of the sculptor or painter?

There is no comparison between the magnificent stone and metal statuary as one enters Ticonderoga from Route 9N, to the welding jobs done in places to the south. I remain appalled when automobile bumpers are joined by the welder's arc into shapeless forms and the resulting efforts constitute to some a form of art. I've seen better sculptures in wrecks I have covered in more than a half century of newspaper experience. Fortunately this type of artistic orgasm has not reached the North County in appreciable numbers.

It is regrettable that the state has not been the leader in portraying, for instance, animal life, both past and present, along the Northway, for such a venture would offer a challenge to any man who works in stone or concrete or bronze. Most assuredly the reservoir of ideas is not dry.

Often I have visualized in fantasy, as I drove the Northway and stopped at rest areas, sculptures of the bear, moose, whitetail, panther, timber wolf, wolverine, the eagle, both bald and golden; even smaller animals such as the mink, otter, fox, fisher — yes, even that amiable pariah of fragrance, the skunk, all with appropriate inscriptions, signifying that these animals once lived, or now live, in the Adirondacks.

If concrete is to be a medium, I have often visualized the astonishment of viewing the giant mastodon, the mammoth, the bison, the musk ox, the caribou, the giant beaver; even the seal, all of which once lived in the Adirondack area. If I may pursue the fantasy I envision a sculpture of what Peter Dubuc caught, the world record northern pike.

We have heroes to immortalize in stone or bronze. Nick Stoner is not the only one. Timothy Murphy, the famous Schoharie County frontiersman who was the rifleman who reportedly shot British General Fraser smack off his horse during the Battle of Bemis Heights, sometimes called the Battle of Saratoga, is one individual who deserves attention. He's not Matt Dillon of "Gunsmoke" nor as well known, but he was an actual part of our history and he deserves better than a full length portrait which hangs in the Old Stone Fort Museum in Schoharie — a statement which in no ways minimizes the importance of this famous museum.

What, pray tell, of Major Robert Rogers, the French and Indian War leader who in his 20's fought up and down the eastern fringers of the Adirondacks? Would he be considered the equal of John Wayne, whose likeness is not in New York, but who adorns medals sold nationwide? What of the remarkable Mohawk Indian chief, Joseph Brant, or, for that matter, the Indian mentioned earlier, King Hendrick?

What of Ely Parker, the Seneca, who attended Rensselaer Polytechnic Institute in Troy, became a noted engineer, and who became confidential aide to Gen. Grant, and who is credited with drawing up the articles of capitulation offered at Gen. Lee's surrender at Appomattox on April 9, 1865? Indians of that day were not citizens and a special action by Congress was needed to enable Parker to obtain a commission. He began as a lieutenant and ended a general.

Men considered villains by early Americans need not be ignored. What of Walter Butler, the infamous Tory of Revolutionary War fame who was killed in a retreat northward in the West Canada Creek area; the army of which he was a leader, discarded its snowshoes during a thaw at a northern lake, and thus Raquette Lake received its name.

Certainly a statue of Ebenezer Emmons, who named the Adirondacks in 1837 would do well as a subject. Or Seneca Ray Stoddard, photographer, author and artist, who was born in the Town of Wilton, Saratoga County and whose pictures of the devastation of the Adirondacks created by clear-cut lumbering, helped institute the move to create the Forest Preserve.

I know of no statue of President Theodore Roosevelt, who technically became President while on a wild dash through Adirondacks to North Creek, where he boarded a train southward because of the assassination of President McKinley.

And what of President Grant, who died on Mt. McGregor, Saratoga County, and who spent his last painful days sitting in a chair, gazing northward, while trying to stifle the pain of cancer with the drug called laudanum?

Is perpetuating the past to be left up to communities or to such institutions as Fort Ticonderoga or Fort

William Henry at Lake George? One failure of our educational system today is a concerted effort to instill into impressionable minds that America indeed had figures of glory, men and women who deserve to be known. Is statuary not one way to accomplish this?

Must one go to a museum in Montreal to see a scene of Mohawks attacking that city? Or to the wax museum in Canada; on that country's side of Niagara Falls, to see famous American figures?

The British know the value of monuments. Visit London if there is disbelief in your mind. They keep legendary figures alive by putting statues in public and heavily traveled areas. I was saddened, while in Germany, to see what I considered merely a wall of concrete dedicated to the memory of American airmen who lost their lives in World War Two. I received a shock of total contrast when I visited East Germany and saw a huge statue erected to honor "Mother Russia" — a realistic sculpture showing a woman holding a fallen soldier in her arms.

No one in his right mind would call for the expenditures needed for giant statuary of this kind, nor for the type seen carved into the side of a tremendous mountain of naked granite at Stone Mountain Park near Atlanta, Georgia, a carving of Southern heroes reminiscent in size to presidential figures carved on Mt. Rushmore.

I speak of smaller creations, of purely state interest, ones to inspire to stimulate study, to educate.

If we are to love New York we must be able to see part of its history. And insofar as the Northway is concerned, it could become the longest, if not the finest, museum in the state.

SEE FOLLOWING PAGES FOR PHOTOS
PERTINENT TO THIS CHAPTER —

No easy moment for Israel Putnam: After Aber-crombie's defeat by Montcalm at Ticonderoga in 1758, French maurauding parties harassed the retreating British. Major Putnam was sent northward from Fort Edward but he and his men were ambushed. The following night Putnam was tied to a tree and con-demned by fire, but a French officer, Marin, rescued him. Monument at left is in Crown Point. Picture above, which shows the rescue, is of painting owned by the Glens Falls Insurance Company, a member of the Continental Insurance Companies.

To the left is the famous Champlain monument at Crown Point, reachable through the public picnic area. This lighthouse memorial was dedicated July 5, 1912.

What is not generally known is that this 73-foot-high structure, made of chiseled Fox Island, Maine, granite, contains a sculpture by one of the world's most famous craftsmen, Auguste Rodin, creator of "The Thinker," one of the best known pieces of art.

The bronze above was the gift of France, and symbolizes "La France," the country in which Champlain was born; specifically at Brouage.

Begun in 1730 by the French, Fort St. Frederic, at Crown Point, was strengthened in 1734 and 1742. The fort was blown up by the French as a British army moved northward and all that remains today is pictured below. Large building, top photo, is the citadel, which contained officers' quarters and stores. Small buildings overhanging wall in foreground (two) were sanitary facilities for the garrison! Bridge in photo at bottom is the Crown Point span which connects New York and Vermont.

Still another memorialization to the area's past is this imposing bit of statuary at the Lake George Battle-ground Park. Figure to right is that of Sir William Johnson, who is pictured with one of the Mohawk Indian chieftains who helped him defeat an invading French army during 1755, in what has been called The Battle of Lake George. It was in this battle that the Mohawk chief, King Hendrick was killed and the noted Mohawk, Joseph Brant, then a comparative youngster, received his first taste of warfare.

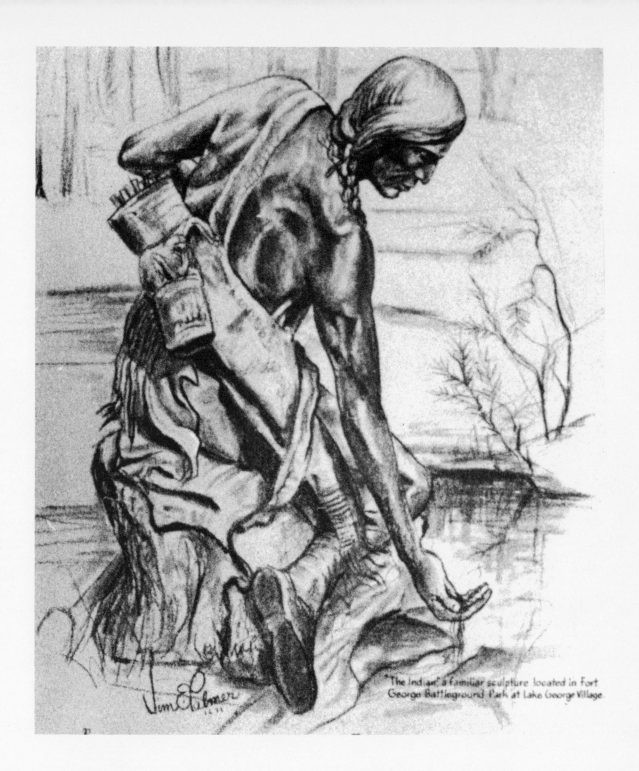

"The Indian" a familiar sculpture located in Fort
George Battleground Park at Lake George Village.

Jim E. Palmer, left, lives on Ridge Road, north of Glens Falls in a home dating back into the late 1880's, which he and his wife renovated and improved. He has been a commercial artist for 35 years and is Art Department Manager, Genpak Corp., manufacturers of plastic containers and plastic houseware. His commercial art is varied with art work as depicted above, a sketch of an Indian warrior drinking from a pool; the bronze statue is in Lake George Battleground Park. Jim and others mentioned in this chapter are part of the varied cultural wealth of the North County.

EnCon Commissioner Robert Flacke delivers words of praise at ceremonies honoring the memory of Winifred S. La Rose. At right, seated, is Howard La Rose, her husband; Assemblywoman Joan Hague; Winnie's sister, Ruth Buckby of Lake George, and Cheryl Young, Winnie's daughter.

Winifred S. La Rose

The monument erected in August, 1980, to Mrs. La Rose by the Lake George Historical Association.

Another view of the dedication ceremonies in the Lake George Battleground Park, during which a memorial to Winnie La Rose was unveiled. Mrs. La Rose was a strong advocate of preservation and beautification of the North Country; was a tireless worker in conservation causes.

This dramatic figure of Isaac Jogues, first white man to see Lake George, is an oft visited monument at the Lake George Battleground Park. Note missing joints on right hand, result of tortures inflicted by the Mohawks when Jogues was held captive in the Mohawk Valley, at Ossernenon, now called Auriesville. His discovery of the lake occurred in 1646.

Photo above, a reproduction of a painting in the Fort Ticonderoga Museum, shows Isaac Jogues with Indian companions, presumably at the portage between Lakes Champlain and George. Possibly the flow of water in the background was the natural outlet to Lake George, which flows some 200 feet downward into Champlain over a gradual course.

An unsuual view of the interior of another type of Adirondack monument, an abandoned iron mine in thè Fort Ann region. In this scene only stalactites of ice are seen – formed by drops of water dripping from the ceiling of the cavern. The one at the right connects both floor and top of cave. The mine probably goes back into the late 1800's.

In this portion of the old iron mine near Fort Ann (Washington County) a full growth of stalagmites made of ice sprout from the cavern floor. Robert Foster of Round Lake is in foreground; the late Kenneth Carr is in background. Unusual here is that water from the ceiling built the growth on the mine floor, but did not, at the same time, create hanging stalactites. There were no broken ones on the stone floor.

The statue of Nick Stoner, (left), in Fulton County could well set an example for a sculpture of Timothy Murphy, Schoharie County frontiersman who fought in the Battle of Bemis Heights, whose portrait hangs in the Old Stone Fort Museum, Schoharie.

As pointed out in this chapter, they built well in the old days. Here is proof: Lock 12 of the original Champlain Canal, which was begun in 1817 and opened in 1823. The lock is 15 feet wide and the bridge was placed by the State Department of Transportation for the curious traveler.

Fort Ticonderoga did not always possess this marble statue of Ethan Allen, leader of the Green Mountain Boys from Vermont, who captured the fort on May 10, 1775 from the British. It was sold to the Fort in 1975 when the Ohio County Public Library in Wheeling, West Virginia, found the statue too high to fit into new quarters!

Bill Hogle, a taxi driver in Ticonderoga, listening to radio station WWVA in Wheeling one night, picked up the announcement it would be sold to the highest bidder and alerted Fort Ticonderoga personnel to the impending sale. The fort won the bid.

Existence of the statue, which stood in the Wheeling library for a half century, was known, but the reason why Allen, a Vermont native, was a prize adornment in a West Virginia community, is not understood. At any rate, it now stands where it belongs.

This inscribed boulder in Ticonderoga commemorates four major events, Champlain's discovery of Lake Champlain, Lord Howe's death in the assault against a French-held Fort Ticonderoga, the invasion by the British under Gen. Amherst, and Gen Burgoyne's march southward to his ultimate fate at Bemis Heights.

Another example of carving by Man and by Nature with Man's help. Photo above, taken by Arnold Le Fevre, Director of Photography, Capital Newspapers, shows the Adirondack hermit, Noah John Rondeau as he appears at the Adirondack Museum at Blue Mt. Lake; sculpture is by Robert Longhurst of Crown Point.

Other photos: A closeup of the head of the famous "Cedar Woodsman" which has been displayed at the museum. Date of its creation and maker are unknown; figure which is constructed of natural cedar crooks, was discovered at a camp near Long Lake. Museum Director Craig Gilborn conjectures the figure may have been assembled by a lumberjack during the early days of logging. Full front and rear views shown in other photos.

Call it what you will — Battle of Saratoga or Battle of Bemis Heights — the 1777 battlefield is now a national institution and historic site. A more unusual monument is pictured, dedicated to a leg, the leg of Benedict Arnold, wounded during the Big Hassle. The sculptor obviously considered the limb, which shed blood for liberty, was the only portion of Arnold's anatomy deserving of honor!

The highway northward into Schuylerville, Saratoga County, contains this unusual monument at its side. To this day the identity of the rider is unknown; presumably he was a courier during the Battle of Bemis Heights in 1777, whether for Gen. Burgoyne or the American forces is not known.

This novel bit of stone stands at roadside on the highway twixt the Town of North Hudson and Moriah. The story goes that when a road was decided upon, crews began clearing the wilderness from North Hudson and Port Henry, and when they met, their foremen shook hands. The monument is the result. Note date of 1870. At one time the block was reportedly "removed" and its whereabouts remained unknown for about ten years, until a Town of Moriah resident spotted it on a front lawn in the Tupper Lake region. He picked it up, returned it to its base!

105

The heating cycle has reached full turn. Here is one of many fireplaces used to heat British barracks at Crown Point, with wood as fuel. Standing alongside is Timothy Titus of the Crown Point Restoration Project.

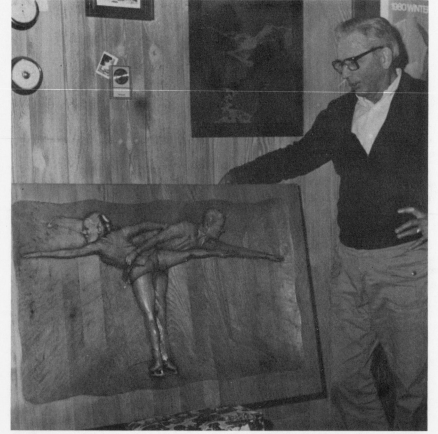

Two examples of works by Paul Twichell, advertising executive turned sculptor. At left is bas relief of Olympic skaters Randy Gardner and Rai Babalonia, now on permanent exhibition in the National Art Museum of Sports, University of New Haven.

Photo by Edwin K. Newcomb, Voorheesville, N.Y.

On next page is a 12-inch nude, an example of skills developed in studies with Canada's famous Jean Julian Bourgault. Paul, a bomber pilot during World War Two, was an advertising executive in Albany, then developed the Whiteface Chalet at Wilmington. After selling the chalet he moved to Keene Valley where he now does commissioned works in portraiture and other forms of sculpture.

While not in the Adirondacks this monument to the past nevertheless is well worth mentioning. The tombstone covers the grave of Amun-Her-Khepesh-Ef, age two, son of Sen Woset 3rd, King of Egypt and his wife, Hathor-Hotpe. The mummy of this child, who would have become a Pharoah had he lived, was stolen from his tomb in Egypt, sold by grave robbers, and eventually ended in a museum in Middlebury, Vt. The boy's ashes were given burial in a cemetery near Middlebury College; it is not known whether the date, 1883 B.C. represents birth or death, but the date itself would bring the child into the past of almost 4,000 years ago.

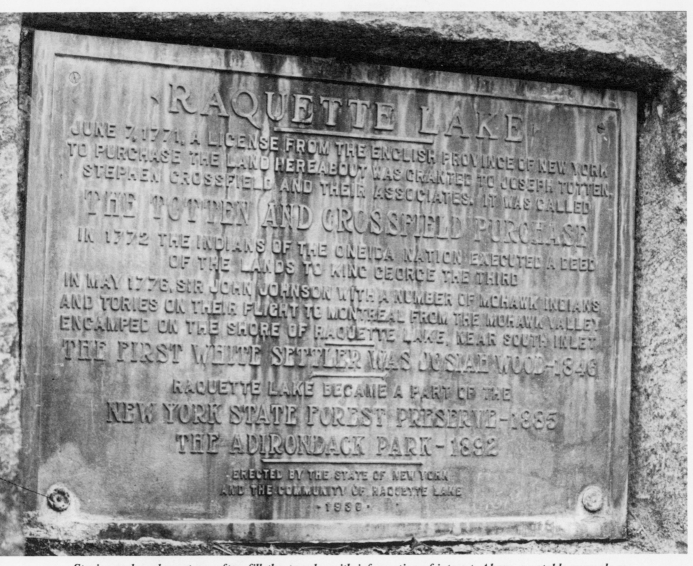

Stories anchored on stone often fill the traveler with information of interest. Above, a notable example on Rt. 28, twixt Blue Mt. Lake and Raquette Lake. The inscription follows:

"June 7, 1771, a license from the English Province of New York to purchase the land hereabouts was granted to Joseph Totten, Stephen Crossfield and their associates. It was called: The Totten and Crossfield Purchase.

"In 1772, the Indians of the Oneida Nation executed a deed of the lands to King George the Third.

"In May, 1776, Sir John Johnson, with a number of Mohawk Indians and Tories on their flight to Montreal from the Mohawk Valley encamped on the shore of Raquette Lake near South Inlet.

"Raquette Lake became a part of the New York State Forest Preserve – 1885; the Adirondack Park – 1892."

The plaque was erected by the state and community of Raquette Lake in 1930. As pointed out elsewhere in this volume, the retreating forces reportedly abandoned snowshoes at the lake; thus this body of water obtained its name.

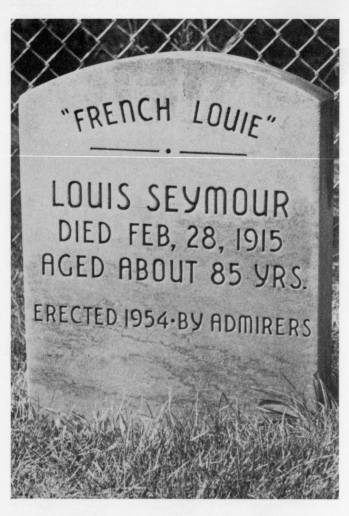

"FRENCH LOUIE"
— · —
LOUIS SEYMOUR
DIED FEB, 28, 1915
AGED ABOUT 85 YRS.
ERECTED 1954·BY ADMIRERS

This unusual tombstone sets in a small cemetery at the "four corners" in Speculator, is dedicated to Louis Seymour, more commonly known as "French Louie," who was reportedly born around 1830 near Ottawa, Canada. After driving mules along Erie Canal towpaths, he became a lumberjack in the Indian Lake region, then constructed cabins at various spots, such as Lewey Lake and West Canada Lake, where he hunted and fished.

When French Louie came to town — that is, Speculator — he sold his furs and with the monies therefrom bought candies for the kids, and a considerable amount of liquid refreshments for himself. When over his binge he would return to the woods for more pelts. He died at Brooks Hotel, Speculator, and the tombstone was erected by admirers who felt such a mountain man should not rest without suitable evidence above ground.

An example of early Adirondack sculpture in wood is this bear, given the author some years ago. Carver is unknown. Craftsmanship is excellent.

MEDICINE MEN

The story goes that a gentleman named Artemas Shattuck took his axe one day in May, 1817, and went into the woods to chop. Chop he did, with hefty blows and mighty grunts.

Once the tree became a log, he began to split it. Somehow as a wedge was dislodged his foot became snagged; he was held in a vise.

"Despairing of receiving aid," read a published state report, "he unjointed his ankle and made a crutch."

I am not sure where this novel happenstance occurred, but if Artemas was a woodsman, it may very well have been in the Adirondack region. Furthermore, there is no indication exactly as to the meaning of "unjointed." It could have meant broken or removed. If indeed he amputated his foot and survived, he must have become a medical wonder. "Unjointing," whatever it meant, is nothing to be alleviated by a mere slug of rum or whiskey — considered, incidentally, to be the first tranquilizer known to Man.

If Shattuck managed to hobble his way to a doctor, he was indeed a lucky man; physicians in the early 1800's were few and far between, especially in sparsely settled areas, and that included the Adirondacks.

Doctors actually began moving into the eastern end of the Adirondacks shortly after the Revolution, to fill a void of about a century-and-one-half.

During that period treatment was pretty much up to the individual and native skills; death and injury were always present shadows.

The first white physician to set foot in the Adirondacks was Rene Goupil, a French Jesuit lay brother. Goupil, unable to take the vows to become a Jesuit priest, did, however, study medicine in France; became a medical missionary, and came to this country where he joined Isaac Jogues, the first white man to see Lake George.

Goupil, made captive with Jogues by the Mohawks, treated both fellow captives and Indians alike. A tomahawk cut his career short in 1642 at Ossernenon, now Auriesville Shrine in the Mohawk Valley, to which place the Mohawks brought him and Jogues for torture. His body reportedly is buried in the Ravine of the Martyrs at that Jesuit Shrine; was interred there by Jogues who recovered the remains from Indian boys playing with the corpse.

René Goupil, memorialized in the statue above at Auriesville Shrine in the Mohawk Valley, was the first white physician in the Adirondacks. He was captured with Isaac Jogues, brought to Ossernenon, now Auriesville, and after torture, was tomahawked. The statue depicts the reason; Goupil made the sign of the cross on the head of an Indian lad, and this roused Mohawk fury.

This work of art denotes use of High Rock Spring, Saratoga Springs, during the days when Indians had exclusive use of the waters. The spring is located on High Rock Spring Avenue in Saratoga. A similar painting, or mural, is in the council chambers of Saratoga Springs City Hall.

More than 300 years after the death of this medical man, mine detectors were used in The Ravine in an attempt to locate Goupil's grave; Father Jogues, in a report, said he had included a silver crucifix with the body. Efforts were unsuccessful.

In 1953, a team of archeologists trenched other possible sites, but met with no success. The author assisted in the search in The Ravine; was an observer on the later 1953 tries, when digging went on under direction of Farther Ewing, world renowned archeologist, an operation which involved other persons such as Robert Whitson, Yale School of Anthropology and George W. Pepper, graduate instructor at Iowa College. Again, no success. Auriesville holds its secrets well.

There were, of course, physicians in the Adirondacks before Goupil — the Iroquois medicine men, who accompanied hunting and fishing parties into the North Country — spots, for instance, such as the Sacandaga vlie, a swampy area which was inundated in construction of the Sacandaga Reservoir. There was Iroquoian trust in these men who became expert in utilization of natural remedies, and who were skilled even in setting broken bones.

Sassafras was one plant often used by Indians, who viewed it as a growth with curative powers for blood problems. Early settlers picked up the plant for similar use, but went one step further; they thought sassafras could cure venereal disease. Tons were shipped to Europe. As a matter of fact, the drinking of sassafras tea became, at times, a "suspicious" move, simply because observers figured the imbiber was taking it for reasons other than pleasure!

The Indians of long ago used dressings of herbs and made soothing brews for internal disorders. During the 1700's Indians used even the common dandelion, which was brought to this country by settlers. This plant is not native no matter what the proud possessor of a lawn feels.

Some of the remedies used by the Iroquois and other nations involved maidenhair fern, the common ground pine, bellwort, bloodroot, white pine and even hemlock; the art of mixing and administering was up to the medicine man. Not to remain unmentioned is plain mud; the Indian was a keen observer of animal life and noted that an injured animal often rested in a swampy area.

[To be noted here is that animals haven't changed much in attitude; some years ago when two buffalo bulls fought at the Miner Institute in Clinton County, the one which had been gored by superior power moved into a swampy area and rested there for several days, until the wound began to heal. At this time, the Miner Institute possessed a herd of 13 buffalo. Today that Chazy institution has a herd of about a dozen.]

If mud packs were used for bad insect bites or more serious wounds, the Indian had no concern about purity; the white man had yet to bring his "civilization" into the picture along with its pollution.

Too widely known to be mentioned in detail are the mineral springs at Ballston Spa and Saratoga Springs —

as well as the waters of Sharon Springs, Schoharie County. It was the Mohawks who passed along word to Sir William Johnson, His Majesty's representative in charge of Indian affairs, that Saratoga waters (and Lebenon Springs waters) might cure his gout. Sir William, a gusty man with the ladies, suffered from more than gout, however, some historians say he had a venereal disease to contend with.

It was between the time of Rene Goupil and the end of the American Revolution that the Adirondacks saw no white physician; that is, a person academically trained in the care of keeping a body operating under full power. One must wonder over the number of trappers and other early frontiersmen who died a lonely, painful death because of injury or from the effects of an infected wound.

After the Hassle for Liberty, the general population of the "Colonies" grew restless and the move was westward. Settlers from Vermont, bedding down in the Bouquet River Valley, inland from Lake Champlain, enticed their former physician, one Asa Post of Panton, Vt., to join them. He did, arriving about 1792. He was 27; served until 1800, then retired to a farm where he died at age 92. For a man supposedly afflicted with "consumption," his years were elastic. Dr. Post is noted as the first physician to settle permanently in the North Country.

In the meantime, a Dr. Alexander Morse came into the picture around the time of Dr. Post's retirement and served the area for a half century. Dr. Morse was one of the first trained individuals, if not the first, to note the benefits of the "effects of the high altitudes of Essex (County) on certain of the more common diseases." As a matter of fact, Dr. Morse in 1809 became a delegate to the State Medical Society and presented a paper on just that subject.

According to Dr. LeRoy H. Wardner, Saranac Lake, who presented an historical outline of Adirondack medicine which was printed in the New York State Journal of Medicine April 15, 1942, "a fringe of small communities grew up in the valleys of the northern and eastern Adirondacks in the fifty years after the coming of Dr. Post."

Continuing, Dr. Wardner said:

"Lumbering, iron mining charcoal making hunting, fishing trapping and farming occupied their rugged citizens. Gradually medical pioneers moved in to make a hard life more bearable.

"Outstanding was F. J. d'Avignon the second, who escaped to Au Sable Forks in 1837 under sentence of death for activities in inciting the Papineau Rebellion in lower Canada."

d'Avignon practiced medicine and surgery; traveled on horseback, operated by lamplight in remote homes, "on any kitchen table," which piece of furniture seemed to more than suffice for almost any kind of surgery.

(I have heard parents in their late years tell the family sprouts that the very table at which they ate, was the

113

The painting above, owned by Wyeth Laboratories, and a copy of which hangs in St. Clare's Hospital, Schenectady, depicts Dr. William Beaumont of Plattsburgh, half kneeling beside the bed of his patient, Alexis St. Martin, whose gunshot wound healed but literally left a "peek-hole" into his stomach! Dr. Beaumont thus was able to keep a day-to-day record of the human digestive process. The copy of the painting was donated to St. Clare's by Dr. Arthur Q. Penta of Schenectady.

table upon which they were born. It never seemed to diminish appetite!)

If the name of d'Avignon sparkles in early mountain medicine, so does the name William Beaumont, Plattsburgh, a surgeon in the War of 1812. Dr. Beaumont was the first physician to accurately trace the process of digestion in the living human body. How he did this is a story in itself.

When Dr. Beaumont served as an Army surgeon at Lake Huron, one of his patients was a soldier, Alexis St. Martin. St. Martin had suffered a severe gunshot wound that opened part of his stomach. Dr. Beaumont did his best to heal the wound but found he had to leave a small section open. Thus he had a "window" through which to look into St. Martin's stomach.

The physician opened an office for private practice in Plattsburgh after the war, at Bridge and Margaret Streets, and so fascinated was he by the St. Martin medical miracle that he brought the man to that Clinton County city for continued observation. Those observations continued for a period of years.

He used the "peek-hole" of the wound to observe digestive processes and his notes gave medical science priceless information on how the human body treats its food intake.

St. Martin married a Plattsburgh woman and raised a family in that city; obviously the wound was not an insurmountable barrier. The story goes that he was increasingly unhappy at the schedule he had to follow on examinations and eventually the unique relationship of doctor-patient ended. A major accomplishment in this was that Dr. Beaumont was able to feed St. Martin different kinds of food and thus was able to time the time of digestion.

The Plattsburgh area is noted not only for Beaumont's experiments and observations on the physiology of gastric secretions but for the inventiveness of Dr. Lyman Guy Barton. Dr. Barton, who began practice in 1891, was the son of a physician and was based in Willsboro.

As a country doctor, he found himself officiating at many births, and also found that an increasing number required forceps curved to prevent cranial injury. He found none on the market. So he devised a sketch, gave it to the village smithy and the Barton forceps thus came into being!

His ingenuity did not end there; he invented a portable operating table to replace the use of the kitchen table.

The story of Dr. Edward L. Trudeau is a well known one, does not bear extensive retelling; what is important is that this pioneer in the treatment of tuberculosis (consumption) spent the winter of 1876-77 in the then "miserable hamlet" of Saranac Lake, and thus became its first resident physician.

Before this, Saranac Lake residents in pain and misery were treated by W. F. Martin, a resort hotel owner who became a famous "amateur doctor," drawing upon the imparted wisdom of Dr. J. Savage Delavan of Albany, a fall and spring visitor.

In writing of Dr. Delavan, Dr. Wardner in his paper before the New York State Journal of Medicine said:

"Dr. J. Savage Delavan was his chief mentor on his spring and fall visits but all gave him suggestions freely and furnished him with authoritative books, pamphlets, and even medicine."

Non-doctor Martin's talents were used within a wide radius of Saranac Lake.

The value of Adirondack air became even better known through such individuals as Robert Louis Stevenson, who possessed the usual lung troubles of the day and spent time at what is now known as the Stevenson Cottage in Saranac Lake. Reportedly he was not too happy during the wild weather of winter, but the noted author of "Treasure Island" unquestionably prolonged his life and vigor — as did thousands of others who came to breathe renewed energy back into their troubled bodies.

The world-famous Trudeau Sanatorium was Dr. Trudeau's monument.

Now in writing of medicine and practitioners of that remarkable art, it would be impossible to write a chapter without mentioning the "Adirondack Mineral Spring" which Dr. John Bell wrote of in the "Medical Times" of January 16, 1871 as Civil War echoes began their slow death.

This spring, which Dr. Bell said "rises in Whitehall," derived its name from the point of issuance from the "base of one of the spurs of the Adirondack Mountains." The temperature of the water, he said, was 52 degrees, a temperature, incidentally which many spelunkers find in their strange wanderings through underground labyrinths.

Said Dr. Bell:

"Its saline constituents are carbonates of lime, magnesia, soda and potassa, with traces of manganese and lithia; also sulphate of lime and chloride of sodium. There seems to be a general concurrence of opinion among the physicians of Whitehall in favor of the remedial power of the water of this spring.

"Dr. Shumway regards it as a stimulant, tonic and diuretic. . .he speaks of its very decided efficacy in chronic rheumatism and also in all chronic cutaneous eruptions.

"Dr. Long prescribed it in Bright's disease with the happiest of results. Instances are related of speedy and permanent relief obtained by drinking it in cases of gravel (gall or kidney stones?), of difficult and painful micturition and even of retention so complete that a catheter had to be introduced."

A pretty remarkable spring. One wonders if it still gushes its miracles from the "base of one of the spurs of the Adirondack Mountains!"

Apparently mountain liquid came in variety.

There was another "water" sold by the bottle called "Adirondack Ozonia." Great things happened when folks drank Ozonia — so read descriptions. It was so "soft and pure" it aided nature "in cleansing, digesting and assimilating the nutritive elements of food, and after carrying this nutrition to every capillary of the body, it turns around and carries back through the depurating and emunctory organs the effete matter of the system for final expulsion, thus eliminating completely and perfectly all poisons, malignant germs and wastes." (The author herewith has put a quotation mark at the end of one of the longest advertising sentences he has seen.)

Ozonia was also recommended for liver troubles, kidney ailments, bladder inflammations and troubles with the prostate glands, as well as with pelvic and generative organs.

And from whence came this most magic of water?

"It flows," read the advertising pitch, "from the bosom of Mother Earth, originally at the base of a pine tree, now a pine stump, standing on the north bank of the St. Regis River."

Again, the author wonders if the Genie of Good Health still springs happily forth at the base of a pine stump.

All this is in the past, of course. Today no Adirondacker or visitor must suffer unduly; no one is isolated anymore, save temporarily; even a victim of injury atop Mt. Marcy may receive aid as fast as weather permits a helicopter and search and rescue teams to reach him or her. Quality hospitals and doctors of quality are within easy reach; times have surely changed.

It remains an interesting note, however, that by the year 1700, world-wide, thousands of drug products had been tested and endorsed for one use or another, but only a few dozen proved effective. Many of these drugs did arrive in America with early settlement.

Even in early days, Indians absorbed some of the teachings of whites, and whites learned much from the Indians.

Once upon a time, earthworms were rolled like fish in flour, in honey, and this weird concoction was used in the treatment of gastritis. A hunter, if he developed a headache, would shoot an owl and use its brain. Sleeplessness called for use of sheep brains; on occasion, the heart of a buck or doe was considered a cure for heart disease.

Bladder troubles? Rabbit testicles were used — how, the author does not know. Those bunny organs also were used for impotency. And many a fox lost his life because his lung was considered an alleviation for tuberculosis.

These are some of the ancient remedies; whether carried over into this country from Europe is not known. Some of them just might have. Who really knows of what the earliest of settlers brought with them in their fertile minds; reservoirs of information that generations before them had passed from one to the other?

The day of the leeches to draw blood, the day of diagnosing diptheria by odor, the day of using whiskey as a medical opiate — those days are gone. Only stories remain. Such as the one concerning two men chopping wood in the northern area of the Champlain Valley.

One held a piece of wood on a block while the other split it with an axe. For the sake of variety the one holding the wood would substitute his foot, drawing it back when the axe began to fall.

The axeman became exasperated, told his partner the "next time he did that, he'd take his foot off." The partner didn't believe the threat; substituted his foot once again, but the axe was too quick; off came the toes and part of the foot.

While it was injury, it was not death. The foot was treated. The victim survived. Matter of fact, the lopped off portion was preserved in a jar of alcohol, and became a community curosity!

SNAKE BITE CURE

The only poisonous reptile in the Adirondacks in early days was the timber rattler. Dr. John Perrigo of Queensbury, who set up his practice about 1800, is believed to be the first physician to introduce to the attention of the public "the prophylactic and curative properties of the rattle-snake weed, (Prenanthes Serpentaria) as a prompt and efficient antidote" to the reptile's venom.

This knowledge, according to an 1885 account, "was in all probability derived from the Indians," who even in that year lingered in small groups around their ancient hunting grounds in the Lake George-Lake Champlain region.

Timber rattlers apparently were a major danger. A British officer in Gen. Burgoyne's Army wrote that Diamond Island, Lake George, "as well as the one close to it," was at one time over-run with the reptiles.

One batteau, he said, loaded with hogs, capsized and the porkers swam to Diamond. So did the rowers — who spent the night in trees. They were rescued, went on to Fort George. Later the owner of the hogs visited the island to claim his livestock, found them "prodigiously" fat, and only one rattler was noted.

One hog was slaughtered for food and its stomach contained snake remains; the pigs had eaten well. This may have been the basis for a later legend that when bacon was made from the hogs, the bacon curled and leaped out of the pan and when pig litters were born subsequently, piglets had rattles on their tails!

Indians were not particularly perturbed. During Montcalm's invasion down Lake George, some of his Indian allies tied the tails of snakes together for amusement and to pass the time of day while camped at Sabbath Day Point!

The snake infestation reached as far south as the rock cliffs found in the Glens Falls area.

WOMAN ENTOMBED

The Death of a College Dean
Brought a Medical Phenomenon
To Light at
Lake Placid

The October, 1964, FBI Law Enforcement Bulletin led an astonishing story in this fashion:

"Two scuba divers, members of the Lake Champlain Wreck Raiders Diving Club of Plattsburgh, N.Y., were sport diving among the ledges of Lake Placid off Pulpit Rock in the early afternoon of September 15, 1963. While exploring the bottom of the lake, approximately 60 feet offshore, at a depth of 105 feet, they saw what appeared to be a store manikin.

"The temperature of the water at this location was around 34 degrees Fahrenheit."

This, then, was the FBI's way to introduce nationally the background of a case which I doubt has any known equal in New York State or, for that matter, in the Northeastern portion of the United States. Although it was a case described by the FBI, that agency did not participate in it. It was, however, one which occupied the attention not only of the New York State Police, but police departments and individuals in many communities.

The "manikin" was not of the store window display type; it was the extraordinarily well preserved body of a woman identified eventually as Anna Mabel Douglass, age 56. also known as Mabel Smith Douglass, founder and former dean of the New Jersey College for Women at New Brunswick, N.J., a branch of Rutgers University.

What made this case remarkable and one that has been described as a "pathological phenomenon," is that Mabel Smith Douglass had vanished in the waters of Lake Placid while rowing on September 21, 1933, a full thirty years before her body was discovered, and her body, when found, was almost perfectly preserved in features and shape and presented what was described as a "classic example of a phenomenon called 'adipocere'." In layman language the term means a gradual substitution of mineral salts and other chemical substances for body tissue. In the words of Dr. James Utterback, a Saranac Lake pathologist: "In effect, forming a cast of the person that existed before."

The penetration of chemical elements, such as calcium salts (found in most natural waters), combined with the extreme coldness of the depth at which the woman was found, created an ideal situation for preservation. The condition might be called, as one observer put it, "partial ossification." Lake Placid cannot be called a large lake in comparison with several others in the Adirondacks, but it can be considered a deep one;

Mabel Smith Douglass (from newspaper photo)

the extreme depth of the twin channels of Placid (each side of the big islands) is due to glacial tongues gouging previous stream valleys. A local glacier lingered on the flank of Whitefact Mt., as on many other high peaks, a considerable time after the main ice sheet had retreated north of the Adirondacks.

When Sgt. Richard Niffenegger, Plattsburgh Air Force Base, and James Rogers, Rouses Point, the scuba divers who found the body, first saw its outlines in the twilight of 105 feet, they swam for closer inspection. One diver told State Police his first impression was that the body was "fully intact." He told police the corpse was resting on its right side in a deposit of silt and the water temperature was 34 degrees Fahrenheit according to his instruments.

The final resting place for Mrs. Douglass, Lake Placid, where her body was found at a depth of more than 100 feet by divers from Plattsburgh. The mountain in the background, touched lightly by snow, is Whiteface.

State Police were told a rope was found knotted around the neck. At the other end of the rope was a "bell shaped" boat anchor. The rope "dissolved" when touched, thereby separating the body from the anchor.

Facial features were visible. There was evidence of shreds of clothing. Shoes of an "uncommon kind" were on both feet.

Niffenegger and Rogers carried the body to the surface where it was secured to a diving buoy. While the body was thus secured, and prior to placing it in a boat, several power boats passed the area at close distance creating large waves. The turbulence caused the complete head and that portion of the neck containing the knotted rope, plus the complete left arm and a portion of the right hand to break from the body and fall to the lake's bottom.

Another diver, identified by State Police as Delmar Faulds of Plattsburgh, went to the bottom and "was able to recover the head, but due to heavy silt deposits was unable to locate the other portions of the body."

The SP report read that when Faulds surfaced with the recovered head, it was discovered the face no longer contained any features and, furthermore, the jawbones had become separated and were still at the bottom. The depth of silt at this location was estimated at an astonishing four feet!

Trooper Mark Cross, while on patrol, received radio instructions from SP Saranac Lake to go to the Grote Boat Landing on Lake Placid "relative to the finding of a dead body." When Trooper Cross arrived, present were Lt. C.A. Stephens, Zone Four Commander, and Troopers R.G. Slingerland and D.C. Gallery, also summoned to the scene.

The search for identity then began, and the author would like to note at this point that titles used in this chapter were the ones used in official reports in the 1963 investigation compiled by Trooper Cross.

Dr. Onslow Gordon, Essex County Coroner, Westport, was contacted by Trooper T.E. McGinnis, SP Saranac Lake, and he said he would appoint Dr. Bartholomew Ring, Lake Placid, as Coroner's Physician. Dr. Ring arrived at the scene and at that time the body was removed from the divers' boat to the dock for examination. At this time the body was found almost devoid of clothing except for portions of an elastic substance "approximately one quarter inch in size, resembling rotted cloth," found on the right leg and shoes. The body was ivory in color and skin surface appeared atrophied to touch.

Dr. Ring, according to the SP report, stated "he had never seen anything comparable to this," and the body was removed to the Clark Funeral Home Lake Placid, for a more complete examination by a pathologist.

Since jaws were missing at that time no identity could be established through dental work. Lt. Stephens and Trooper Cross interviewed Thomas George Lake Placid, operator of the George and Bliss Boat Landing; Mr. George told police the body might possibly be that of Mrs. Douglass.

This suggestion was followed; Lt. Stephens and Trooper Cross consulted old newspaper files at the Lake Placid Public Library and found reports of the missing Mrs. Douglass as filed by her daughter, Edith. State Police then interviewed Patrolman Bernard Fell of the Lake Placid Police Department, and that department's files were opened. Information therein revealed rescue attempts were continued through Oct. 15, 1933, and discontinued. State Police also found that the lake not only had been dragged, but dynamite had been exploded in its depth in an attempt to bring the body to the surface.

Dr. Utterback conducted an examination of the body at the Clark Funeral Home and present for the post-mortem and assisting were Troop Commander Capt. H.T. Muller, Lt. Supervisor W.B. Surdam, Lt. Stephens, Sr. Inv. R.R. Gaffney, Inv. L.A. Stoffel, Trooper J.F. Cotter and Trooper Cross. Prior to the post-mortem Trooper Cotter took black and white and color photographs.

Dr. Utterback's examination disclosed the subject to be approximately five-feet, five-inches tall; that she weighed about 140 pounds, "that the body had been well cared for in the sense of personal hygiene," and that there was no obvious external evidence of violence in tissues examined. There was, however, evidence of an old clavicle fracture. Portions of undergarments were found wedged between the thighs, and at the time it was presumed the woman had not borne more than one child. That was a probability; it was later found Mrs. Douglass had borne two; both were dead at the time of the discovery of Mrs. Douglass' body.

State Police interviewed Chief of Police Lawrence MacDonald, Lake Placid, and additional records revealed no other females were reported missing or drowned in the lake except Mrs. Douglass.

Trooper Mark Cross, left, and Trooper Paul Endersee are two of several members of the State Police who investigated the drowning of Mabel Smith Douglass. They are pictured at the Wilmington station.

At this point, officials were certain of the identity in their own minds, but the investigation went on. Other interviews with other persons followed. One woman told police she knew Mrs. Douglass when she had been the dean of the New Jersey College for Women, and that pressures grew as the college developed, and Mrs. Douglass was forced to retire for reasons of health sometime in 1933; that after retirement, she came to Lake Placid to recuperate at her camp. The woman, who had been a student at the college, gave police a physical description that matched the one given by Dr. Utterback.

Police then contacted Henry Vincent who had reportedly seen a "woman in a rowboat" near Pulpit Rock while he and Kenneth Bliss were transporting lumber in their boat to a short camp. Vincent said the "row boat" was a St. Lawrence skiff and that in his experience as a boat builder, this particular craft was very treacherous in the hands of someone not skilled in its use. Mr. Vincent also told State Police that when the daughter of Mrs. Douglass had been notified that her mother's boat had been found capsized, the daughter made a statement "to the effect that she believed an anchor was missing from the boathouse."

On September 18, three days after divers found the body, Frank Pabst and Thomas Tucker Plattsburgh, members of the Wreck Raiders Diving Club, made another descent near Pulpit Rock and despite heavy silt, found a jawbone and some teeth. These items were turned over to Inv. Stoffel and Zone Sgt. W.L. Shurter. They were given to Dr. Utterback. Discovery of the jawbone and teeth, however, did not help since it was found the dentist who had treated Mrs. Douglass had died and his records had been destroyed.

This question in the minds of many had surfaced: Was it an accidental death or suicide? At this time, the picture of Mrs. Douglass as a despondent person, began to emerge. One woman told police Mrs. Douglass had suffered financial loss in the stock market, and that was "common knowledge."

State Police Manhattan moved into the picture and it was disclosed that her husband had died in 1916; she had had two children, one of whom had died in an accident in 1923, and a daughter, who was killed in a fall in 1948, 15 years after the disappearance of her mother.

"Further investigation," said the SP report, "revealed that prior to the retirement of Mabel Smith Douglass as Dean of the New Jersey College for Women, and later known as Douglass College, in May, 1933, Mrs. Douglass had taken a year's leave of absence because of ill health."

Intensive efforts by SP brought medical records to view.

Dr. Utterback's medical findings during the post-mortem, in addition to those mentioned, supported SP evidence.

Furthermore, despite the death of the dentist who had treated Mrs. Douglass in former years, and the destruction of his records, the jawbone found by divers Frank Pabst and Thomas Tucker provided the final link in identification. A detailed examination made of the jawbone by Dr. George Wilson, Lake Placid dentist, revealed the teeth were gold inlays. And Troop B Commander Capt. Muller had received correspondence from a resident of Haworth, N.J., who had known the deceased, and who recalled the fact that she had inlays.

There were other bits to consider — the anchor found by divers, for instance. It was a "horse anchor" of the type used when those animals were the power sources of everyday travel; they were shaped like a bell, and such an anchor was found to be missing from the Douglass boathouse. To top it off, the shoes found on the victim's body were shown to Parnell LaTour of Saranac Lake, who was in the shoe business and an expert in shoe types; he said they were of an expensive make and were the style in the early and late 1930s.

Finally when all evidence was analyzed, Trooper Cross was informed by Coroner Gordon that in his opinion, an opinion based on evidence and discussions with Dr. Utterback, the death was due to accidental causes and SP were advised no inquest would be held. On September 26, Trooper Cross contacted Essex County District Attorney Daniel Manning and informed him of the coroner's decision. Mr. Manning said he had consulted with Dr. Gordon previously and "could see no reason for a formal inquest."

As a result, this statement was issued as a news release by the BCI out of Saranac Lake:

"State Police investigation into the recovery and identification of an unknown body from Lake Placid by members of the Lake Champlain Wreck Raiders Diving Club, has identified the body as Mabel Smith Douglass, who vanished Sept. 21, 1933. The investigation reveals no evidence of a criminal homicide.

"The investigation does reflect ill health and an extreme nervous condition of Mrs. Douglass, but since positive factual evidence is lacking, and the rope the skin divers saw around the neck disintegrated when touched, examination of a knot or accidental entanglement in an anchor rope cannot be determined.

"Therefore, the official coroner's verdict is accidental death."

Douglass College claimed the body as no living relatives of the deceased woman could be located. Burial took place October 2, 1963, in the Greenwood Cemetery, Brooklyn.

She Found Her Peace
Within Cold Depths;
After Despairing Prayer
She Heard a Voice,
She Felt a Touch,
She Rested, Finally in His Care.
— BF

THE DISEASE CALLED ACID RAIN

**The Killer Stalks Quietly,
Inexorably, From West
To East, And The
Mountains Suffer**

The awesome problem of acid rain, killer of life in Adirondack ponds and lakes, is in no way diminishing. It remains a growing evil not only to marine life but a threat to North Country forests.

It is not just the rain.

Acid snow, in its own insidious way, delivers a more shattering blow than rain. Snow accumulates in Adirondack lake watersheds until depths of several feet are reached. Within the snow blanket are the poisons which are released almost at once; as the spring snow melt starts, it overwhelms the delicate balance of life.

The killing process continues day and night, as industrial wastes pour from giant smokestacks in America's mid West. Airborne sulfur dioxide and nitrous oxides form diluted sulfuric and nitric acids in solutions, the winds from West to East bear the poisons into the Adirondacks. The process of death thus becomes inexorable.

Acidity is measured by what is called a pH factor. A pH of 7 is considered neutral. The next unit lower, 6, represents a tenfold increase in acidity. A two-figure drop from 7, therefore, would mean an acidity increase of 100 percent, and so on down the line! In other words, the lower the pH factor, the higher the acidity.

Because the problem is of such tremendous proportions, New York State cannot handle it alone. The elimination of industrial wastes, shooting heavenward from mid West smokestacks — literally being "shot" into the air, to be picked up by the winds — is a Federal matter.

New Yorkers are concerned. Vastly so. One prominent Adirondacker, William Roden, representing the Adirondack Association, appeared before the Environment and Public Works Committee of the United States Senate in Washington, Sept. 23, 1980. I am privileged to quote his testimony, since Bill has long studied the problem.

Bill and his wife operate the Trout Lake Club, a cottage resort on a lake in the southeastern Adirondacks; his family has been at this location since 1924 and his children are the fourth generation of Rodens to work at the resort.

Bill has another attribute: He is a newspaper columnist, writing an outdoor column known as "Adirondack Sportsman," carried regularly in many mountain newspapers. He is a hunter and fisherman; an astute observer of the North Country scene, and a person well able to put the situation into factual status. His testimony follows:

Our lake, Trout Lake, still has a pH of over 7 and is, therefore, not yet affected by acid precipitation or what we laymen call acid rain. However, just 30 miles to my north a friend of mine owns a camp on a small body of water called Lincoln Pond. Out of curiosity he took readings of his pond. In '77 it was 7.2; in '78 it was 7.0; in '79 the pH was 6.8 and, fortunately, it has held this level in 1980.

To the west of me is Canada Lake, a body of water with a surface area of some 525 acres, formerly known for its bass fishing. It is a very popular recreation lake with a number of resorts and many summer cottages on its shore. Today the bass are gone. The reading is down to 5.2 and the fishermen from that area are understandably angry. The winds from the west that cross Canada Lake cross Trout Lake and I must, therefore, ask myself how long before our lake turns. This past summer guests at my resort had fantastic fishing — bass, and lake trout for those who knew how to catch them in the cold deep water. Dozens of bass were weighed at our Snack Bar in excess of 2 pounds and three were over 5½. As I'm sure you have been told, bass are one of the first species to disappear as the pH of a body of water drops.

How long will it be before those who vacation with us for the family activities and the fishing will begin to think of going elsewhere? The warning is already there in my backyard — a brass bell that glistened in the sun for 25 years shines no more — it has turned green during the last 3 years.

You have asked me to present the viewpoint of the small businessman and give you some idea of the economic impact of acid rain on our area. It is difficult to

121

cover all aspects and you must tolerate rough figures. We do have some studies which indicate the value of fishing to the New York State economy. In 1979 it was estimated that there were 1,375,000 anglers who fished in New York State. The value of this activity to our economy is estimated by our Department of Environmental Conservation researchers at somewhere between 518 million and 601 million dollars in 1979.

It is impossible for me to give you a specific figure for the part of that fresh water fishery that is Adirondack-oriented — it would be substantial, for in the Adirondack area there are a total of 2877 individual lakes and ponds encompassing 282,154 surface acres. New York State's portion of Lake Champlain is not included in this figure but world-famous 28,000-acre Lake George is. So you will appreciate the significance of our problem, the latest count we have is that 264 lakes and ponds with 11,518 surface acres no longer support aquatic life of any sort including fish, crayfish, mussels, salamanders, etc.

Please understand also the rate at which this problem is assaulting us — 52 ponds with a total of 1,158 acres were among those measured that turned acid in the last year!

Because the acid situation was first discovered in the Adirondacks in remote, high-elevation ponds, there is a tendency to think that they are the only ones affected. This is not so. We now have a number of lakes in the 1,000-acre category at lower elevations which are sterile. There are a number of resort lakes which are presently on a rapid down-trend and are expected to lose their ability to support fish life in the near future. Canada Lake, mentioned before, Big Tupper Lake and Cranberry Lake (fifth largest in the Adirondack Park) are three well-known Adirondack resort lakes that are currently seriously threatened.

One of the largest bodies of water with a serious acid problem is Big Moose Lake in Herkimer County in the western part of the Adirondacks. The surface of Big Moose is in excess of 1300 acres. It once had an outstanding fishery including brook trout, lake trout, and bass. President Grover Cleveland was very familiar with Big Moose Lake and fished it. He visited Dart Lake Lodge which was a small lakeside resort on the outlet stream of Big Moose Lake. The pH reading for Big Moose Lake today is 4.17. I'm sure you've been told by professionals who have testified before you previously such waters will support no fish life. Said one of our fishery biologists recently:

"With that kind of a pH, I would expect no sport fishery to be possible for all practical purposes. Much too large for a liming program. As far as the Department of Environmental Conservation is concerned, *nothing* can be done."

I have here a book from my Adirondack library. It was published in 1941. The author, Leighton Brewer, is unknown to me but the title, "Virgin Water," caught my eye as a fisherman. Mr. Brewer was in the High Peaks of the Adirondacks. He writes:

Lake Tear (sometimes called Tear of the Clouds) is open to dispute as the source of Hudson's River, but it is commonly known as such. This lake, high on Marcy's slopes, is not only acid, but is the victim of pollution by humans.

"The story of the Flowedlands is also instructive. As I have already mentioned, it was formerly a swamp, but converted by a five-foot dam into a lake some three quarters of a mile in length. Through this lake flows the Opalescent River, which is, in fact, the main branch of the Hudson, only a few miles below where, as Feldspar Brook, it bubbles out of the ground at Lake Tear-of-the-Clouds.

"For some time no signs of fish appeared, although Lake Colden, just above, was overstocked with trout. Then one July morning about five years after the dam had been built, someone passing across noticed large trout rising, whereupon he put his rod together and proceeded to take five fish totaling 15½ pounds. These fish multiplied very fast, for in a few years the lake was just boiling with trout from 1 to 2½ pounds and a certain number of bigger ones.

"They grew rapidly, for all those caught were very fat and had small heads, indicating that they were young fish. This lake was soon fished without respite from the first of June until the last day of August, with an average of three rods a day; and I have estimated the annual toll was more than five thousand trout. Yet it continued to yield more and better fish than any other lake in the whole region."

Bill's testimony now continues:

The New York State Department of Environmental Conservation is repairing that dam at the Flowedlands that Brewer mentions and in order to do so, has drained the water from the pond. There was no delay or hesitation for today there are no fish. You should know, too, that Lake Colden, Lake Tear-of-the-Clouds, the upper Opalescent River and, in fact, all of the High Peaks ponds are sterile and have no fish. When you climb New York State's highest mountain, Mount Marcy, you cannot catch your dinner of brook trout in a pond along the way as I did as a young man.

The ramifications of acid rain are only just beginning to surface in some respects. I told of the fishery of Big Moose Lake. Last week I spoke with a resort owner on Big Moose Lake and heard one of the most troublesome reports that has yet come to my attention. There was a report one morning of an odd taste in the tap water. He tasted it and had to agree. Since his was a spring water supply, he checked it out immediately and found nothing. He took a faucet sample and sent it to the laboratory. The analysis showed there were high concentrations of copper and lead in the drinking water. He called in a biologist and a chemist and they tested the spring water and found a low pH reading. Further testing has shown that many neighbors and neighboring resorts using both spring water from the lake basin and Big Moose lake water have the same low pH. What this acidified water is doing is leaching copper from the copper water pipes and lead from the soldered joints into their drinking water. A few days after this incident my friend had trouble with the septic system of his resort. Investigation disclosed that the anerobic bacteria which are the main factor in the proper working of the system were not functioning and the septic system was sterile.

My friend tells me the bacteria are especially suceptible to copper and this metal was coming into the system in sufficient volume to kill them and make it non-operative. This problem is also surfacing at other locations. There is no way I can put a dollar value on this. My friend has corrected his problem by filtering his water through crushed limestone at considerable expense. This situation was discovered and corrected but I ask myself is it happening elsewhere and is there any danger to people? And how do you interpret these problems in terms of the economy? Now and in the future?

The other day at the annual meeting of the New York State Conservation Council a friend from Rome, New York, stopped to tell me a story he found quite upsetting. He is an experienced trapper. Incidentally, in New York State trappers have an annual income of more than 12 million dollars and there were some 22,000 trapping licenses sold last year. During the last trapping season, my friend had gone back into an area he had trapped frequently in the past with success. His sets were for weasel, mink, otter, fisher and raccoon.

His success was zero. And then the reason dawned on him. This was in an "acid rain disaster area" as the local people call it. There were no fish; therefore, the animals that feed on fish had to leave. How can you put a dollars and cents value on that? The environment will support only so much wildlife. You can't move a population from one area to another populated area and have them all survive so there must be a tragic loss of wildlife numbers and an unmeasurable decline in the quality of life.

At the Syracuse College of Environmental Science and Forestry we have a group of scientists and biologists who are conducting an ongoing research program on the effect of acid rain on plant life and trees. Their findings are not yet conclusive. But their implications are frightening. The acid in rain and snow scour tree leaves, causing what the scientists call "cuticular" damage which, in turn, greatly increases the tree or plant's susceptibility to disease. Laboratory studies have demonstrated that plants in grounds saturated with acid rain suffer from a lack of nutrition. Research indicates that the acid content of rain and snow leaches nutrients out of the soil and, therefore, they are not available to the growing plants. Certain species of trees may be particularly susceptible to this action.

For the Adirondack area, this is a direct attack on our principal year-round industry — the wood products industry. Most of our forest land that is privately-owned is managed in some fashion. Several paper companies have large holdings in the area and have their lands on a sustained yield basis. Most other private landowners periodically cut for lumber, pulp, and firewood on their lands. If the trees are destroyed, the loss would be obvious and would need no explanation from me and this is a real possibility at some time in the future if nothing is done. But perhaps more insidious would be a substantial reduction in the growth rate which might be caused by this nutrient loss. Foresters tell us this is a very real possibility in the near future if the acid rain situation is not corrected.

I can't correct this measure — you must. When our forefathers established our Constitution they devised an incomparable formula for living together and they gave the Congress the authority to enforce it and keep it effective. In the suburbs, if my neighbor has a dog that barks all night or a stereo that disturbs the peace, I go to my Town Government and the problem is corrected. To live together we have to consider each other. Where there is a national problem, such as this one, you — the members of Congress — are the ones we turn to and the ones we expect to correct a bad situation. We know and you know what is causing the acid precipitation and where it originates. It can be corrected — I only hope that you will accept and understand the importance of what is presently happening and what is about to happen and take the necessary steps to stop this environmental degradation before it becomes a national disaster.

That, then, is Bill Roden's testimony and, as pointed out, he speaks with authority. His knowledge of the outdoors is state-wide; he is a former president of the New York State Conservation Council, as well as the Adirondack Conservation Council. He is not a man given to exaggeration.

He has mentioned several areas. Hopefully, it would not be presumptuous of me to add somewhat to the overall picture.

Twelve years ago, in the isolated West Canada Lake area, Brooktrout Lake was highly productive. This 77-acre lake is now dead; stocking has been discontinued; fish cannot live in its waters. Spruce Lake is on the verge of death rattles; this 179-acre lake, once the producer of lake trout and brook trout, now verges on the acidity of vinegar, which has a pH factor around 2 or 3.

It is estimated more than 25 percent of brook trout and other cold water fisheries resources are as dead as moon rock.

In tests made in the South Branch of the Moose River, below Old Forge, hatchery trout died within a few hours when held in cages in stream waters between the spring run-off and early May. This is the time when waters are hit heavily with the full impact of melting acid snow.

While rain and snow are to be considered, so is content of clouds. In one cloud which covered the summit of Whiteface Mountain at Wilmington, the top of the mass hovered over the 4,867-foot peak, and the bottom was at the 2,500-3,000-foot level.

The higher portion of the cloud, says Raymond Falconer of the Atmosperic Sciences and Research Center, contained little contamination. This is where the rain formed. But after falling through the cloud layer, the raindrops had scavenged out the contamination or cloud droplets, lowering the pH factor from 6.1-6.3 from near the top, to 4.1-4.2 under the base of the cloud at 2,000 feet.

Looking at it another way: In this instance, trees and other vegetation from 2,000 feet up to the summit were literally bathed in acid.

In the so-called Perkins Clearing area, reachable northward from Speculator and southward from Indian Lake, and which borders the West Canada Lakes wilderness, is Pillsbury Lake. It is dying. Acidity is no discriminator; it affects both public and private bodies of water. Lake Madeline on the privately owned Litchfield Park estate between Long Lake and Tupper Lake, is marginal.

Heaven Lake on the same property, is dead.

The overall picture begs questions about large bodies of water such as Lake George and Lake Champlain, both at low elevations but fed by mountain streams containing acid. These lakes seem to be in pretty good shape. So do Paradox Lake and Eagle Lake, but these, like Lake George and Champlain, are on the eastern perimeter of the Adirondacks and therefore are not as hard hit as the western slopes; Cranberry Lake, mentioned by Bill Roden, is in the northwestern Adirondacks.

Thus the grim picture. Nero, hardly the greatest of Roman emperors, had something of a reputation for offering poisons to the unsuspecting, but he was a novice to the industries now offering diseases ravaging our mountains and forests.

How long do we fiddle while the patient is expiring?

West Canada Lake, part of whose expanse is seen in the background, rests at approximately the 3,000-foot level, and is considered a lake sickened by acid rains. Once planes could land on its surface, but no longer is this true; the lakes in this region are part of a wilderness area, closed to motorized traffic, even brief landings and takeoffs by aircraft.

Brooktrout Lake, once healthy, once productive, is now considered terminal because of acid precipitation. The author and his son a few years ago fished this lake for more than a day and the result: One trout.

A scene familiar to many — the summit of Whiteface Mt., Wilmington. On days when rain clouds cover the summit and precipitation is generated, the top of the mountain, as well as the area downward to the 2,000-foot level, is literally bathed in acid rain.

"By the Rockets' Blue Glare"

Adirondack Iron, Resting on the
Bottom of the Atlantic,
Marks a National
Historic Site

In August, 1973, Duke University's vessel, the East-ward, loaded with electronic gear, put out to sea to explore a six-by-sixteen mile rectangle about seventeen miles southeast of Cape Hatteras, North Carolina.

Its objective: To discover a vessel measuring 172 feet overall, with a beam of 41-1/2 feet, a draft of 10-1/2 feet, buried 220 feet below the surface of the Atlantic Ocean.

It was no ordinary vessel.

It was a ship of iron, a great deal of which was extracted from Adirondack Mountain mines, a "floating battery" which within a few hours in 1862 had changed the entire worldwide concept of warfare on sea.

It was, of course, the Monitor, the ironclad used by Union forces during the Civil War.

The search was successful; the Monitor was pinpointed in the liquid grave in which it had been slowly disintegrating for over 100 years, with dead men and a black cat aboard. The cat was stuffed into a turret gun.

The ship still rests off Cape Hatteras and is now off limits to divers in search of souvenirs. Because of its fragile condition there is little likelihood of raising it for modern generations to see. It is a tragic loss to the visual concept of America's history.

In its brief existence of less than ten months from the time it battled the Confederate ironclad, the Merrimack, during the Battle of Hampton Roads, it became known as the "cheesebox on a raft." Seamen who served aboard this floating juggernaut had another name for it, the "Hell Box," because temperatures within sometimes rose to 110 degrees.

The ship was the brainchild of John Ericsson, a Swede of genius stature, who tried to interest the navy of the North but failed. Later, he turned to Abraham Lincoln and when he did events had shaped a course for acceptance. Lincoln was intensely concerned over rumors that the South had constructed an ironclad to break the blockade of Southern ports by the wooden ships of the North.

Ericsson was given 100 days to complete the vessel, an astonishingly short time in those days when technology was not as we know it today. Furthermore, it was stipulated that the inventor was to pay for the construction out of his own pocket and would receive nothing from government unless the vessel proved itself workable in all respects!

Ericsson accepted the challenge and delivered the Monitor in 101 days, just in time for the ship to defeat the Confederate ironclad, Merrimack, on March 9, 1862. Obviously he was paid, since the North ordered additional ironclads.

John Ericsson, inventor of the screw propeller, was the genius who designed the Monitor, which he called an "Iron Steam Floating Battery."

Above photo from the U.S. Bureau of Ships National Archives; shows the Monitor flush deck, with turret, pilot house and ventilator shafts. Smokestack, which artists of the day pictured at rear of turret, was capable of being drawn into the hull. Canopy over turret offered much-needed shade on the "Hell Box."

In building the ship, Ericsson used the screw propeller, his own invention. He also devised a revolving turret, the machinery for which was manufactured in the Cluett Machine Shops in Schenectady, N.Y.

With this turret the Monitor could direct its field of fire without maneuvering the entire ship. The Merrimack, by contrast, could not; that ship, a former frigate, sunk in 1861 and raised, had merely been coated with iron. And guns were in fixed positions. The Merrimack carried eight 80-pound rifled guns besides two capable of throwing a 120-pound shell or a 100-pound solid shot.

It was propelled by two steam engines, possessed a large furnace for heating shot and, almost unbelievably, was equipped with an apparatus for throwing hot water at the enemy! What the idea was behind the hot water baffles some historians; and some believe it was to diminish enemy enthusiasm by scalding as well as to weigh down the vessel under attack.

The Monitor was constructed at the Continental Works, Brooklyn, and she carried two eleven-inch Dahlgren guns, the heaviest that had, up to that time, been mounted on any vessel. The Dahlgren cannon was a cast iron, smooth-bore weapon, invented by Admiral John A. Dahlgren, and much used by the U.S. Navy.

Her deck was almost flush with the sea; only a few inches separated it from the surface. The deck contained nothing save the wheelhouse, the turret and a smokestack capable of being withdrawn into the shell of iron, much as a turtle withdraws its head.

She possessed a ventilating system which on occasion refused active duty and the heat of the boiler fires, concentrated within the congested interior, gave rise to the mentioned "Hell Box" designation.

The plates for the Monitor were made under contract with Corning, Winslow and Co., Troy, N.Y., and the Rensselaer Iron Works nearby. Corning, Winslow also manufactured steel-rifled guns.

The flat-bottomed Monitor was launched Jan. 30, 1862 at Greenpoint, Brooklyn. Its turret worked. Its 11-inch tapered Dahlgrens performed their acts of violence. The vessel proved capable of moving under its own power, although at times during its brief career it was towed to battle areas, then turned loose to create its path of destruction.

There has been some difference of opinion as to whether the iron used in the Monitor was totally Adirondack in origin. It was not. But, as stated, a great deal of mountain iron went into the craft.

Some of the ore came from pits at Hammondsville, owned by the Crown Point Iron Company, located in the western portion of that township. The ore from this digging was processed in a blast furnace organized about 1845 by C.F. Hammond, John C. Hammond, Allen Penfield and Jonas Town.

There are shipping records still in existence in the Penfield Museum at the historic spot known as Ironville, showing shipment of iron to Troy for fabrication into plates and rivets. The blast furnace operated until 1870.

(The reader will note that Ironville also was the site where Thomas Davenport conceived his idea of the electric motor — the chapter in this volume called "Mountain Genius").

There was ore also dug from mines in the Fort Ann area of Washington County. And this writer was informed in 1977 by Ralph A. Marino, Waterford, that ore was dug from Mt. Greylock in Massachusetts. This basic ingredient was smelted in a foundry in North Adams, then shipped to Troy.

There were other areas, I am sure, since Ericsson's purchasing policy was to spread orders around. Fort Edward historians say a blast furnace in that community, built in 1854, also converted ore into pig iron for the Troy works. That ore also could have come from the Fort Ann region.

So the honor went not only to the Adirondacks but to other regions as well. The point to be made is that Adirondack treasure added to the glory of the famous ironclad.

The Battle of Hampton Roads between the Monitor and the Merrimack was short lived. John Ericsson's thundering innovation, which he called the "Iron Steam Floating Battery" was commanded by Lt. John Worden and no casualties occurred, although three men were stunned by shock waves when solid shot hit and dented the Monitor's turret. Lt. Worden was temporarily blinded by power or "cement," according to an account issued some twenty years after the battle, and this happened while he was at the peep-hole in the pilot, or wheelhouse, directing efforts of his ship.

Lt. John Lorimer Worden commanded the Monitor during its battle with the Merrimack; was temporarily blinded during the sea fight.

An artist's conception of the Battle of Hampton Roads in which the Merrimack, lower left, was stopped in its efforts to destroy blockading ships of the North. Monitor pictured protecting the wooden ship like a mother hen. Ship at right has been hit; note lifeboat pulling away.

This was illustration used by the Atlanta "Constitution" in that newspaper's description of the battle. Direct hits could be scored only on the turret and the few inches of iron of the Monitor above water level. The Monitor could swing its guns in all directions; the Merrimack, with fixed cannon, had to be maneuvered.

The Merrimack's depredations were cut short by the battle and that converted ironclad was blown to pieces later by a Confederate demolition team to prevent Union forces from capturing it.

The end, however, was nearing for the Monitor.

It did blockade duty (boring times for seamen) and at the end of its career was being towed to Beaufort, South Carolina, by the steamer Rhode Island to join in a land and sea attack on Wilmington. The ship was then under command of Commander John P. Bankhead.

Perfect weather was met in rounding Cape Henry at the mouth of Chesapeake Bay. But on Dec. 30, in the afternoon, the sea began to heave in giant swells; Cape Hattaras was evidencing its notorious muscle. The seas increased. Waves poured over the ship. The vessel began to pound. The strain on towlines increased; a port hawser parted explosively. The Monitor became unmanageable. Two sailors attempted to cut the remaining towline. They were washed overboard. A third stalwart managed to do the job. The Monitor floated free.

Seas poured into its interior through ventilator shafts and hawsepipes eight inches in diameter. The engine room became inundated; fires were extinguished; power was lost. The crew struggled to bail with buckets, a useless gesture.

At 11 p.m., as the New Year approached, a red lantern, denoting distress, was hung from the turret. At 11:30 p.m., the anchor was let go; this device, released from the bottom of the ship, tore away its packing and more water gushed in. The Rhode Island and the stricken Monitor by this time were an estimated two miles apart.

But the distress signal had been seen and Rhode Island lifeboats were on their way, with the entire scene lighted by the blue light of rockets. Men were taken off; one group, too terrified to leave the vessel, clung to the turret. They were ordered to save themselves. They did not. A seasick sailor was left moaning in his bunk.

Commander Bankhead was the last to leave.

Sixteen men perished.

Sixteen men and one black and frightened cat. A sailor spotted the ship's pet atop one of the Dahlgren cannon and figured if he put it out of its misery it might mean bad luck. So he stuffed the howling animal into the cannon and plugged the opening.

The slow descent of the Monitor followed only minutes later; as the last boat was rowed away, the red lantern sputtered out and only the noise and scene of the boiling seas were seen and heard.

Artistic license was used in this imaginative drawing of the last moments of the Monitor. The Rhode Island, which was towing the ironclad actually was a good two miles distant after towlines broke and were cut in the stormy seas. The entire scene was lighted by blue-light flares or rockets. Note rescuing lifeboat; note also that the Rhode Island was a side-wheeler, while the Monitor was powered by a screw propeller.

Another version of the dying agonies of the Monitor off Cape Hatteras, this one from "Harper's Weekly" of January 24, 1863. Note smokestack. Once again it might be mentioned the Monitor and Rhode Island were two miles apart; the artist put the ships closer together for dramatic effect.

131

A leisurely moment on Adirondack iron, following the Battle of Hampton Roads. Dent in turret sheathing can be seen at lower left. At one time the Monitor was visited by President Lincoln, but word came that a Confederate ironclad was approaching and Lincoln and his inspection party left only an hour before ships were joined in combat. Sketch from U.S. Bureau of Ships, National Archives.

ADDENDUM

Proof of the fact that the ship found by the Eastward is the Monitor was established in March, 1974, with the support of the National Geographic Society and the U.S. Navy in cooperation with the U.S. Army Reserve and the research vessel Alcoa Seaprobe. Underwater pictures were taken, both movies and stills.

There was need to transport the unprocessed films to Washington. At Cape Hattaras at the time, as visitors, were E. Gilbert Barker, long interested in the Penfield Foundation and Museum at Ironville, Crown Point, and his wife, Joyce. With them were Norma and Jim Carrier; Norma and Joyce are sisters. The Carriers live in the Schenectady area.

The research group, knowing Barker's interest in the Monitor, asked the visiting group to transport the films to Washington. The Barkers and Carriers did just that, but recognizing their priceless cargo, never left the car in which the films were packed out of sight. Even in stopping for food from Cape Hattaras to Washington, at least one of the foursome remained locked within the car!

"When we finally delivered the films to the destination," Barker told this writer, "you could have heard the sigh of relief for miles around!"

E. Gilbert Barker, left, and author at Penfield Museum.

Vignettes

ON TURTLE THUMPING

The fine art of Turtle Thumping was practiced in Adirondack swamps by early settlers who migrated from New England. In Turtle Thumping, a man used a long pole, sometimes shod with an iron point.

During winter, when turtles were buried in swamps, the hunter would jam the pole into any area which interested him; if he hit an object, he dug. If it was a turtle he kept it for meat. Many a snapper has vanished into Colonial pots in this fashion.

Turtle thumping? One result of this unusual practice might be the acquisition of a snapping turtle, pictured, a delicacy much prized in early days, as it is at present — unless the reptile comes from the Hudson's PCB's-filled waters.

STRANGE DUCK

Not all hunters know their prey well enough. A Conservation Officer, working the Warren County area, arrested a duck hunter for transporting wild waterfowl without wings or heads attached. One of the carcasses, plucked clean of feathers, looked pretty unusual; matter of fact, it looked like a plucked hot dog.

The carcass was, indeed, that of a waterfowl, but not a duck. It was a sea gull, protected not only by state but federal law!

MID 1700 MILITARY MENU

In the early and mid 1700's soldiering needs were the same. Men in uniform fought and they had to eat. And they ate whatever they could get in the form of issued rations and what the countryside about them furnished.

Archeologists, digging in the area embracing Fort Amherst and Fort St. Frederic along Lake Champlain's shores, found soldiers consumed a variety of wildlife. The now-extinct passenger pigeon was often a dish. Bones from these birds have been identified in the trash areas of the forts.

(The last passenger pigeon recorded for Essex County, according to the High Peak Audubon Society, was a specimen collected at Willsboro on October 9, 1891. Peter Kalm, the Swedish naturalist, 1750, found a great number of these pigeons in the Champlain region. Said he: "The French shot a great number of them, in which we found a great quantity of the seeds of the elm.")

In addition to the skeletal remains of the pigeons, archeologists found remains of cattle, fish, deer, bear, elk and moose. At times soldiers even ate crow. The fish remains may prove to be that of sturgeon which once lived in the giant lake.

THERE'S A LIMIT

State Police do indeed receive unusual calls for assistance. Try this for size: There was no mouth-to-mouth resuscitation effort made by Trooper O. H. Byrne, Pulaski, when he answered a frantic call for assistance from a woman who said her baby had stopped breathing. Reason: The "baby" proved to be the lady's pet cat!

EARLY DUTCH "PROBLEM"

The early Dutch settlers who traded with Indians who drew much of their furs from the Adirondack hunting grounds, were not familiar with the American species of the mountain lion, or panther. It was the Indians who introduced the animal to the early Dutch in the 1600's by offering them skins for trade.

What puzzled the Dutch was that none of the hides had the large manes they associated with the African lion, about which animal they knew. Therefore the Dutch came to the conclusion that all hides belonged to females, and the Indians killed only this sex!

The mistake in judgment was a natural one. The mountain lion is not native to the Eastern Hemisphere, which includes Europe.

THE SCALPED OX

In a minor Indian attack along the shores of Lake Champlain during the French and Indian War French-led Indians slaughtered not only humans but oxen. One ox was found with its horns literally hacked from its head, bellowing in pain. It was shot by an American group which took after the raiding party. Another ox was scalped, and this beast was driven to Lake George where its wound completely healed and where it became a notable local celebrity.

The animal ended up on the farm of Col. Schulyer in Albany a year later and from the Schuyler farm it was shipped to England where it became widely known as the "scalped ox." Weird happenstance, but a matter of record.

CASE OF TEMPORARY SHOCK

I must admit I was startled at a phone call received from a well known political leader in the Adirondack region. I was invited to a wedding.

"Who's?" I asked.

"My father's!" was the reply.

The gentleman must have sensed my astonishment.

"I'm sure," he said a bit stiffly, "that you understand the marriage is a *second* one for him."

MIND DOES TRICKS

Strange things happen to the mind of those lost over a period of time in the Adirondacks. LaRue Thurston, age 67 at the time he became lost in the Elk Lake area, was rescued by four hikers and was hospitalized in the Glens Falls Hospital for several days. He had spent seven days and six nights in the woods.

At one time he hallucinated. On the second night of his wanderings he saw a "large man, dressed in green, carrying a flashlight which did not work." Another night he saw another man, huge, carrying a handgun. And there was one night when from the top of a mountain he fancied he saw the lights of a village or lodge. But these sights proved mirages of the night. There were times, he told this writer, that he literally blacked out but kept moving.

ON TREE DISEASES

The Dutch elm disease is not only a blight but a catastrophe. The first report of the disease in the United States occurred during the 1930's, and the blight arrived on imported elm logs, peeled into veneer. It was first noted in the New York City area in 1933, and had reached into the Lake George-Warrensburg area by 1950.

It is known as the Dutch elm disease simply because it was Dutch scientists who isolated the fungus causing it; this was in 1919. The fungus is carried by a beetle.

Thus today throughout the Adirondacks, skeletons stand where once elms spread their generous canopies. As pointed out in another chapter in this volume, the gypsy moth, also an import, is devastating thousands of Adirondack timberland acres. The beech, which furnishes food-nuts for both deer and bear, is afflicted with a blight; on a trip into Murphy Lake one day former EnCon executive Ed Littlefield pointed out a hillside of dying beeches to this writer. The birch has become the victim of a disease called the birch miner. More recently oak is suffering from disease.

The white pine also is falling victim. And in the winter of 1979-80, certain areas of the Adirondacks were quarantined because "Christmas trees," grown for market, were carrying disease. Where will it all end?

RARE TID-BIT: MOOSE NOSE!

Craig Gilborn, director, Adirondack Museum, offered this tid-bit from "How to Hunt a Moose," an article in the museum files. It may not appeal to your gastronomic tastes, but here it is anyway:

"Moose nose is cooked by cutting off the upper jawbone just below the eye. Drop this jawbone in a kettle of water and boil it for about thirty minutes. Remove, cool and skin it, taking the hairs and bristles and dark skin off.

"Now wash it well and place the skinned nose into a fresh kettle of water. Cut the white and dark meat into thick slices and pack them into jars. Cover with the juice from the boiling. This will jell when chilled, and it can be sliced and eaten like sandwich meat."

The gentleman who wrote the article on how to prepare the gastronomic delight of moose jaw would have lost his enthusiasm for the delicacy if he desired it from this monster. This remarkable photo of a bull moose in the act of charging was taken by the late Walter Schoonmaker, who miraculously escaped with his life. The animal is quite obviously in a fighting mood!

"MEDICAL" NOTE

Would the following have been a note on the first "sword swallower"? These are quotes from the journal of Van den Bogaert, a traveler in the 1634, as he moved from one Mohawk Indian village to another:

"Dec. 24 — It was a Sunday. I saw in one of the houses a sick man. He had invited two of their doctors who could cure him. They call them 'Simachkoes,' and as soon as they came they began to sing and light a big fire.

"They closed the house most carefully so that the breeze could not come in, and after that each of them wrapped a snake skin around his head. They washed their hands and faces, lifted the sick man from his place and laid him alongside the fire.

"Then they took a bucket of water, put some medicine in it, and washed in this water a stick about a half a yard long, and kept sticking it into their throats so that no end of it was to be seen, and then they spat on the patient's head and over all his body."

What Van den Bogaert did not mention was whether the patient recovered!

WINDOW ART

A visitor to the Adirondack Museum at Blue Mt. Lake told me upon his return that the museum possessed "one of the finest paintings of the lake" he had ever seen. I was puzzled; I know of no such painting. Upon closer questioning this developed:

The individual had seen what he THOUGHT was a painting. But it wasn't; it was a window at the museum which looks over the famous lake!

A NATIONAL PARK?

If the Adirondack Park Agency comes under criticism on occasion, memory should hark back not too many years ago when the proposal was made to turn the Adirondack Park into a National Park. Gov. Nelson A. Rockefeller was governor of New York State and the idea was that of his brother, Laurence Rockefeller.

Had the National Park project turned into reality, it would have meant the end of private property as we know it. Holdings of more than three acres would have been prohibited and eventually these would have been eliminated as owners died off. Hunting would have been prohibited, and the federal government would have been in total control. The National Park idea was opposed by many, including this writer.

And Laurence Rockefeller himself seemed a surprised man when, at a meeting of the Adirondack Mountain Club at Sit'n Bull Ranch near Warrensburg, the mountain club considered the proposal and turned it down cold. His was a startled face. I saw his reaction.

NOT RECOMMENDED PROCEDURE

Many individuals who travel mountain trails become frightened when meeting up with a wandering bear — even though a cautious, slow withdrawal from the scene will solve the situation.

Three years ago another method of scaring off a bear was evolved, when a group of youngsters from Camp Chingachgook, Lake George, took a field trip with a counselor over to the Avalanche Pass way in the High Peak region.

They camped overnight and upon investigating a noise, found a mother bear and her cub on the scene. Mama was up a tree where the group had hung a pack containing more than thirty sandwiches. "Just to keep it safe from such animals as bears."

There was considerable shouting and stomping, but the big sow continued to attack the pack to get at its contents. Stones were thrown. They made no impression.

Then one of the sprouts had an idea. He passed it around. They "mooned" the bear. The unexpected gesture startled the sow and her cub to such an extent they took off.

And what, pray tell, is "mooning"? In this instance, it meant several of the boys slipped their pajama bottoms down to around their knees, turned, and displayed their bottoms!

Legends are born in this fashion.

A LIFE IS SAVED

My Sunday column in The Times-Union Nov. 3, 1974, started in this fashion: "Rev. Burnham H. Waldo, pastor of the North Creek United Methodist Church, has been named 'Fireman of the Year' by the Warren County Chiefs and Officers Association."

Behind that brief statement rested the story of an incredible act of heroism; Rev. Waldo has since been transferred to parishes in the Schenectady-Schoharie County areas, but the feat at North Creek remains unparalleled.

On June 28, 1974, he was lowered head first into a cesspool, his feet held by Charles Shuman, Patrick Cole, Harris Hewitt and Robert Shumsky and, held thusly, he took a deep breath, held it and thereupon went head-first and waist deep into the mass of filth to rescue a three-year-old boy.

The boy, Harold Tucker, had broken through the cover to the cesspool, was out of sight. Fourteen-year-old Tom Ordway was with Harold at the time, and Tom, with rare presence of mind, let a chain into the pool and literally talked the frightened youngster into hanging on — while the child's mother called for assistance from the North Creek Volunteer Fire Co.

Help arrived within minutes, but Harold's strength had given out and he went under. When Rev. Waldo was lowered into the mess he felt around with his hands, touched the boy's hair, grabbed it, and both were pulled to safety.

Today Rev. Waldo still minimizes the incident; says the entire operation was successful because the entire company of the North Creek fire group cooperated, that the whole thing was a team effort. He praises Fireman Pat Cole for his successful efforts in mouth-to-mouth resuscitation; offers credit to the emergency and intensive care units of Glens Falls Hospital.

What of Tom Ordway? He was nominated to the National Court of Honor, Boy Scouts of America. The author heard of this story while attending an open house at the North Creek Fire Company, with conversations with Chief Frank Morehouse and others, including Tom Pierson, Jarvis Dunkley, Don Filkins, Rodney Sargent, Melvin Waldron and Ernie Johnson of the Schenectady area, a company member who has a camp at North Creek.

I wonder even today, if faced with a similar emergency, if I would have the courage to do what Rev. Waldo did so willingly.

FRIENDS MISSED

I would be negligent in this volume if I did not express sorrow at the departure of a number of personal friends who have passed from the Adirondack scene, and who will be sorely missed.

In June Francis Donnelly, Town of Minerva Supervisor for 46 years, a man I much admired, died at Glens Falls Hospital; an amazing man of great talent who lived in Olmstedville in a 100-year-old home. One of my memories: The invitation to attend the golden wedding anniversary of Supervisor Donnelly and Nora Phelps Donnelly, his gracious wife. A pleasant and heartwarming event indeed.

Arthur Knight at linotype machine.

Patterns are hard to break. Even today, with the passage of years, I miss the opportunity of picking up the phone and talking to Art Knight of Lake George, former publisher and editor of the Lake George Mirror, a two-fisted newsman never afraid to speak his mind, and whose "Idiotorials," aimed at abuses, were wonders to read. Without people like Art Knight and former State Senator Nate Proller, who now lives in the Glens Falls area, there would be no Memorial Highway up Prospect Mt. at Lake George, and thus the elderly, the infirm, the handicapped, would have no opportunity to view from a mountain top the area they love so well.

The death of Cyrus Woodbury, one time guardian of the sanitation committee of the Lake George Park Commission and the Lake George Association, proved an abrupt shock. Cy Woodbury was my kind of gentleman, outspoken, straight to the point and a man imbued with love of his area. His death was instantaneous; occurred while he was doing a volunteer job, cutting the lawn of a church.

Charles H. Tuttle is another man I miss. This unusual gentleman, who founded Top O' the World vacation resort, left few legacies as valuable as his love for the Lake George region, which he described in this fashion when he was ninety years of age in a book called "Memorabilia for My Children":

"At Lake George Nature had unrolled a large canvas and thereon had painted her own portrait in lineaments of awesome beauty and the majesty of the ages, for it was the oldest part of the Continent."

The author had occasion to speak at a testimonial for Charles Tuttle. As as attorney he had few equals. The amount of community work he accomplished was enormous. He pioneered in the battle against discrimination; he was recognized by many religious groups as a champion of all faiths.

VALUE OF A SMILE

The Bouquet River Lodge of the Schenectady Y.M.C.A. is a monument to the indifference of a leader of a youth group.

At the same time, it is evidence of the dedication and kindness of P. F. Loope, formerly an executive with the Schenectady organization, and former executive secretary of the Adirondack Mountain Club.

The story goes back many years. An elderly and lonely gentleman who owned about 35 acres along the Bouquet River, south of Elizabethtown, bordering on Route 9, made a practice of dropping in at various establishments in downtown Schenectady, mostly to pass the time of day.

One day his trip had an unusual purpose. He had decided to donate his property, which contained an old hunters' hotel, away, lock stock and barrel.

He entered the downtown office of a well known organization which caters even today to the young. There is no need to mention the name, since it could be a source of embarrassment; the organization remains worthwhile in all respects. It was one of the executives who missed the opportunity, and this he did by refusing to talk to the old gentleman. That worthy, rebuffed, then visited the Y.M.C.A. and was welcomed by Loope. After chatting for a few minutes, the man made his offer. Loope jumped at the chance. The Y.M.C.A. accepted it with gratitude.

There was, of course, the question of money. But this was forthcoming from various civic minded individuals. Enough was collected to build a fireplace of native rock. More was spent on planting trees — now fully grown. The old hotel was painted and repaired. The interior was redone — all of it by volunteer labor. The water supply was fed by a mountain stream, high above the building.

Groups began using it for Adirondack outings. It became once again, a familiar landmark.

And the remarkable fact remains: The Y.M.C.A. acquired the property as a gift because of the courtesy of Loope to an old man! Strange is the way gratitude was expressed for the kindness of companionship.

P.F. Loope, the man whose interest in an elderly man's company and conversation sparked off the creation of the Bouquet River Lodge is pictured at right during signing of a contract for construction of a fireplace.

CLINTON PRISON'S
FIRST ELECTROCUTION

The hand of fate and the lens of a camera linked two men together during the summer of 1890 and as a result, one of the men became the first man to die in the electric chair in Clinton Prison, Dannemora.

This is the electric chair, long unused, at Clinton Prison, Dannemora, where Cal Wood was the first to be electrocuted. Wood shot his father-in-law.

The background to this story is one of enmity between one Cal Wood of Stony Creek and his father-in-law, Leander Pasco, who lived in the same area of Warren County.

The basic reason for the ill feeling is not known, but Wood, over a period of time, had built up several grievances against Pasco; one novel complaint was that Pasco "broke up a goose nest where Wood had two geese sitting on their eggs!"

Whatever the reason, the situation exploded one rainy day in May, 1890 shortly after both Wood and Pasco tried to obtain warrants against each other from Justice of the Peace Dunlop. The judge refused telling each man to settle their differences amicably.

Pasco lived on what was known as Aller Road. His son-in-law lived not far distant in a cabin on an old logging road.

At 5 p.m., the bell from the Stony Creek tannery pealed the hour, and approximately a half hour later residents along Aller Road heard two shots. Few paid any attention, since gunfire was not uncommon; the supposition was that someone was collecting meat for his meal.

The next day, however, the body of Leander Pasco was found alongside the road. He was quite dead. He had been murdered with buckshot. An autopsy revealed ten punctures, four in the left arm near the elbow, five in the back and one in the jaw, fracturing the lower mandible and knocking out several teeth.

The corpse was not touched all night and it lay in the dirt until late the following afternoon, when District Attorney Charles R. Patterson and Coroner Frederick B. Streeter arrived from Glens Falls, with Sheriff Mills from Pottersville.

Among the curious who gathered to see the dead man was Cal Wood and his wife, Mattie. Others in the group noted that Wood seemed "pale" and kept glancing nervously at a fragment of cloth caught on a bush near the corpse. Another piece of similar cloth lay on the ground.

Wood had good reason to be nervous. The pieces of cloth had come from the lining of the coat he was wearing. There apparently had been no struggle. Pasco was killed in ambush. The cloth fragments had been used, it was determined later, as wadding for Wood's gun.

District Attorney Patterson called upon a Pinkerton detective, and the case against Wood rapidly materialized. Footprints at the death scene matched those of his shoes. It was learned he had washed his shot gun with hot water to eliminate traces of it having been fired.

But the evidence that put Wood in the electric chair was the cloth.

A good seventy miles to the south, in the City of Schenectady, at Union College, Professor Maurice Perkins was a member of what was Schenectady's first camera club. Eight men comprised the group. Professor Perkins was among the outstanding. While history does not record his skill, it most assuredly involved close-up camera work. He was called into the picture. Wood's coat, along with the cloth fragments found, were put into his care.

What method he used is not known even today, but apparently he photographically matched the fragments with the tears in the lining and the textures matched. As far as the jury was concerned, that was conclusive proof. Wood was tried twice. The Court of Appeals reversed the first conviction. In the second trial Judge Francis E. Smith, Essex County, prosecuted the case and the defense offered in Wood's behalf by his attorney was insanity. There was testimony that Wood had fallen from a roof in earlier years and cracked his skull and that the injury had disturbed his brain. However a physician's testimony, coupled with that of an alienist from New York City, stated that he was sane. He was convicted once again and the Court of Appeals did not contest the decision.

The above, taken from an old newspaper photo, shows members of the Schenectady Camera Club, first of its kind for that city. Seated, second from right, is Prof. Maurice Perkins of Union College, whose camera skill led to evidence presented against Cal Wood of Stony Creek, convicted of murder.

Cal Wood was removed to Clinton Prison and suffered the same fate met by William Kemmler at Auburn Prison on August 6, 1890. Kemmler was the first man to die in "the chair" in New York State. Wood followed him by almost exactly two years but in another prison.

DEATH WAS THE PENALTY

Much has been written about the ravaging of the Adirondack Forest Preserve in the early days.

What isn't generally known is that there was a time in the 1700's that the cutting of certain trees meant death to the chopper — even if the trees were on his property!

When England controlled what was then America, her Navy had been built into the world's greatest sea force. To maintain a navy of sailing vessels meant a supply of masts had to be found. The forests of England were almost exhausted of timber tall enough to stand over her ships.

The Adirondacks loomed as a vast and inexhaustible reservoir. The tall virgin white pines were ideal; they towered and grew straight. They were massive enough in girth, strong enough in growth, for any of England's forces of the sea.

So the British king, with his limitless power, sent his King's Rangers to the Adirondack area and these hardy souls prowled the wilderness of the north and marked suitable pines with the "mark of the arrow." That meant one simple, hard fact. The tree was not to be cut until England needed it.

The penalty was death.

As the Revolution approached, naval authorities in England realized their predicament. Huge trees were felled by the scores, by the hundreds, and piled along the St. Lawrence River, ready for shipment overseas.

But the move came too late. Angry Colonials, striking at England's Achilles heel, moved to the storage areas and burned the logs. England was left with ashes.

And to compensate, she had to devise masts which were not solid single trucks, but overlapping. The sailing abilities of her ships lessened and while the cutting off of the supply by the Colonials did not win the war, the gesture contributed to the weakening of Britain's sea forces.

SHOULD HAVE STUCK TO SALMON!

All fishermen are not always gentlemanly behaved. In 1977 State Police while investigating a reported "burglary" arrested a 30-year-old "sportsman" on a charge of criminal mischief.

The so-called "sportsman" had planned a weekend of fishing for salmon in the Salmon River, leading into Pulaski, but part of that weekend was spent in breaking church windows. He gained entry into the structure, tipped over pews, punched holes through the walls and ended his spree by throwing books through a set of stained glass windows.

He reckoned without the anger of parishioners; a group surrounded the church until Trooper D.B. Grossman, Pulaski, arrived to make the arrest!

John P. Bowman

Mrs. Bowman and daughter Ella.

TOMB OF NO RETURN

John P. Bowman was an unusual man as the reader will, I am sure, agree.

He was a complete realist in life and a theorist in his view of after-life.

He arrived from Vermont in 1852 and opened a tannery at Stony Creek, Warren County, an area then rich in hemlock bark, which was used in processing hides. Within a short time his company had twenty-five men and was turning out 40,000 "sides" of sole leather annually.

His firm operated for decades, until the resource of hemlock ran out on the 6,000 acres of timberlands he owned. The acreage did not, however, run out of wood felled for the bark; that wood, in many instances, was left to rot on the forest floor!

Bowman retired after amassing a fortune and moved to Cuttingsville, Vt., where he constructed a huge "and elegant Victorian mansion" for his wife, Jennie, and his daughter, Ella. Tragedy stalked the move; Ella died at age nineteen only a few years after the move to Cuttingsville. This was in 1879.

Less than a year later Bowman suffered another heavy blow. His wife died. He was left alone.

It was at this time his unusual theories about after-life became evident. He ordered a mausoleum constructed which even today is considered one of the most remarkable of such memorials. For more than a year 125 sculptors, granite and marble cutters, masons and laborers were employed in its building.

Bowman spent $75,000 on the tomb without batting an eye.

A Vermont newspaper story, in describing the structure, said:

"Outside of the mausoleum is a larger-than-life statue of Bowman, bent with grief and burdened with a mourning cloak, silk hat, gloves, a huge funeral wreath and a key.

The grief-stricken man is shown mounting the marble steps; the key is in his hand to open the door to join his loved ones. His face is one of a man who suffered much."

Even while Mrs. Bowman and daughter Ella were entombed, Bowman was convinced they would return. He kept the mansion and all of its rooms ready for their return. When he died in 1891 the belief of their return was still strong. He left a will filled with details and money "to make sure his wife and daughter would be comfortable when they returned!"

Even more astonishing, if such is possible, is that Bowman thought he would return to life and the entire family would be rejoined in an existence even happier than the one once lived.

His will provided for a caretaker and cook to keep the big house in shape. And the story goes that even bed linens were changed regularly for the Bowman family — when they returned.

Some say the story is "laced with embellishments." Perhaps. What isn't is that money finally ran out and the house was sold. The mausoleum remains an attraction for tourists and many liken it to a Grecian temple.

I have been told that the structure is covered during late fall and winter for protection from the elements. It is located in what is known as the Laurel Glen Cemetery. Cuttingsville is on Route 103, not too long a distance southwest of Rutland.

It is silent and somber. There is no life within. The hopes of Bowman never came to pass.

CITY FELLA' GOES SMELT DIPPING!

I don't know about the fellows over Indian Lake way in Hamilton County, but I guess some of the smelt in this lake are still splitting their fins laughing over an "expedition" the "City Fella" was on one midnight.

I had expressed interest in smelt dipping at Indian and Brian Farrell took me up on it. A date was set. I met Brian and checked into Don Ellis' Adirondack Trails Motel, but before the Big Dip attended a meeting at the Fireside Inn run by Mrs. Helen Clark. Met quite a few people, including Fred Turner, chamber prexy; Dick Fruilla, Supervisor; Town Councilman LeRoy Spring and Town Justices Franklin Mitchell and Ed Stores. There were many others, including Mrs. Cynthia Kluin, Mrs. Fran Wells and Bob Geandreau, chamber directors. Ted Aber, well known Hamilton County author, was on hand; so were Fran Reilly, Forest Ranger Gerry Husson and Dan Eldridge.

The Big Dip started later; met Brian, Don, Ranger Husson, Fred Eichler, and tried the Squaw Brook outlet. Water too high, went to another brook. What happened to me is one of the reasons I remember the occasion so well.

I found my boots leaked. Also that the water was bitterly cold. Rocks were slippery, and while others leaped from one to another with the agility of antelopes, I did an elephant act, slid off one, landed waist-deep in Indian. **To top it off, my glasses fell into four feet of water. In retrieving them under the glare of searchlights, I used my left arm. And that was the arm which contained a newly-purchased watch.**

Ernie Blanchard, town water superintendent, saved the day (or, rather night) when he ran his outboard to the spot and anchored its prow to the shore. That, I found, was more stable than slippery rocks. . .

Well, everything has to end and this trip did and I imagine there was a lot of silent laughter on the way to Indian Lake, a trip interrupted only briefly when I emptied my boots of about ten gallons of water. The happy ending was at the restaurant once run by the late Marty Harr, a good friend, now run by Walt, his son. Therein, about 3 a.m., we had the smelt, deliciously rolled in egg and flour batter and deep fried.

Then to the motel for sleep. I still wonder: Did I hear the echoes of silent laughter permeating the crisp Adirondack air as I left?

You see, nobody else fell in. Only the character from the city.

A
REPORTER'S
ALBUM

THE ST. JAMES WINDOW

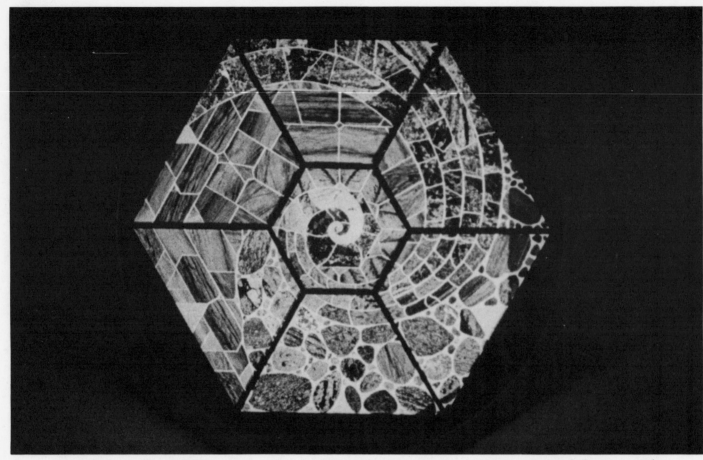

Dr. Vincent J. Schaefer, left in lower photo, retired director of the Atmospheric Sciences Research Center, scored a big hit in the world of art when he created the above window, panes of which are made from thin slices of Adirondack rocks. A full description is contained on the adjoining page.

Schaefer, in performing this remarkable feat, used a diamond-edged saw, did this work of love for St. James Church, North Creek, in his workshop at his Rotterdam home. Fifty years ago Schaefer helped form the Mohawk Valley Hiking Club, of which the author was a member. Lower photo was taken in earlier years while inspecting masonry in a historic building in the Mohawk Valley.

WHAT THE WINDOW MEANS

In describing the extraordinary window, panes of which are made of slices of Adirondack rock, the words of Dr. Vincent J. Schaefer of Rotterdam, creator of the work of art for St. James Church, North Creek, are the best.

Says Dr. Schaefer, who installed the six-foot-high creation behind and above the altar with his brother, Carl Schaefer:

"The window has been designed to relate to the North Creek area of the Adirondack Mountains. Its exterior shape and a related inner hexagon symbolizes the hexagonal snow crystal which is an important part of the environment and economy of the region.

"From the central core a spiral shaped in the Divine Proportion unwinds toward the outer edge of the window. The pointed tip of a hexagonal quartz crystal is a symbol of The Creator. Extending from this is a single spiral stream which divides into three representing The Trinity. The spiral then has a fourth stream added to symbolize Creation.

"All the rocks in the window are native to the Adirondacks. The single stream of white is crystalline limestone. The oldest rock of the mountains having an age of 1.2 billion years. The three streams are Marcy and Whiteface anorthosite. Gneiss, the dominant rock of the Adirondacks, follows as the spiral streams become four.

"Garnet bearing rock from the Gore and Ruby Mts. mines flows beyond to reach the edge of the hexagon. Potsdam sandstone outlines two edges of the large hexagon. This rock is from the ancient sea which invaded the mountains more than a half billion years ago. The final sequence are rocks ground by the Continental glacier which flowed across the mountains 50,000 years ago."

The basic themes of the St. James Window:

1. *The Creator (hexogonal quartz crystal)*
2. *The Trinity (three lines of anorthosite)*
3. *Creation (fourth stream added)*
4. *The Divine Proportion (the Golden Spiral)*
5. *The Snow Crystal (inner and outer hexagon)*
7. *Chronological sequence of Adirondack rocks:*

   a. *Crystalline limestone*

   b. *Marcy anorthosite*

   c. *Gneiss*

   d. *Garnet (Gore and Ruby Mts.)*

   e. *Sandstone (Potsdam)*

   f. *Glacial drift*

145

When Paul Schaefer of Schenectady offered the suggestion that more open space for deer could be obtained by forbidding trapping of beaver in designated areas of the wilderness for designated periods, his point is well made.

Man cannot cut timber legally in the Forest Preserve but beaver can; matter of fact, this water-loving rodent eats what he cuts. In this photo, and the two which follow, it can be seen how the beaver goes about the job of opening his own clearings in defiance of the state constitution.

As a starter, note the gnawed-off stump, surrounded by water impounded by the beaver dam.

As the beaver pond is enlarged, water rises, spreads deeper into surrounding territory, inundating and eventually killing trees. Some, less savory, may be left standing but they will die. In above photo note smaller saplings, white in color; these have been stripped of bark and twigs for food, which might hike a few eyebrows about the beaver stomach — but Nature has set the dietary course and the animals follow it diligently. As nearby supplies diminish the beaver move farther afield, often digging ditches which they use as highways for protein, or whatever a birch bark sandwich has to offer.

The scene is now set for the final stage, which may be seen on the following page.

We now have before us a portion of a beaver meadow, upstream from the animals' dam. The rising water has created a bog and the area is clean of all standing timber except trees noted.

A beaver colony sometimes will remain in one area for years, with its population controlled; if the group is too large, the young are driven elsewhere to start their own domain. When it is obvious the food supply is exhausted, beaver will travel overland to another stream, there to construct their own version of the Hoover Dam.

In the meantime, the original dam may slowly disintegrate; the swamp may slowly drain and new vegetation will take over. Once this occurs, deer will move into the area to eat new browse. What Man cannot do, these rodents can. These remarkable photographs were taken by Walter Schoonmaker, a friend of the author's, a gentleman who passed away a few years ago.

Top: Four "sports" of yesteryear, dressed in the latest hunting fashion! Lower photo: More suitably dressed is this riverman astride logs during a drive on Big Marsh Stream, near Piseco Lake.

A happy group during the 1970's: Once a year the late Harry McDougal, best known as "Mr. Republican" of Essex County, invited friends to his cottage alongside a trout-filled brook in the Lewis area, near Elizabethtown. Harry is pictured seated, at left. These were informal affairs and were often referred to as McDougal's annual "Conservation Day" outings. The group often contained nationally known political friends, including former Lt. Gov. Poletti, pictured next to Harry. It was a fun day, geared to relaxation and discussions on problems and the future of the mountains. The author felt privileged to be invited.

A familiar figure at the annual canoe races at North Creek-North River is Hank Rose, proprietor of the North River General Store. The gentleman, who left Florida to live in the Adirondacks in 1971, is pictured with a collector's item — a grizzly bear trap, weighing a good thirty pounds, which can be set only with use of mechanical devices. The grizzly never roamed the Adirondacks, but the black bear of prehistoric times is believed to have approximated them in weight — up to 1,000 pounds!

The 1974 White Water Derby at North Creek on Hudson's Upper River was the last competition in that contest for Dr. Homer Dodge, considered the dean of American canoeists. But it wasn't the difficulties of actual participation, says the 92-year-old former president of Vermont's Norwich University. It was, however, the "hassles" of traveling; Dr. Dodge, who lives in Maryland, spent four days in travel for the event. The 1974 derby was his 14th at North Creek and that community honored him with a formal program, "Homer Dodge Days." Up to that year he had canoed for eighty years and insofar as can be ascertained he is the only man on record to successfully shoot through the 40-foot high foam of the North Channel of the Long Sault Rapids, a six-mile stretch on the Canadian side of the St. Lawrence River.

Photo by Walter Grishkot

Above ski photo, taken by Capital Newspapers photographer Fred McKinney, a devoted follower of the sport, illustrates the difference between bureaucracy and private enterprise. The photo was snapped October 24, 1980, when snow making machines had covered privately operated Killington Peak, Vt., with four feet of snow, while New York State was cutting back on operating expenses for Gore Mt. and Whiteface.

An aroused citizenry of North Creek and Warren County residents, however, forced the state into retracting cutbacks. There is now considerable talk of amending the state constitution so that Gore and Whiteface could be leased to private operators.

Walt Grishkot of Glens Falls, left, is a photographer with infinite patience. Some years back when he heard that rainbow trout were attempting to leap the high falls in Hague Brook, a tributary of Lake George, he set his camera up and this outstanding photo was made within a period of the four hours he remained in one spot. During this spring period the rainbows made valiant attempts to swim upstream during their spawning runs.

The photo was reproduced in a full page spread in a national magazine. Grishkot's activities still include photography but his interests have broadened; he is the originator of the nationally famous balloon festival held annually in the Glens Falls area and has several photographic awards to his credit.

Stark's Knob, near Schuylerville, is famed as a volcanic core, but it never served an Adirondack volcano. It was deposited at the site when the African and North American continents collided millions of years ago; the core is African in origin. At left two youngsters enjoy the Hudson River in the distance as they rest atop the small peak.

Where do old trolleys go? One at least, found its way to Bolton Landing, and is now run as a restaurant by William Gates and his wife. The trolley, says Bill, pictured, once ran the route between Glens Falls, Hudson Falls and Fort Edward; two Glens Falls men purchased and did work on it as a hobby. In 1937 Chris Liapes of Glens Falls brought the trolley to Bolton Landing and placed it on land leased from Mrs. Walter Gates, Bill's mother. It was run as a restaurant and Bill bought it in 1949, and has run the popular business ever since.

One might call Crumley's Drugstore in Fort Ann, Washington County, the last bastion of the old-time soda fountain. Which it is, and the cheerful dispenser of such tasteful dishes, Paul F. Crumley, is pictured at right. Photo above was taken many years ago when the drug store was run by E. Ferrie Crumley, Paul's dad, a dedicated outdoorsman whose disappearance in 1951 created a mystery of several years.

Mr. Crumley vanished while fishing Bear Brook in the Raquette Lake region, and heavily manned searching parties failed in several quests. His bodily remains were found six years later by a hunter. Mr. Crumley is the gentleman seen in the photo above.

The drug store has been a landmark in Fort Ann for a century and its current proprietor has a background not only in pharmacy but is a former newspaperman who was once city editor of the Endicott Bulletin. He also worked for the Binghamton Press and the Knickerbocker Press, Albany.

Few can see it today because of its inaccessibility, but you're looking at the cave along the Hudson at Glens Falls made famous in James Fenimore Cooper's "Last of the Mohicans." The river can be seen at the end of the tunnel. It was here that Uncas and Chingachgook and the party guarded supposedly sought shelter. The cave is on the S. Glens Falls side of the river.

Fun and tragedy mix in the Adirondacks. Above, Ed Lewi, of Ed Lewi Associates, Latham, N.Y., a public relations firm which handled PR work for the 1980 Winter Olympics, is pictured in novel situation which had nothing to do with the Olympics. Lewi and companion (front seat) were creating a picture for photogs at Storytown, Lake George. Passenger in rear seat is unidentified; wouldn't talk, and nobody was about to try force.

When Trout Pavilion, oldest hotel at Lake George, burned during the late 1970's, this was the tragic scene of the total destruction. With the fire the famous hotel passed into memory.

One would guess from these photos it all depends on how you look at the world. Above is a great horned owl, a protected bird of prey who takes a dim view of the cameraman. Other photo shows a comparative rarity in the feline field, also expressing interest in the click of a shutter!

Osborne's Inn, Speculator, was a training spot for Max Schmeling, first German to win the heavyweight boxing title. Photo above shows the six-foot, one-inch fighter in the ring at Speculator. Photo, right, shows Schmeling before taking off from the Schenectady County Airport for his fight with Joe Louis in New York. Man at his right is Dick Merrill, pilot; man at top, with cigar, believed to be Joe Jacobs, Schmeling's manager. Other individual not identified.

Schmeling, in a stunning upset, knocked out Joe Louis on June 19, 1936 and in a return match an angry Louis knocked him out in 2:04 of the first round on June 22, 1938.

At Speculator he varied his training by chopping wood and for relaxation, shot the bow and arrow.

At Schenectady, where his party boarded a chartered Eastern Airline plane for New York, after having motored southward, Merrill sensed the aircraft was too heavy, and ordered it lightened by one individual. The selection was made and the author remembers well seeing this person, standing forlornly, watching the plane disappear!

Trolley systems once criss-crossed portions of the Adirondacks. Today they are long gone but trolley buffs can, on occasion, still find the berms, or embankments upon which track was laid. The berm being viewed in this instance is south of Glens Falls; crosses a farmer's field.

If trolley berms are a thing of the past, so is this type of lumber camp, which once dotted the interior of the Northern Wilderness. Lumberjacks and two females, probably cooks, are pictured before a log camp, the roof of which is made of spruce bark. Note man at right with double-bitted axe and similar axes impaled in tree at left.

161

Nature can change the course of a river. So can Man. In 1954 Man did just that with a portion of the Upper Hudson. A new channel for the river was blasted out at the Tahawus workings to enable the National Lead Co. to create a new reservoir for slurry water wastes. The move was made to avoid dumping such into the Hudson itself. The channel is three-quarters of a mile in length. Portion of Hudson visible in background.

A placid scene of a waterway, the Champlain Canal Division of the Barge Canal. Of note is the old "potato" house along the shore, where farmers once stored the tubers for shipment by boat to hungry cities. A long standing joke is that many an insurance claim was put in for potatoes "ruined" by high water; the "evidence" usually vanished.

162

The sadness of the final days of President Ulysses Simpson Grant is reflected in these photos. Above: The Grant Cottage atop Mt. McGregor, Saratoga County, where he died in 1885. Left: Grant, pictured on porch. Note wrapping about his throat; he was the victim of throat cancer. The ailing gentleman often sat at a nearby lookout, taking in a view of the Adirondacks, a region he could see but not visit. Interesting note: Grant was baptized Hiram Ulysses Grant, and he wrote his memoirs at Mt. McGregor — later published by Mark Twain.

163

In 1969 the mountains were combed for a suitable Christmas tree for display in Washington, D.C. One was found in the Chestertown area, and when mounted and lighted for all to see in Washington, Glens Falls photographer Walter Grishkot journeyed there to take this excellent photo.

An exhibit of craft and art work, created by inmates of Clinton Prison, Dannemora, was held before a Christmas-New Year's show staged by prisoners. This painting of Christ, approximately six feet in height, was among outstanding works of art. The artist worked in oils. Prison art, from Clinton and other institutions, often reflects remarkable talents and skills.

165

This tranquil scene was a health hazard in 1669. The name of this ravine, located in the Town of Glenville, Schenectady County, is Wolf Hollow. It is a geological fault and displacement of 1,000 feet in the earth's surface rocks. In 1669 the Mohawk Nation of the Iroquois ambushed Algonkian invaders, drove them from the Mohawk Valley forever, and until the coming of the white man with his guns, liquor and diseases, retained control. The ravine is a passageway from the Mohawk River to the north; was once an Indian trail for hunting parties seeking food in the North Country.

Test your eyesight and powers of discernment by looking closely at this photograph and locating the deer. Clue: It is looking directly at you, with head turned, body broadside. Photo credits goes to Finch, Pruyn, Glens Falls, and picture was printed in The Conservationist Magainze, 1968. If finding the animal drives you up the wall, you have company; it did the author!

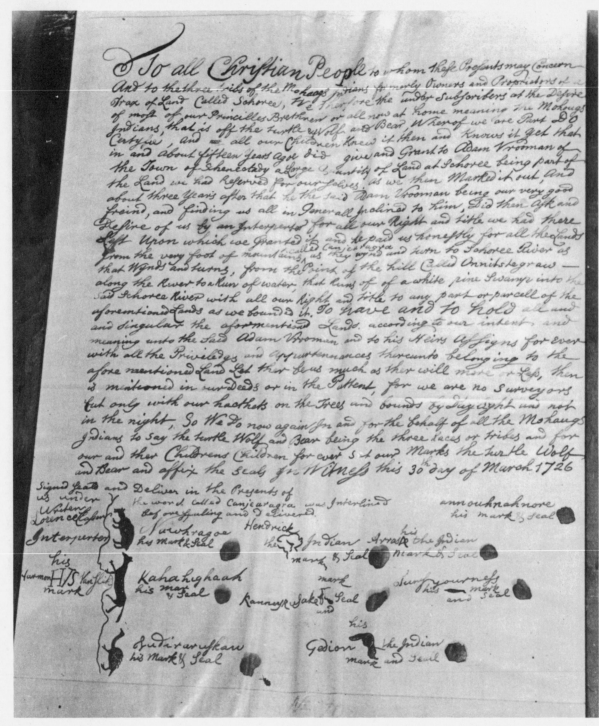

An interesting transfer or reaffirmation of a transfer of lands owned by the Mohawks to Adam Vrooman in the Canajoharie and Schoharie region. Vrooman was considered a good friend and an honest man by the Mohawks who termed themselves Mohaugs in the transfer, which was made in 1726. The river today called the Schoharie is noted as the "Schoree" River in the grant paid for by Vrooman.

The Mohawks during this time constituted a strong and powerful force not only in the Mohawk Valley but in the Adirondacks, which they controlled for hunting and fishing.

As pointed out in Volume No. 1 of Adirondack Album, Major Robert Rogers once desired 25,000 acres in the Lake George region from the Mohawks, but was thwarted by Sir William Johnson. This grant is a copy of an original; is at the Old Stone Fort Museum in Schoharie.

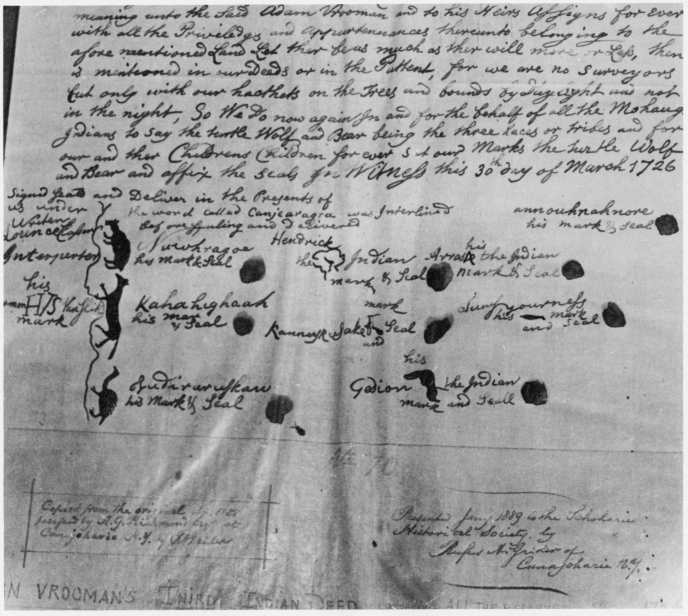

A camera closeup of the grant to Adam Vrooman, pictured on the opposing page, shows Indian signatures and marks and seals. Three "clans," or, as the grant describes, "races or tribes," are to be noted. At left, top animal is the bear, representing the Bear Clan. Middle animal represents the Wolf Clan; lower, the Turtle Clan.

Of exceptional interest in this grant is the signature following the Bear Clan, that of "Hendrick." Could this have been King Hendrick, the Mohawk who assisted Sir William Johnson in the Battle of Lake George, and who was killed in that fight?

This Mohawk, a chieftain, was one of several who visited the site of their ancestral home near Fonda, called Caughnawaga. The Indian group lived at Caughnawaga, Canada, and visited several areas in the Mohawk Valley. In this photo the chieftain points to the expanse of land once occupied by early Mohawks; the stakes at his feet were placed by archeologists who at the time of the photo were mapping out the village area. It was at this spot Kateri Tekakwitha, recently beatified by the Roman Catholic Church, was baptized.

170

Two of the Mohawks visiting the Mohawk Valley from Caughnawaga, Canada, were kind enough to the author to accompany him to a monument near the Lower Mohawk Club in the stockade area of Schenectady. On the marker are words describing early Schenectady, destroyed in February, 1690, by the French and Indians, some of the latter Mohawks who had left their valley years before to live in Canada.

When Schenectady was burned Mohawks from the area west of that settlement offered assistance to the bereaved settlers. Such were the fortunes of war in those by-gone days.

Considered one of the outstanding "camps" of the Adirondacks is the pretentious stone building built in 1893 by Edward Litchfield, a retired Brooklyn attorney. Above is the great hall, containing hundreds of animal mountings. Litchfield, in building the French chateau, brought scores of masons and stone cutters to the building site, where they remained until the stone shell of the building had been erected.

The structure, which has walls varying in thickness from three to six feet, is backdropped by Lake Madeline. Litchfield obviously liked his privacy, since the chateau sets about five miles from the highway between Long Lake and Tupper Lake.

The Litchfield Park estate, which comprised about 9,000 acres when created, also served as a scene for an experiment by its owner. Elk, moose and beaver were brought in for restocking and a generous area of the estate was fenced and kept under watch of guards. But storms and poachers wrecked sections and the animals either escaped or were shot.

Above photo taken during Adirondack fact finding tour of legislators; Assemblyman Glenn Harris is at lower left.

Not only are trophies of game from throughout the world mounted in the great hall at the Litchfield Park chateau southeast of Tupper Lake, but there are art treasures such as medieval armor, an example of which is shown above. Standing next to the German-made suit is John Stock, Superintendent of the Park and the man who directs its lumbering operations.

CANNON
TAKEN FROM JOHNSON HALL BY
SIR JOHN JOHNSON ON HIS
FLIGHT TO CANADA MAY 1776
SPIKED AND ABANDONED NEAR
TRAIL IN ADIRONDACKS
STATE EDUCATION
DEPARTMENT 1935

Self explanatory is the historical marker over this cannon, pictured at the baronial estate of Sir William Johnson in Johnstown. Sir John Johnson, son of Sir William, was driven from his home domain by the Colonials; the Revolution was then about a year old and spreading rapidly.

174

One of the finest aerial views of the historic island called Sagamore in Lake George. That is the name usually applied today because of the presence of the Hotel Sagamore, seen at lower left. In the late 1880's the area was called Green Island; is often referred to by that name today.

In 1882 Seneca Ray Stoddard said it was "partially cultivated," and was owned by F. Thieriot.

The value of Green Island in 1882 is not known. But Dome Island, visible from Green, in 1856 was purchased from New York State for $100! Today it is owned by the Nature Conservancy and its value could be put at well over $150,000.

Stoddard said Green Island was ideally suited for a hotel. The original Sagamore burned and the current one pictured is considered one of the outstanding resorts in the nation. A portion of the northern end is used by EnCon.

The basic idea here is that everybody can, on occasion, make a "mistake." The rear of this car is all that's visible after the driver hit a weak spot on frozen Lake George; the story goes that he was a "stranger in those parts" and thought that crossing the lake eastward from Bolton Landing would be a "short-cut" to Vermont. Sign in photo erected by an area gagster.

Photo by Walt Grishkot

One of the author's favorite photos, taken at Lake George during a local celebration. The look on the little girls' faces is not one of dismay, but wonderment at the doleful-eyed creation being held by this writer – a monkey, dressed for the occasion and one of the animals displayed at Animal Land. The look on the costumed girls' faces is, in my opinion, a priceless moment caught on film!

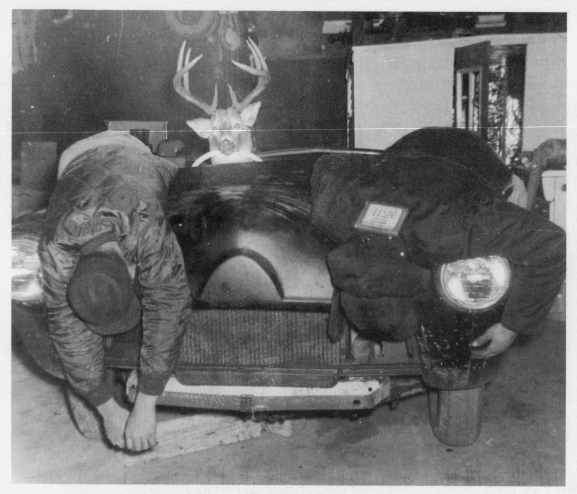

A column I did a few years ago illustrates that Nature, inscrutable, mysterious and innovative, can sometimes turn the tables on hunters.

During the big game season, in the Speculator area, a deer, determined on self preservation, cruised the woods, spotted hunters, nabbed two, then foolishly checked into a deer checking station to report his catch. The above photo was the result and, I am told, there was consternation among EnCon personnel at the sight when Wally Whitetail drove in to have his "catches" tabulated.

It is to the undying credit of EnCon personnel that they promptly arrested the deer and revived the two men, brothers, Rickie and Reggie Bonner of Couse Corners, East Greenbush. The whitetail was charged with violating Human Game Laws; only one hunter at a time!

Of course there's another side to this story. Bud Bonner, brother to Rickie and Reggie, and the gentleman who shot the 12-pointer, figured the catch should be presented in an entirely different way. Blessed with a good sense of humor, the Bonner Boys cooperated and the above photo, taken by Bud, was the remarkable result!

This historical marker stands in front of the Fulton County Jail in Johnstown and is self explanatory. While there have been additions and renovations made, much of the original building is in stable condition. The sign, however, does not denote the fact that the jail was closed on orders of New York State because "it did not meet state standards," and prisoners are now boarded at the Montgomery County Jail. When the author visited the Johnstown installation, boarding was costing Fulton County in the neighborhood of $28,000 a month, and a new jail's cost was estimated in the millions — one fourth of Fulton County's annual budget!

The author, after inspection, saw little reason for closing the jail; it was serviceable and clean, but the state, in its "wisdom" said it had to close.

The ground traveler cannot see such a scene as this; it takes flying on wings manufactured by Man. This unusual photo shows the southern start of the Champlain Division of the Barge Canal at upper right, and displays in remarkable fashion the exact point where the canal leaves the Hudson River in the Fort Edward area. The flow of the Hudson is to the south, that is, toward the bottom of the photo. The canal rises gradually northward through a system of locks, then levels off and descends eventually into Whitehall. It is fed by feeder streams, one of them from the Glens Falls area.

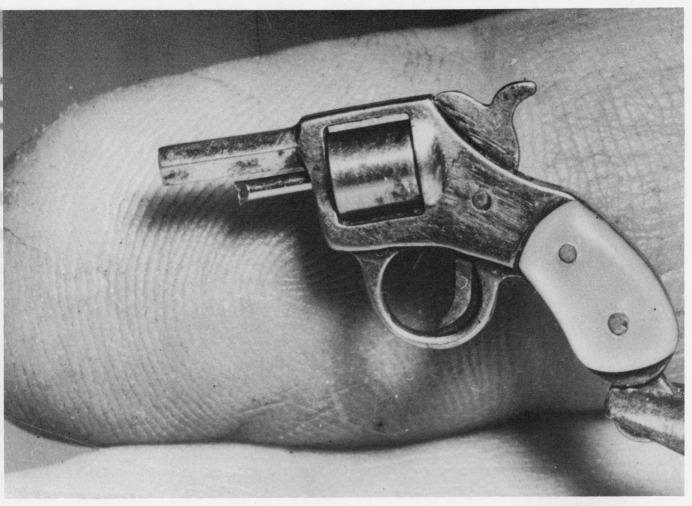

The revolver pictured is outlined against the tip of a human forefinger; it is pearl handled, and the trigger mechanism worked when the photo was taken. This novel masterpiece of skill and patience was made by the late Col. Hammersley of Saratoga County, who told the author he had created the remarkable revolver at the Watervliet Arsenal. To gain an idea of its size and precision work, merely look at the tip of your forefinger and realize that the weapon is even smaller!

The huge and stately elm tree that stood outside Monty's Elm Tree Inn, Keene, is pictured with the sign it once held. It was one of the most notable landmarks in the mountain region. Great care was taken to preserve its life, but the ravages of time and disease took their toll and the tremendous tree is merely a stump of its former self. If it were alive today it probably would rank as one of the largest and oldest — if not the giant of all elms — in New York State today.

One must grow continually amazed at changes in well known Adirondack towns and villages. Here, for instance, is the main street of Warrensburg in the late 1800's. Note abundance of picket fences separating private properties from street; they may have been, in those days, protection against wandering domestic stock. An enlargement of this photo can be seen in the Adirondack Museum at Blue Mt. Lake. The tall poles with cross pieces — do they represent home delivery of power? An interesting question.

What happens when a dam is thrown across a river? The result is what some call a "flow." In this case, the dam you see made of concrete, has replaced the old crib-work barrier, and holds back the Cedar River, creating in the meanwhile, the Cedar River Flow. The barrier can be seen near the entrance to the Moose River Plains area, past Wakely's, reachable through Indian Lake.

Not uncommon in the North Country are scenes such as this, taken of a mountain stream in Hamilton County.

Arto Monaco is a man not to be doomed by the Ausable River. His extraordinary Land of Make Believe, at Upper Jay, exists no longer as such because of flooding by the Ausable, but Arto, who once worked for the Disney studios, is now busily engaged in designing toys – and creating working models of them at his workshop. Repeated assaults by the Ausable proved too much for the Land of Make Believe, and Monaco closed his tourist attraction in 1980.

No game of "peek-a-boo" is this. The car is parked for effect; the photo, snapped in the North Hudson area, shows how quickly Nature will take over an abandoned road. The road in this case was of macadam, led into the Moriah area. Unmolested, Nature would smother the entire length within a few more decades.

How long this bottle remained in Lake George, or how it got into that basin of water is unknown. It was found by a skin diver from Troy. The inscription reads: "Vitreous Stone Bottle, J. Bourne & Son, Patentees, Denby Pottery near Derby — P. & J. Arnold, London, England." Could this article have been dropped into the lake during the Revolutionary War or even earlier?

Lake George is a creation of many moods, many scenes. This is one of winter beauty, when windblown snow created an unusual pattern of ripples on its frozen surface.

When the old dam across Hudson's River in the Fort Edward-Hudson Falls area was breached a few years ago, not only did thousands of yards of accumulated debris behind the dam wash downstream and clog channels, as well as the entrance to the Champlain Canal, but the lowered level of water disclosed what you see in the photo. The "jutting mounds" are log and rock cribs, apparently used in the days when timber was floated down the river. A new dam for power is planned for the area.

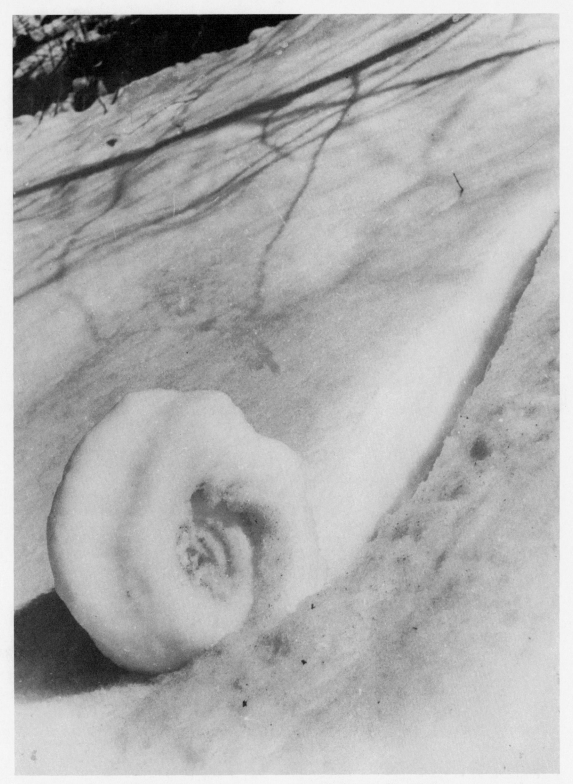

A scene of unusual beauty and not rare when weather conditions are just right is the "snow roller" pictured above. This one was photographed on a hill north of Warrensburg. They form during thaws, when snow is loosened, picks up a pepple and rolls downhill, with the pebble in the center. As the roller continues its course it picks up layers of snow.

Life, Injury, Death, are pictured on this page. Top photo: Before stocking rainbow trout by helicopter became fashionable fish were tossed into bodies of water such as Lake George by netting them from hatchery tanks and "shoveling" them into a better and more natural life.

Lower left: The raw flesh seen on this dog's neck is indicative of indifference. This dog was "raiding" camps in the North Point area of Long Lake and Conservation Officer Irwin A. King was notified. The animal, frightened of people, was found to be half starved, but worse, a nylon rope tied around its neck had cut deeply into its flesh. It was removed surgically; then King found a home for Molly. The dog, it was felt, had belonged to campers or hikers.

Lower right: Washington County tragedy. A buck, hit by a car, dies slowly along Route 149.

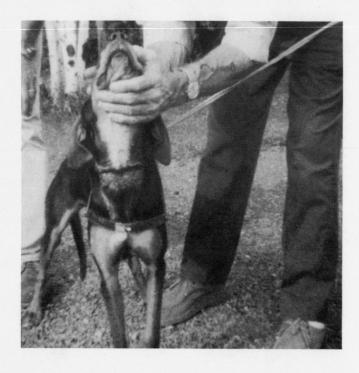

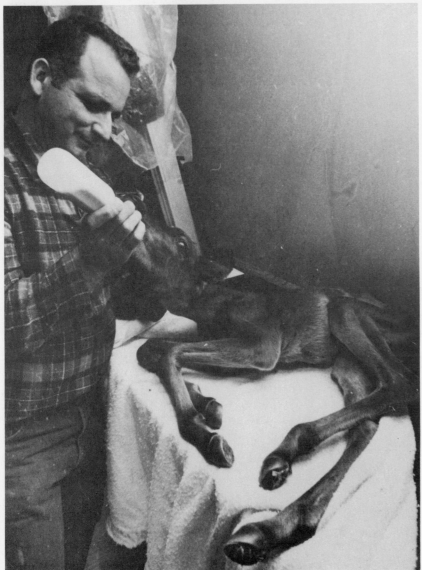

Another example of contrast: Top photo shows a dying deer, victim of winter kill. . .stravation and bitter cold, a not uncommon occurrence in the Adirondacks.

But in the Plattsburgh area this remarkably tiny creature, a foal, or colt if you will, gets bottle fed by a considerate owner. This little fellow drew lots of attention in the Platts-burgh area when Mama presented the welcome opportunity of facing the outside world.

The first snow train run to North Creek back in the early 1930's presented this view at the station, when hundreds of skiers, some equipped with toe strap "bindings" converged on the village to enjoy what was then non-state-developed slopes. It was at this station that Theodore Roosevelt boarded a train to take him to the presidency of the country.

The early Iroquois were more fortunate than other Indians because they lived near the earliest settlers of the Mohawk Valley, the Dutch, who furnished them with firearms in receipt of furs. Indians molded their own musket balls from lead obtained in trade. These came from archeological diggings at Caughnawaga, near Fonda. The Mohawks from this area ranged far into the Adirondacks for game and fish; Father Jogues, a Jesuit captive, once penetrated as deeply as ninety miles to the north — which would have brought his hunting group into the Lake Placid-Saranac Lake area.

195

Trail compaction is often mentioned as a hazard to oft-used trails in the High Peaks area. What it means is what you see above; so much foot traffic has moved along this route to Mt. Marcy that erosion has occurred and tree roots are exposed. Once soil is removed, rains and winter snows do the rest, and erosion continues at an accelerated pace.

196

With the wild turkey back in circulation in many counties, both south and north, this scene would not be an unusual one. In this sketch, done by the late Walter Schoonmaker of Rensselaer, a bobcat is seen about to pull a turkey into his clutches. Members of the cat family, domestic and otherwise, are experts in catching winged prey before such have the chance to get airborne to safety.

HUNTING TYPES

At left: DAN'L BOONE WEIGHT LIFTER TYPE,
the Incredible Bulk of the woods. Dressed in buck-
skins he usually lasts about a half hour before other
deer hunters mistake him for a buck and send him to
nearest hospital for treatment and observation.

Lower left: I'LL-DRINK-TO-THAT-TYPE. Distains
saloons. Brings own brand of panther juice; starts day
in manly fashion with belts of coffee royals, pops a
cork throughout the day, forgets what he did with his
rifle and usually snores out the rest of the trip.

Lower right: NEWCOMER. Usually a desk man
who has dreamed dreams. Stalker of rare lack of skill.
Only kind of hunter who can make a grown bear
laugh until tears flow. His exploits will be dramatical-
ly reported in company newspaper. An easy task. He
edits the thing.

BURIED GUN TYPE: City-bred. Heard of Adirondack weather, so dressed the part. Pictured shortly after sighting a 20-point, 300-pound buck caught in a balsalm thicket and suddenly realizing his rifle was still buried under his underwear with the safety off.

Upper right: OVERNIGHT NOVICE: Essentially a squirrel and chipmunk hunter looking for a trophy head. Ordinarily a suave, man-of-the-world type when engaged in his business as president of a plant manufacturing wart remover, but a man torn by killer instinct when in the wilderness. Pictured as he waits for first peep of his prey.

NATIVE-FROM-JUST-AROUND-THE-BEND-TYPE: Habitat of this gentleman, at right, usually neighborhood pub. Complacent look as he views unlucky hunters submerging sorrows in brew denotes a not unusual fact, to wit: His freezer was filled with venison six months before the season began.

Above is a new species of fish, as yet unnamed by ichthyologists, but possesses notable traits for many Adirondack waters. Lives only in acid rain lakes and ponds. Grows on the stuff, but will vary diet only on insects which breed in waters with a PH factor of 2, which approaches vinegar. Tastes well if fried in a batter of flour and hydrochloric acid. Is expected to completely rejuvenate the Adirondack fishing scene.

This unusual bit of fauna dwells in caverns, has powerful mandibles. Eats paper, preferably the tougher kind. Can be enticed from cave during daylight hours by opening a looseleaf notebook and rattling the pages.

NYS Museum scientists have been baffled over this new species, now called E. Pluribus Pliers. Eats only a new species in the field of entomology, called the hinged butterfly. Powerful jaws on occasion can crack a nut better than a squirrel on vitamins.